Reflective Practice in Forensic Settings

A Cognitive Analytic Approach to Developing Shared Thinking

Edited by Jenny Marshall
and Jamie Kirkland

Reflective Practice in Forensic Settings

© Pavilion Publishing & Media

The authors have asserted their rights in accordance with the Copyright, Designs and Patents Act (1988) to be identified as the authors of this work.

Published by:

Pavilion Publishing and Media Ltd
Blue Sky Offices
25 Cecil Pashley Way
Shoreham by Sea
West Sussex
BN43 5FF

Tel: 01273 434 943
Email: info@pavpub.com
Web: www.pavpub.com

Published 2021

All rights reserved. No part of this publication may be reproduced, stored in a retrieval system, or transmitted in any form or by any means, electronic, mechanical, photocopying, recording or otherwise, without prior permission in writing of the publisher and the copyright owners.

A catalogue record for this book is available from the British Library.

ISBN: 978-1-914010-84-2

Pavilion Publishing and Media is a leading publisher of books, training materials and digital content in mental health, social care and allied fields. Pavilion and its imprints offer must-have knowledge and innovative learning solutions underpinned by sound research and professional values.

Editors: Jenny Marshall and Jamie Kirkland

Cover design: Emma Dawe, Pavilion Publishing and Media Ltd

Page layout and typesetting: Tony Pitt, Pavilion Publishing and Media Ltd

Printing: CMP Digital Print Solutions

Forthcoming titles in the *Innovations in CAT* series:

Therapy with a Voice
(Lucy Cutler and Steve Potter)

Embodied Therapeutic Presence and Relational Space
(Tim Sheard)

Working Relationally with Children, Young People and Families
(Nick Barnes and Lee Crothers)

Contents

Series preface
Foreword
Acknowledgements
Contributors

PART 1: Introduction to forensic work, reflective practice and the relational model 11

   Chapter 1: The challenge of working in forensic services
      Jenny Marshall and Jamie Kirkland 13

   Chapter 2: Traditional approaches to reflective practice – history, aetiology, evidence and approaches
      Jon Patrick, Katharine Russell and Adam Polnay 21

   Chapter 3: Cognitive Analytic Therapy – the model
      Jenny Marshall and Jamie Kirkland 35

   Chapter 4: Relational mapping – an alternative approach to reflective practice
      Steve Potter 47

PART 2: Facilitating reflective practice – considerations and practical steps 63

   Chapter 5: What are the core competencies needed to deliver reflective practice?
      Jamie Kirkland 65

   Chapter 6: Steps to reflective mapping
      Steve Potter 79

   Chapter 7: Reflective practice – case studies from forensic settings
      Jenny Marshall, Louise Yorke, Alison Bickerdike, Clare Bingham, Nicola Kemp, Vicky Millar and Mark Ramm 95

   Chapter 8: Crossing and uncrossing the line – using CAT reflective practice to think about the reciprocal role enactments encountered in critical forensic situations
      Jason Hepple 111

Chapter 9: Helping the helpers – the experiences of reflective practice from the perspective of facilitators
    Jamie Kirkland, Heather Tolland, Emma Drysdale and Steve Jefferis 121

Chapter 10: CAT-informed Supervision of CAT-informed reflective practice in a forensic setting – 'Map and Talk'
    Alison Bickerdike, Nicola Kemp and Clare Bingham 133

PART 3: Reflective practice and the wider organization 151

Chapter 11: When forensic services go astray – what can CAT offer at a system level?
    David Harvey 153

Chapter 12: Leadership and Cognitive Analytic Therapy
Part one – relational dynamics and culture
    Jenny Marshall 167

Chapter 13: Leadership and Cognitive Analytic Therapy
Part two – a personal and professional journey
    Jenny Marshall 183

Chapter 14: Concluding thoughts
A dialogue between the editors
    Jenny Marshall, Jamie Kirkland and Steve Potter 195

References

Appendix 1

Appendix 2

Series preface

The *Innovations in Cognitive Analytic Therapy* book series aims to offer helpful but also challenging accounts by practitioners in various fields of theoretical development and clinical work based on Cognitive Analytic Therapy (CAT). The editors and contributors are experts in their fields who have undertaken innovative and exploratory work using the CAT approach – the presentation of which, in our view, is long overdue. We hope that these books will make important and compassionate contributions to our understanding of and approaches to a range of clinical and other problems and presentations – contributions that will be helpful and thought-provoking not only for colleagues already familiar with CAT, but also for many others. The series builds on and complements previous overviews by the late Anthony Ryle, creator of the CAT model, and other wide-scope multi-author volumes.

A distinctive feature is a predominantly relational and socio-cultural conceptualisation of mental health problems, or of distress and 'disorder', and correspondingly of therapeutic approaches to them. A fundamental emphasis throughout, based on understandings derived from years of psychotherapy outcome research, Vygotskian activity theory and more recent research in infant psychology, is the importance of a (genuinely) collaborative and co-creative approach to treatment. This long-standing emphasis in CAT will be evident in, for example, descriptions of the co-creative process of reformulation, both written and diagrammatic ('mapping'). These in turn will emphasise recognising and working on enactments of internalised early relational patterns ('reciprocal roles') in life generally, but also between both clinicians and clients. They will also emphasise the gradual internalisation of new, more benign relational experience. This is regrettably far from being the case for many individuals currently in therapy or, especially, undergoing treatment within public health services, despite its recognised importance as a key 'common factor' in outcomes.

As well as offering practically helpful accounts of developing and innovative work in often challenging clinical fields, we aspire for these books also to contribute to the ongoing development of the CAT model, including as a general framework for understanding and treating mental health problems. This will be important for its own validity and vitality as well as more generally to advance the field of mental health. Anthony Ryle, who created the CAT model during a long and avowedly integrative evolutionary process, certainly always welcomed such developments. We look forward to the *Innovations in Cognitive Analytic Therapy* series promoting productive debate, and being part of an open, creative dialogue between practitioners of CAT and colleagues from other approaches and disciplines in support of a versatile, integrative and relational approach to mental health in general.

Ian. B. Kerr and Steve Potter
Series Editors

Foreword

"Trust in the model" have been the wise words often repeated by my co facilitator (or more affectionately and respectfully, my "wingman"), Jenny Marshall, when faced with live mapping with a group of senior leads in an organization, and the knot of anxiety in my stomach begins to twist...

Contextual use of the CAT model can be anxiety-provoking for practitioners. Our training focuses on therapy cases and it can feel exposing to put ourselves into the larger arena to offer a relational perspective to clinical teams, managers or senior leads. Risks can lurk in both our own maps/histories ("Will I be exposed as the imposter?") and the realities of potential attack if the reflection and accurate relational description of CAT threatens powerful dynamics/investment in the status quo. This book is a timely encouragement to develop reflective practice in our systems whilst also highlighting the importance of support and dialogue with like-minded colleagues given the challenges involved.

My starting point began in the late 1990s, with a passion to share the model with any staff team who would listen, fuelled by positive feedback from service users, and the early work of Ian Kerr, Mary Dunn, Glenys Parry and Sue Walsh. They demonstrated that CAT was far more than a talking therapy, but a model that could develop relational thinking and mentalisation in services, helping to reduce the likelihood of iatrogenic harm, enable more therapeutic interactions with service users, and support the wellbeing of staff. I repeatedly heard feedback from staff following introductory CAT skills training that they found the model accessible: they quickly 'got it', were able to put it into practice in their day-to-day work, and valued a reflective space. The last time I heard Tony Ryle speak at a conference, he encouraged us further with his view that the more contextual/organizational use of CAT would be a key way forward for CAT in the NHS.

It is a great pleasure to see this book come together – the first from the CAT community on the contextual use of the model. I have been lucky to witness some of the development, such as Ian Kerr's contextual work with community teams in Sheffield, CAT skills training in forensic settings with Jenny Marshall and Steve Potter, and the many authors of this book who contributed to the first Forensic CAT conference in 2019 and then worked hard to reach this point of fruition.

It is a testament to shared working that Jenny is joined in this book by Jamie Kirkland (another wingman) to pull together a variety of different, innovative and engaging 'voices'. As a result, they have skillfully worked together to let us hear about the range of possibilities CAT is bringing to reflective practice in forensic settings.

The challenges of living and working in forensic settings are immense and the intensity of emotion linked to trauma, risk and loss of liberty can make it very difficult to step out of the dance and open our minds. Reflective practice is potentially most difficult to do in these environments, and thus most needed. When a supervisee came to me with the case of a male patient who had murdered his 18-month-old child, I initially doubted whether I could effectively supervise. I experienced a tiny window into the challenges faced by forensic staff on a daily basis. "Trust in the model" enabled a formulation of his trauma history behind the murder and a more compassionate perspective was possible for me, my supervisee and the ward staff. Similarly, when facilitating CAT skills introductory training on a forensic ward, I felt angered and (covertly) critical of staff who complained about a patient 'kicking off' after he had been refused a sandwich from a dispensing machine when hungry as it was ten minutes after the scheduled lunchtime. My frustration and inner judgement of their provocative control shifted to more understanding when we later CAT mapped what it was like for them to work on the ward. They spoke of their need to retain tight control in order to avoid their 'dreaded place' of the ward being out of control, in chaos and with the very real threat of physical injury and denigration. Trust in the model, or "map and talk" as Steve Potter would say, enabled all involved to hold different/multiple perspectives in mind.

In true CAT spirit, this personal and heartfelt book has been written by the clinicians at the coalface, not as 'experts', but encouraging dialogue through sharing their work to develop a more compassionate and relationally aware therapeutic culture. Tools such as The Helper's Dance List and The Covid Struggles List are further examples of increasing the accessibility of CAT ideas for staff and normalising/sanctioning the exploration of what we bring to the dance. This book has much to offer for the development of reflective practice in a range of settings, not just forensics. I hope it will encourage you to 'have a go' (if you are new to this) or to extend your practice, and find support from relationally minded colleagues.

Trust in the model (and your wingman!).

Kate Freshwater
Consultant Clinical Psychologist and Trustwide Lead for Cognitive Analytic Therapy

Acknowledgements

This book grew out of a collaboration between many of the chapter authors and the book editors; they were brought together by Steve Potter; we are indebted to him both for creating the network of practitioners working relationally in forensic services and for his support for both the first conference on 'Shared Thinking Space' in 2019 and the opportunity for this book. As series editors, Steve Potter and Ian Kerr have been supportive in, firstly, asking us and then encouraging us to push our own boundaries in writing and editing this book. We would also like to thank the CAT community who have joined us in this endeavour, given up their own time in writing and therefore expanded the number of voices we have been able to hear. We would like to thank Darren Reed and Louisa Robertson at Pavilion Publishing, for guiding us on the journey. Finally, we would like to thank Natalie McNulty for her diligent reference checking.

Jenny

I have been extremely lucky to have had the support I have throughout this journey. When I started my journey of CAT training, Kate Freshwater was my supervisor. She has been much more than this over the years and I have no doubt that I would not be the therapist, supervisor or person I am today were it not for her endless belief, compassion, knowledge, support, role modelling, containment and much more. Her influence will be heard throughout this book although not directly referenced as has been the mark she has left on the many people she has supervised and supported over the years. Steve, as mentioned above, has been a mentor to me over the years, building my confidence as a co-trainer and reflective practice facilitator. Again, I have been heavily influenced by him and his thinking which can also be heard throughout my work and this book. Everyone on the CAT practitioner course in Manchester – without doubt the best training course I have been on and the one which has most influenced my work. All those within Ridgeway Hospital, Roseberry Park who have supported the development of CAT over the years, working hard to sustain it, particularly frontline staff and managers supporting with rotas!

Finally, I thank my family without which I could not have done any of this; my husband Jamie who is my rock and has endless patience and belief in me. And my two babies (not so little now!), Sam and Henry, for their energy and ability to keep me grounded in the moment when I need it most.

Jamie

I have been influenced and supported by a range of CAT colleagues over the years. I am particularly indebted to my first CAT supervisor, Maggie Gray, for encouraging my development. I am especially grateful for the gentle way Mark Ramm has championed the development of CAT in forensic services in Scotland and allowed me to be part of this journey. I would like specifically to thank James Mead and Ruth Stocks who have given vital management support to reflective practice in Glasgow and allowed me to develop my work in this area. I would like to thank George, David, Keith and Dougie at HBT13 for regular reflective moments and restorative conversation that maintained my sanity. Finally, to my lovely family, Orlagh, George and Alice, who put up with my need to take time to think without complaint. I am very lucky.

Contributors

Dr Alison Bickerdike is a Clinical Psychologist and CAT Practitioner. She has worked in East London NHS Foundation Trust (ELFT) Forensic Directorate since 2007, in both the Medium Secure Service (John Howard Centre) and since 2018 as Lead Psychologist in the East London Community Forensic Service (ELCFS). She has a particular interest in the use of CAT formulation in teams and organizations. Along with Nicola Kemp and Clare Bingham she is one of the Project Leads for the 'Map and Talk' Reflective Practice Project in the ELFT Forensic Directorate. She has also developed applications of the CAT model in group and individual work with men who have committed sexual offences.

Dr Clare Bingham is a Consultant Clinical Psychologist and Head of Psychology at the John Howard Centre Medium Secure Service in East London NHS Foundation Trust (ELFT). Along with Alison Bickerdike and Nicola Kemp she is one of the Project Leads for the 'Map and Talk' Reflective Practice Project in the ELFT Forensic Directorate. She has been running 'Map and Talk' sessions for ward teams and supervision groups for facilitators since 2014.

Dr Emma Drysdale is a Consultant Clinical and Forensic Psychologist in the Directorate of Forensic Mental Health in NHS Greater Glasgow and Clyde. She is currently the Psychology Department lead for research and has supported evaluations of the reflective practice input to the service. She was also involved in the development of the Directorate's therapeutic milieu training. She regularly facilitates reflective practice sessions for a low secure inpatient unit and provides staff and patient support following significant incidents.

Dr David Harvey is a Consultant Clinical Psychologist and Cognitive Analytic Therapy Practitioner. He has worked for 17 years in services supporting people with complex mental health needs, who may pose a risk of harm to others or themselves. He has done this in the NHS, Probation, Courts, Children's Services, Prisons and the voluntary sector. He has a particular interest in how clinical presentations that challenge services, such as those likely to attract diagnosis of 'Personality Disorder', can disrupt effective system working and proportionate risk management as a result of powerful emotional reactions to the work in professionals, teams and organizations. He has become increasingly attracted to the idea that the application of psychological theory, including CAT, outside of the therapy room may be one way in which the multiple and complex needs of many stakeholders can be considered and carefully balanced.

Dr Jason Hepple FRCPsych UKCP reg is a retired Consultant Psychiatrist in psychological therapies for Somerset NHS Foundation Trust where he still contributes as an honorary psychotherapist and mentor. He is a CAT trainer and supervisor and a life member of ACAT. He has published books and papers on later life, CAT in groups, CAT with obsessionality and on the dialogic heart of CAT.

Dr Steve Jefferis is a Clinical Psychologist, ACAT-accredited CAT practitioner, supervisor and trainer. He leads the CAT Service for Cumbria, Northumberland, Tyne & Wear NHS Foundation Trust at the Centre for Specialist Psychological Therapies, Walkergate Park, Newcastle upon Tyne. He is also Course Director for the Newcastle Practitioner Training in Cognitive Analytic Therapy and has a particular interest in organizational and consultation applications of CAT.

Dr Nicola Kemp is a Clinical Psychologist and CAT Practitioner. Along with Alison Bickerdike and Clare Bingham she is one of the Project Leads for the 'Map and Talk' Reflective Practice Project in the ELFT Forensic Directorate. She has been the Senior Clinical Psychologist for the Women's Forensic Service in East London NHS Foundation Trust (ELFT) since 2011, during which time she has implemented CAT as one of the core therapies. Her key interests include reflective practice, staff support after traumatic experiences in the workplace and trauma-informed care in complex settings.

Dr Jamie Kirkland is a Consultant Clinical Psychologist, CAT practitioner, supervisor and trainer. He works across two services: a medium secure service in NHS Greater Glasgow and Clyde where he is reflective practice lead, and NHS Fife Learning Disabilities team where he is supporting the development of a CAT-informed service. He is co-director to the CAT practitioner training course in Scotland. He is interested in the application of CAT in team, consultancy and creative settings.

Dr Jenny Marshall is a Consultant Clinical Psychologist, CAT therapist and supervisor. She works in medium and low secure services at Ridgeway Hospital, Tees, Esk and Wear Valleys NHS Trust. She has developed an overarching relational model based on CAT principles and embedded reflective practice for frontline staff. She hosted the first forensic CAT conference on shared thinking space in 2019 and has developed reflective practice beyond frontline staff to managers and senior leaders. She has a longstanding interest in using CAT and relational principles to influence culture.

Dr Victoria Millar is a Consultant Clinical Psychologist working in the Forensic Clinical Psychology Department at the Orchard Clinic, a Medium Secure Unit within NHS Lothian. She has recently qualified as an accredited Cognitive Analytic Practitioner. Interests include working therapeutically with people with psychosis while recognising the value and being actively supportive of the therapeutic milieu.

Dr Jon Patrick is a Consultant Forensic Psychiatrist and Psychotherapist. He is also a BPC registered Psychoanalytic Psychotherapist and Anna Freud Centre accredited MBT Tutor. Jon has spent much of his career helping to set up, run and supervise reflective practice groups (RPGs). More recently he chaired a Scottish group to lay out a framework for the training and delivery of RPGs in forensic settings. He sees reflective practice as vital to the work of any functional, healthy organizational system.

Dr Adam Polnay is a Consultant Psychiatrist in Psychotherapy and a member of the Scottish Association of Psychoanalytic Psychotherapists (SAPP). He is an Associate Fellow of the Higher Education Academy and an Anna Freud Centre-accredited MBT practitioner. Adam works at The State Hospital (Carstairs), Scotland's high secure forensic hospital, and leads the NHS Lothian psychotherapy department. Adam is involved in the Scottish Forensic Network, particularly in developing Reflective Practice Group (RPG) services and teaching psychodynamic concepts. His current main research area is the evaluation of psychodynamic reflective practice groups.

Steve Potter is a Psychotherapist based in London working with a variety of multidisciplinary teams in the UK and internationally developing relational awareness and reflective practice through the process of relational mapping. He teaches and supervises Cognitive Analytic Therapy. He is committed to developing an integrative and educational approach to developing relational awareness using the methods of psychotherapy. He is author of *Therapy with a Map* (2020) and co-editor of the *International Journal of Cognitive Analytic Therapy and Relational Mental Health*. His website www.mapandtalk.com offers various resources and events for the application of Cognitive Analytic Therapy.

Mark Ramm is a Consultant Clinical Forensic Psychologist. He is a CAT practitioner and trainer. He was the co-director of the first ACAT practitioner training course to be run in Scotland. He currently works in the Serious Offender Liaison Service in NHS Lothian and is an accredited risk assessor with the Risk Management Authority. He also works with various other organizations where the CAT model appears to have useful application.

Dr Katharine Russell is a Consultant Clinical Forensic Psychologist. She currently leads the Forensic Clinical Psychology service in NHS Lothian. For many years, she was co-lead of the Serious Offender Liaison Service; involved in creating and developing this unique service to provide clinical expertise to criminal justice agencies managing high risk and complex offenders. She has developed and run training for multidisciplinary and multi-agency groups on numerous issues related to working with offenders including risk assessment and working with offenders with personality disorder. She has chaired a Forensic Network Working group on Structured Clinical Care. She has also published research in these areas.

Dr Heather Tolland is a Research Assistant for the Directorate of Forensic Mental Health and Learning Disabilities in NHS Greater Glasgow & Clyde. Her recent work has focused on risk assessment, challenging behaviour and staff wellbeing. Prior to this, Heather completed a PhD in Criminology at the University of Stirling, focused on the mentoring experiences of women who had offended.

Dr Louise Yorke is a Consultant Clinical Psychologist and since 2015 has been head of Inpatient Psychology across the Regional Secure Unit at Langdon Hospital in Devon. As part of a practice involving cognitive, trauma focused and dynamic trainings, Louise is a CAT therapist with a longstanding interest in cognitive analytic therapy (CAT), relational ways of working, clinically and associated mechanisms affecting organizational culture and clinical change. In addition to these roles, Louise has previously held the post of co-editor of Reformulation, the Journal of the Association of Cognitive Analytic Therapy (2015–2019). In 2016, working with colleagues from a range of disciplines, Louise developed Relational Discovery, a relationally organized, trauma-informed philosophy of care and model of culture change, operational management and practice, applicable to organizations within and beyond healthcare environments.

PART 1: Introduction to forensic work, reflective practice and the relational model

Chapter 1: The challenge of working in forensic services

Jenny Marshall and Jamie Kirkland

Introduction

Human beings are complex; we do not fully understand them and working in any area, whether health or any other sector, requires us to form relationships. At their best, these relationships can be containing, supportive, compassionate and nurturing. But at their worst they can be traumatizing and distressing. In this book we aim to discuss the complexities of caring relationships within forensic services and the unique challenges that working in this area brings. We will argue why reflective practice is a core requirement for working in forensic services and we will hear from a range of innovative clinicians on how they are applying ideas originating from the field of cognitive analytic therapy.

The challenge

> 'Few organizations are more emotionally challenging than those tasked with the care of highly traumatic and traumatizing forensic patients.'
> (Tuck, 2009, p43)

If all human relationships are complex and working in organizations involves navigating networks of relationships, what is it specifically about forensic services that is described as more emotionally challenging than other areas?

The nature of the client group

Forensic services care for individuals who are a risk to others, perpetrating acts of violence or harm to others. In addition, many of these individuals are also a risk to themselves, engaging in serious acts of self-harm or attempts at suicide.

All too often, the lives of individuals in forensic services are characterised by abuse, trauma and neglect, impacting on their ability to feel safe, trust others, their relationship with authority, control and power and the way emotions are regulated. Trauma and emotional distress is a common thread throughout forensic services, not only part of the story individuals tell about their journey into forensic services from childhood to adulthood but reverberating through communities harmed by offences committed, and through staff groups traumatized by bearing witness to it.

Relational security

The aim of forensic services is, therefore, to manage risk and to safely rehabilitate. At the heart of doing this is the therapeutic relationship which has been identified as critical (Johnson *et al*, 2010), as there is a need to engage individuals to start the long journey of reintegration back into society. However, it is often addressing difficulties in relationships that is central to any rehabilitation.

Relationships developed in early life influence the way we relate to others throughout our lives (Ryle & Kerr, 2020) and such patterns are often unconsciously repeated in relationships with people caring for us. For those with experiences of care, they will learn what it is like to be cared for and learn to both care for others and for themselves. However, for those who have experienced trauma or rejection, particularly by powerful or important others, expected to care and protect, forming trusting relationships and feeling safe is especially difficult. Building therapeutic relationships when trust and safety are areas of difficulty is hugely challenging even for the most experienced and skilled clinician, particularly taking into account the need to balance risk alongside. In addition, it often falls to those staff who have the least training and experience to have the most frontline contact, walking the tightrope of emotional (relational security) and physical containment (security) (Marshall *et al*, 2014).

If staff manage to navigate these complexities, it then falls to them to have both the privilege of hearing their story, the pain and emotional impact of hearing about both the hurt caused to others and the hurt and loss experienced by them. Holding both the experience of the individual as a victim alongside them as perpetrators can be extremely challenging for even the most experienced staff members. This is the case not only in relation to historical events whereby service users may have been both victim and perpetrator, but the real everyday situations staff are expected to manage. It is not unusual that staff may go from responding and containing an incident of violence, to engaging in benign activities, such as colouring, with the same person in a short space of time. If there is not space to consider the challenge of holding multiple positions of both being hurt and hurting others, individuals in teams may end up identifying with only one part of the individual's experience. For example, a staff member having been assaulted might naturally be more focused on risk management, observing early risk signs and being cautious in decision making. Another staff member who hears about the service users' shame following the assault or is aware of their difficult early experiences, might be more focused on their vulnerability and may be more willing to take therapeutic risks. The result of this can be team conflict and splits as interventions are driven by differing views. These dynamics are not only unhelpful and damaging to patients but can also lead to untoward incidents, frequent demoralisation, team conflict, communication difficulties, poor job satisfaction, sickness and burnout in staff (Onyett *et al*, 1997).

Much has been written about working with complexity in forensic settings. However, caution should be exercised when considering both the impact of working with 'complex presentations' or considering the impact of working with violence and aggression, to ensure that clinicians, services and organizations do not solely locate 'difficulties' or 'complexity' within service users. The trauma and violence staff are exposed to will affect individuals emotionally in different ways. In this way, staff not only bring their 'professional' selves to work but also their own personal experiences, backgrounds and characteristically different ways of coping. In addition, it must be taken into account that care and treatment of people in forensic services takes place in a context. The physical environment has a huge impact on service users, staff, teams and the wider organizational context.

The physical environment and physical security

Those people that find themselves in forensic services are not there voluntarily. The majority are under a legal framework related to the severity of their offending. Locked doors and keys are characteristic and become the symbol of power as environments are tightly controlled and details of lives are scrutinized as part of daily care and risk assessment. This pervades the whole system from the physicality of the locked door to the control of personal items. As a service user once said to me, 'I am a 52-year-old man but I have to ask for a razor every day to shave my face'.

The reality of working in such a highly controlled environment is that service users, staff and teams will respond to the environment in their own unique ways based on their experience of power and control. In the experience of powerlessness, we will all find ways of surviving. Some may respond by becoming compliant, others might be pulled to rebel. However, others might experience it differently altogether and perceive the control to be protecting, and in response feel safe.

The diagram below illustrates common responses to the forensic environment.

Figure 1

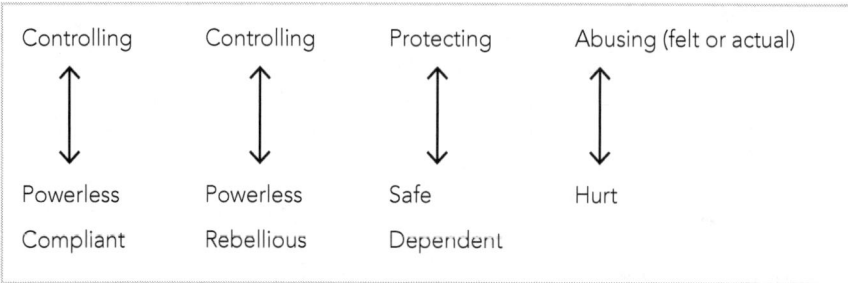

The environment creates many challenges for clinicians, primarily in relation to side stepping the control and creating meaningful engagement; distinguishing between compliance and meaningful engagement and collaboration; recognising rebellion, and the pull to respond by becoming increasingly restrictive and punitive through a battle of wills. For example, an individual who had experiences of punitive control growing up, may have learnt to survive by rebelling and taking some control back. In forensic services, this may create a challenge; if this individual is pulled to fighting the system, the initial risks which brought them into services may not be the same factors which maintain their prolonged stay in services, as they 'fight the system'.

When an individual is responding to the controlling environment with anger and rebellion, they are in the short-term trying to take back some control. In such situations, staff have several choices though can feel at times as if there are only two; engage in a battle of wills by restricting further and overtly displaying their powerful control, or to pacify, and give in to the control. An alternative middle position is to observe; notice the dynamic, map it out loosely on paper, acknowledging the anger (and possibly underlying hurt) which is triggering the rebellion. This may allow some thought about the temporary control that this rebellion might give the patient but also the potential longer-term negative consequences.

These dynamics may be a strong invitation for staff or teams to become more punitive or rescuing but require the ability to notice, step back and most importantly think about the dynamics at play. This is the heart of reflective practice.

Those working in nursing roles will not only be working in a physically restrictive and controlled environment, they will often be providing physical containment and managing violent and aggressive behaviour. At times, in order to maintain safety and prevent harm, physical intervention will be required. At its most serious, seclusion or solitary confinement may be needed. The impact of working in an environment where violence and aggression is likely takes its toll on staff, leading to increased levels of stress

(Coldwell & Naismith, 1989; Reid et al, 1999). The issue of violence-related stress is a particular problem in forensic mental health settings (Mason, 2002). There is an expectation that staff will have to manage traumatic incidents involving interpersonal violence, self-harm and suicidal behaviour.

Figure 2

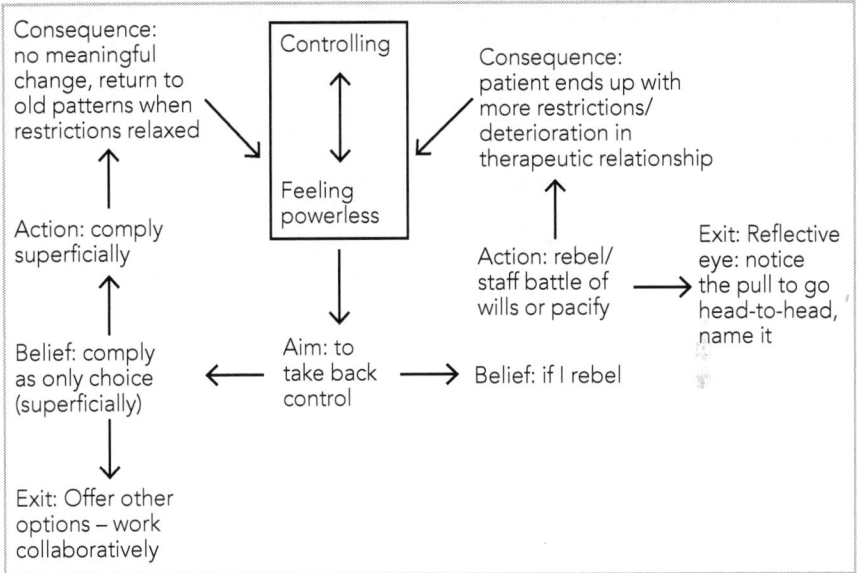

Cognitively, it may be easier for staff to reconcile themselves to the physical environment of secure hospitals, prisons or physical interventions. Such environments and interventions are a last resort and only used to keep people safe or reduce risk. However, the emotional experience of enforcing environment controls or carrying out a physical intervention can be harder for staff. Just one example is the impact of interventions such as physical restraint on those with a history of trauma. In such situations, staff can end up intervening to protect while being aware that the felt experience for the service user can be that of reliving abuse. The alternative is that they don't intervene, fail to protect and the lack of felt safety can further escalate cycles of self-harm. Either way they can feel they are unwittingly recruited into relational dynamics of 'abusing' or 'failing to protect'. The complexity of these emotions which staff grapple with on a day-to-day basis goes to the core of our humanity and, in order to ensure best care for service users and staff, these dynamics need to be thought about.

As well as acknowledging the challenges of trying to provide care which is perceived as traumatic and abusive, it is important to acknowledge those situations where care does become clearly abusive. Serious incident reviews such as the Mid Staffordshire enquiry (2013) and Winterbourne View (2012) have common features, in that the abuse does not happen as isolated incidents. The blame is not solely located within individuals but instead is understood as occurring within a wider organizational culture. With this in mind, it can be argued that when working within forensics, clinicians cannot focus solely on service users or individual staff members, locating complexity and challenge within them; instead there needs to be reflection upon the interactions and complexity of challenges that staff are negotiating within the environment and that these dynamics take place within a wider organization and sociopolitical culture.

Figure 3

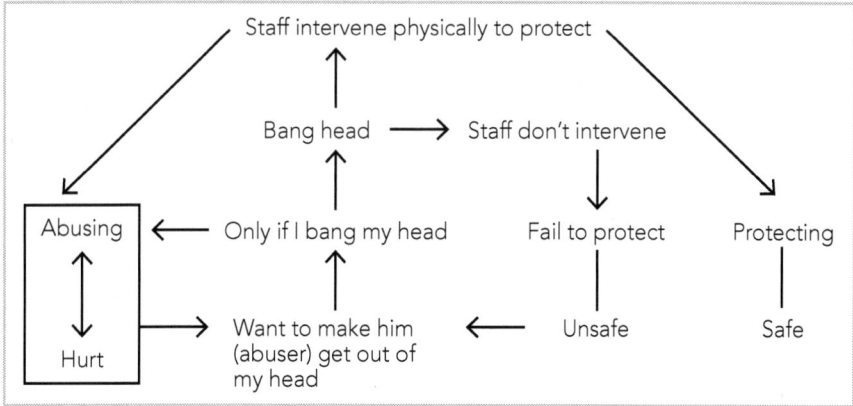

The organizational culture

Although forensic services have expanded over recent years, it is the case that some have been around for many years and carry with them histories of the institutions and their cultures. Even with newer forensic services, to truly understand the experience of working in such services, is to not just focus on the client group but on the broader context both within the health service and within the history of the service.

The wider sociopolitical culture in which forensic services operate has changed; in the United Kingdom, public and statutory services have been experiencing prolonged austerity for a significant period of time now. Alongside this, services and the NHS are subject to greater scrutiny from the media and from regulatory bodies. Within forensic services, this has led to increasing tension between, on the one hand, balancing public safety in the context of increased media attention, with attention to least restrictive practice and on the other hand, recovery and the need to rehabilitate people more quickly into community settings. In essence, services are being asked to do more, to a higher standard, more quickly; there is greater emphasis on measuring this performance both privately within organizations and publicly.

Gerada (2014) describes both the industrialization of health care and unprecedented change over the last 20 years as having changed the working environment for staff. Naturally, the pressures and the expectations on staff has led to increasing attention being given to the culture and wellbeing of staff, but whereas policy documents often focus on the impact of complex service users, certainly when referring to the health service, the staff survey indicates that some of the causes or contributing factors to staff stress relates to relationships at work with both colleagues and managers. There has been increasing recognition of the need to invest and develop occupational health services for staff in the NHS and it is important that these services do not focus solely on individual staff but attend to the wider team and organizational culture in order to promote staff and team wellbeing. Indeed, it is the organizational culture with specific reference to senior leaders that is increasingly written about as impacting directly on patient care.

A note on multiple positions…

If we simply described all the challenges of working in both organizations and forensic services, this would only be part of the picture and would raise the question: *Why work in forensics if it is so difficult?* Therefore, it is important to acknowledge the other aspects of the work. Working with people in any area and being trusted to hear someone's story is a huge privilege. In forensics, I have been struck by the courage and bravery of so many people. From the service users with histories of horrific trauma who have still not given up on humanity and who have the strength to trust in sharing their stories both of their abuse but also their abusing of others, with the hope that the future can be better. From the staff members who can still hold a sense of humour whilst cleaning up faeces smeared over a seclusion room door, or who can tolerate life-threatening violence but still have compassion enough to take care of someone, or from the leaders who share their vulnerability, not as faceless people making decisions but as human beings who are still moved and affected by what they see and hear and carry the burden and weight of expectation, responsibility and blame.

Working in forensics might be challenging, but if we remove the labels of service user, staff member, leader, we are quite simply human beings primed for relationships and often showing huge bravery in how we embrace this when given the opportunity.

What happens when we don't have a space to think?

The ability to think requires us to be able to hover over different feeling states, taking into account a sense of time and history alongside the intensity of emotion. This 'reflective eye' helps us not to fall into being emotionally overwhelmed and unable to see a way out. It helps us not to act solely on emotion. This ability develops in childhood with the presence of an observing, containing other. Experiencing stress and trauma can compromise reflective capacity. In therapy, we are often developing the reflective or observing eye, the ability to notice feeling states and patterns of relating as a precursor to change.

Within forensic services, on an individual service user level, trauma has often compromised reflective capacity. This can be further compromised if the ward or wing does not feel safe and feelings can get acted out. In relation to staff working in an environment with high levels of violence and aggression, stress can similarly compromise reflective capacity leading staff to be more likely to make decisions driven by high levels of emotion and leading to splits within teams, as described earlier. Within the wider organizational and sociopolitical culture, the impact of austerity on financial pressures and increased scrutiny on services can also impact on senior leadership teams, potentially leading to similar stressors and inhibiting reflection.

Applying a relational model within forensic services allows for thinking space about some of the unique challenges faced by staff working in these areas. Without reflective capacity or an observing eye within the system, these power struggles or enactments are likely to impair or limit therapeutic relationships and progress. A compassionate and emotionally containing therapeutic environment is developed from having individuals, teams and organizations who can think and reflect on relational dynamics, in themselves, others and the wider system.

This book aims to explore reflective practice, describing traditional models of reflective practice, and introducing an alternative model based on principles of Cognitive Analytic Therapy (CAT). Skills and competencies for delivering reflective practice will be presented alongside applications of reflective practice within and across teams before exploring how this can fit within a leadership and organizational culture. We have been privileged to have drawn upon a wide range of services, clinicians and thinkers in presenting this work. Our aim is to present many pieces of a reflective jigsaw which seeks to build capacity for reflection in teams across different settings. We hope to inspire others to add to the voices by suggesting 'this is one way of doing it' rather than 'this is how you do it'.

Chapter 2: Traditional approaches to reflective practice – history, aetiology, evidence and approaches

Jon Patrick, Katharine Russell and Adam Polnay

Introduction

In this chapter, we will hopefully guide you through some of the background evidence and approaches used traditionally within reflective practice in the UK. I, Jon, will start by reviewing the landscape that we are placed in to be reflective, then Katharine will illuminate the evidence base before Adam takes us on a tour of how psychoanalytic ideas are applied in reflective practice.

1. The landscape we find ourselves in – Jon Patrick

Across the UK's professional social care and mental health disciplines, the idea of being reflective as an integral part of a clinician's work and responsibilities has increasingly shaped the topography through which we move on a daily basis. For example, within nursing, the *Review of Mental Health Nursing* (Department of Health, 2006) and the *10 Essential Shared Capabilities for Mental Health Practice* (NHS Education for Scotland, 2011) both acknowledge the importance of professionals being reflective practitioners. The recently revised Nursing and Midwifery Council Code is also hugely focused on requirements for nurses to be reflective, and providing evidence of being a reflective practitioner is now an essential requirement for future professional revalidation. The General Medical Council's *Good Medical Practice* (General Medical Council, 2013) also states that all doctors should regularly reflect on their own practice. In an influential document, *New ways of working for applied psychologists in health and social care*, psychologists are encouraged to lead on reflective practice provision (Department of Health, 2007).

Within this wider geography, the literature, which Katharine will helpfully describe below, reflects a growing recognition of the importance of this work in mental health settings more specifically. On acute inpatient wards there has been a particular emphasis on reflecting in groups since the policy implementation guidance for Adult Acute Inpatient Care Provision came into being. This states:

> 'It is essential that staff have the opportunity to jointly reflect on the impact of the day-to-day work with users and their families in order to feel informed and empowered to make the most effective interventions.'
> (Department of Health, 2002, p33)

This guidance draws a clear link between staff being able to jointly reflect and being able to deliver the most effective interventions. This idea has been further promoted in the *Ten Essential Shared Capabilities Framework* (Hope, 2004), which identified an ongoing commitment to personal and professional development through supervision and reflective practice as a necessary part of workforce development.

Sadly, as forensic practitioners will be all too aware, things do not always go smoothly or well in forensic environments. Bad things can and do happen when containing some of the most complex and disturbed people in society. A number of enquiries into the care and treatment of patients who have offended or are contained within forensic settings have all either alluded to the importance of staff engaging in a reflective process or have recommended it directly. These include the Fallon Inquiry into the Personality Disorder (PD) unit at Ashworth Hospital (Fallon, 1999), which deals with how staff and patients became caught in a pernicious, toxic and dangerous dynamic that led to serious breaches of security. Similarly, *Falling Shadow: One Patient's Mental Healthcare 1978–1993* (Blom-Cooper, 1995) and *Too Close to See* (Mental Welfare Commission, 2009) both illustrate how staff teams that are not being asked to formally reflect on both their relationships with and treatment of patients can lead to catastrophic, fatal consequences.

As well as these more troubling episodes, there have been a number of positive developments within forensic mental health in the UK that have provided the backdrop and impetus for development of reflective practice in Forensic Services. Locally and more latterly in Scotland, the Scottish Group of Forensic Clinical Psychologists' *Position Paper on Psychological Approaches to Personality Disorder in Forensic Mental Health Settings* (Russell, 2016), outlined the need for a comprehensive, considered and reflective approach to the care and treatment of PD – something which reflective practice could be considered integral to.

Hovering above our Scottish relational geography, there have been a number of UK documents that have outlined the need for staff to have access to reflective practice. These include the Royal College of Psychiatrists *College Centre for Quality Improvement – Standards for Psychotherapy in Medium*

Secure Units (Macallister & Jacobs, 2012). This helpfully synthesises some of the evidence with regards to the importance of provision of reflective practice in forensic settings. A second document that stresses the importance of relational security aided by having staff team's come together and engage in reflective practice is the Royal College of Psychiatrists and Department of Health's *See, Think, Act – Your Guide to Relational Security* (Royal College of Psychiatrists, 2015). Similarly, this is also recognised in the Royal College of Psychiatrist's *Standards for Low Secure Services* (Tucker *et al*, 2012).

Reflection itself is regarded as a good thing in forensic mental health settings: from a hypothetical standpoint; from anecdotal staff report; as well as what is available in the literature (Craissati *et al*, 2015; Macallister and Jacobs, 2012). We will outline more about the latter in the middle of this chapter and then Adam will write about the process of reflective practice itself from a more traditional psychodynamic viewpoint after I outline some of what we feel this kind of process can help with. For our purposes, we are looking primarily at reflective practice groups (RPGs) as the key vehicle for helping staff to make sense of their experiences in forensic mental health settings. The group provides a unique opportunity to allow different perspectives to be heard and to allow alternative facets about patients, staff and the patient-staff system to be made sense of.

The aim of RPGs is therefore to encourage staff to discuss and consider the relationships that patients are having between each other, which may be causing conflict in the environment, as well as relationships between patients and staff, which may be causing conflict on the ward or within the staff team. Additionally, RPGs should consider the relationships between staff, where there may be conflict between staff members about how particular patients or patient groups are managed. In addition, staff are encouraged to consider how patients relate to themselves, ie how do they tolerate distress, their levels of self-esteem and self-efficacy, and how they manage moods. Staff are also encouraged to think about how they manage or cope themselves in relation to their work. Alongside this, RPGs should be able to facilitate reflection about the organization and how it is functioning as a whole as well as its relation to staff, teams and patients.

This may seem like a lot, but it encapsulates the wide range of interpersonal and intrapersonal dynamics that staff are having to manage when they come to work. Importantly, they may not be consciously aware that this is something they are doing. Rather than other aspects of staff supervision and management which focus on task-related activities that are pertinent to the fulfillment of job roles, ie the activities often laid out in job descriptions, RPGs are a space to think about the fundamental role of managing relationships with others that is necessary to the fulfillment of many of these tasks, but that is often not clearly stated or recognised as being required. Schön (1983) noted that the knowledge implicit in some of the actions taken is hard to describe as it has been developed intuitively and internalised.

The explicit purpose and hope therefore when working with RPGs is to allow a space where staff can notice how they are affected by patients and process communications from patients rather than 'act out' with them. Hopefully, this will allow staff to minimize splitting and reduce the negative emotional impact of forensic work, in turn creating more resilient and caring teams. Such teams are more able to make sense of patient communications and notice risky situations developing and work to minimize and obviate these.

Together with this explicit task there is an implicit set of outcomes for RPGs also; these are to reduce staff sickness and burnout, improve morale and, importantly, to work on increasing the team's empathy towards patients. Hopefully, this allows for greater amounts of structured clinical care to take place and ultimately help the patients engage and respond to treatment.

2. The current state of play of the evidence base for reflective practice groups – Katharine Russell

As a group of practitioners, we are comfortable providers of, and participants in, reflective practice groups. However, we are also aware that RPGs are relatively poorly researched in terms of quantitative data and rigorously controlled studies. In writing this chapter it has been interesting for me to again review the literature and examine the studies and data that are available. It does appear that the increasing focus in policy documents on the importance of RPGs is resulting in the increasing use of RPGs and associated evaluation of the implementation of new RPGs in terms of evaluating different models and looking at different outcomes.

When looking at the literature it is clear that researchers have looked at a range of methods to assess effectiveness; these, however, are predominantly qualitative, eg survey, semi-structured interview and thematic analysis. Whereas most studies in mental health focus on outcomes for patients, in the limited research that has been done, the primary focus of research into RPGs, in terms of change outcome, is staff wellbeing. The benefits for patients are not presumed to be absent but are seen to be affected indirectly; for example, improved staff wellbeing will ensure a more empathic, effective workforce.

From my reading of the literature, it is clear that within reflective practice groups there are a number of different formats. This can vary from closed groups meeting regularly once a week to reflect on ongoing staff–staff and staff–patient dynamics and how different patients can impact on team functioning, to processes that last two to three days set up to reflect on a recent incident or event. A good summary of different models is summarized in a paper by Jones (2014) on models used in social work but that also reflects models used in health settings. This latter model, *Critical Reflection* (Fook & Gardner, 2007; 2013), was developed to encourage staff to reflect in small group discussions, to challenge assumptions and look at potential changes in thinking and implications for practice. In my experience, the motivation for reflective practice can often increase after some critical incident but the issue with introducing RPG as a response to an incident is that the energy and motivation to maintain this can be lost over time.

The first variation has been described by Warman and Jackson (2007) as an opportunity for staff to share concerns, difficulties and challenges about their work with clients. The purpose is not necessarily to make changes or find solutions, rather to build a reflective capacity in the participants and the team by looking at the underlying meaning of client behaviour and communication, the ways in which clients can impact on staff at an emotional level and how this impacts on how staff engage and care for clients, the impact of past adverse experiences on the development of future experiences and relationships, and how particular client populations groups can impact on wider staff and organizational culture (Warman & Jackson, 2007).

A different model developed by Ruch (2007a; 2007b; 2009) in child and families work is organised where a participant presents a case and then the group members discuss; initially without posing questions. The groups are asked to stay in 'wondering mode' rather than 'problem solving mode' in order to encourage members to maintain a reflective stance (Jones, 2014). Many of the evaluations of RPGs have been done on pilot groups, presumably to evidence that they will be beneficial in the long-term. For research purposes some of these groups are time-limited and only open to certain staff members whereas in our real-world experience, RPGs are just regular features in a weekly or monthly diary and manage different staff changes and service developments.

Perhaps most well known in psychiatric care is the Balint group. Developed in the 1950s to support GPs in their work, these groups were set up so that participants could present cases with a different kind of focus. These groups were developed to support doctors to consider their patient beyond what they presented in the consulting room and are a closed group that meets regularly with a psychoanalyst leader. The cases that the group were encouraged to present were patients that were hard to engage or that had an emotional impact on the doctor. Once the participant has presented their case, the leader encourages discussion in the rest of the group about the emotional impact of hearing the case on the group and encourages discussion about what may be going on for the patient. Towards the end of the session the presenter will be encouraged to re-engage and discuss what has been helpful or not helpful in listening to the groups process.

These groups are now run all over the world. Research on Balint groups has indicated that participation in the group improves the communication skills of the participants (Bascal, 1972) and changes the types of patients the doctors say they have difficulties with (Dokter *et al*, 1986). Kjeldmand *et al* (2004), in a comparative study, found those doctors who were in a Balint group reported better control of their work situation, had less frequent thoughts that a particular patient should not attend for a consultation and were less likely to presume that psychosomatic patients were a time-consuming burden (Rüth, 2009).

We have, of course, noticed the similarities between these models in terms of reflective stances but the differences in practice can also impact on the potential for research in terms of clarity around memberships, frequency, intended outcomes and how they relate to actual outcomes. Groups set up around a particular event that are 'one-off', may have different intended outcomes to those that run regularly and frequently around the day-to-day difficulties of working with particular clients, which capture events as and when they arise, particularly in the long-term. We did not find a study that compared the effectiveness of these different types of formats on outcomes such as staff wellbeing, team cohesion and empathic understanding of clients.

Overall, there are a number of positive outcomes associated with RPGs for staff (Harley, 2017; Heneghen *et al*, 2014). Creating a safe space is a theme that appears in a number of studies (Heneghen *et al*, 2014). This was one of the findings of O'Neill *et al* (2019), in a study with liaison psychiatry nurses in an Emergency Department. Similarly, McAvoy (2012) found that creating and maintaining a safe environment was a key task for the facilitator but also that staff actively participate in the RPG in accordance with how psychologically safe they feel in the group.

McVey and Jones (2012) similarly conducted a study looking at themes in feedback from five RPGs in cancer care services and found that feeling safe was an important theme. They described that this was associated with a protected space, nonthreatening/non-judgmental stance and feeling able to admit imperfections. The issues of staff feeling safe within the group again arose in a staff survey on attitudes conducted by Hartman and Kitson (1995). Staff that found the RPG unhelpful were more likely to note concerns about the safety of the space and the contribution level of other participants.

The facilitator competence and stance are closely linked to creating a safe space. Lees (2017), in an independent evaluation of an RPG project in Brighton and Hove Children's Services, using qualitative data, described RPGs as providing 'time and space to think' as part of several findings but also highlighted that facilitation was key and noted the important functions of maintaining the structure as well as managing group dynamics and 'challenge'.

Improving capacity to manage the emotional impact of work is another theme that I found was frequently highlighted. Powell and Howard (2006) conducted an initial evaluation of RPGs in a group of trainee clinical psychologists and reported participants frequently cited the group as being helpful in managing the emotional impact of work but there was less evidence that there was a behaviour change as a result of this insight.

Platzer *et al* (2000a, 2000b) looked at two cohorts of postgraduate nursing students in their study and focused on processes as well as outcomes. Their outcomes showed that staff felt more confident, more able to empathise with others and were more assertive about offering challenge to poor practice. Furthermore, they reported being able to think more critically about their own practice, found improvements in applying theory to practice and having greater awareness of their professionalism and value base. The processes identified as helpful were receiving validation, encouragement and reassurance from the group, having the opportunities to learn from others' experience and perspectives, being more constructively challenged or criticised and feeling less isolated.

Similarly, Lees (2017), in the study described above, looked at processes for reflection as well as outcomes and found the positive key themes to be: expressing and examining emotional experience, acknowledging and expressing shared experience and resonance, expressing and hearing personal perspectives from others (which could highlight diverging views), wondering and listening and drawing out.

The combination of providing a safe space and improving capacity to manage emotional impact of work underlines the importance of Reflective Practice in supporting staff with achieving the balance of both working in a professionally competent manner at work whilst also allowing the space to be open and honest about the impact of the work on themselves as an individual and a professional, and to process that in a meaningful and helpful way. It allows staff to reflect on the interaction of their professional life and personal experience.

Further studies have also highlighted positive outcomes for staff. Dickey *et al* (2011) used a mixed-methods study and found that staff of all grades and experience positively rated an RPG. Positive consequences were noted to be increased personal resilience, increased team cohesion and increased ability to deliver high quality care as a result of attending. Vachon *et al* (2010a) found improvements in critical thinking in a study looking at the use of RPG to help occupational therapists utilise research evidence in their practice. An improvement in team functioning was also noted in studies by Dawber (2013a, b). Finally, Heneghen *et al* (2014) found that common positive outcomes in RPGs run by clinical psychologists were staff wellbeing, service cultures and teamwork. Common challenges were engagement, group dynamics and a lack of management support – all trials we have faced in our own reflective practice at various times!

Overall, there is moderate qualitative evidence for RPGs with largely positive findings about effectiveness for staff wellbeing but a lack of quantitative data about this. This is clearly an area that requires further study alongside more rigorous studies looking at the impact and process of RPGs for staff. Where there are continued increases in numbers of RPGs being delivered around the country there would seem to be significant opportunities and need to look at the evaluation of the impact of groups on staff, patients, teams, organizations and the milieu.

Nevertheless, I think it's important to stress that absence of evidence does not mean evidence of absent effect. The summary of studies in terms of process and outcome clearly highlights the value staff place on RPGs. Increasing ability to manage emotions, solve problems, increased reflection-in-action and improved team cohesion are recurrent themes. There were also similarities in the challenges identified, ie conflict between work demands and being freed up to attend RPG, the role of the facilitator and their ability to create a 'safe space'. Few studies were able to evidence changes in ward atmosphere or patient outcomes. However, there is an acknowledgment that this is harder to measure in a controlled way given the many variables that can affect patient outcomes. We all feel that more comprehensive and longitudinal research is required – and this has become an increasing priority in our work settings.

3. Key principles of multidisciplinary team reflective practice groups – Adam Polnay

In view of the dynamics described in Jon's introduction, analysis of patients' relationships with clinicians as caring figures and clinicians' responses, both helpful and unhelpful, needs to be a primary focus of treatment. This work is a central aim of multidisciplinary team RPGs. To create a safe and well-functioning clinical team, it is vital that staff are:

- aware of emotional responses to the work
- recognise that these are normal
- make time to reflect on and process these responses in appropriate settings.

(Johnston & Paley, 2013; Thorndycraft & McCabe, 2008).

These are all factors that have been remarked on by Katharine in her section, above, about the evidence base. Led by appropriately skilled facilitators, multidisciplinary team RPGs can provide a regular, safe, confidential, non-judgmental and supportive setting for the whole clinical team to reflect together on their interactions with patients and understand some of the dynamics that they are part of.

Practical principles for reflective practice groups

Prior to going ahead and setting up an RPG, we have found that initial teaching about interpersonal dynamics is helpful to generate interest in this area and to increase clinicians' sense that making time to stop and reflect is a priority. These teaching sessions may then facilitate the clinical team, in due course, to request a more regular reflective practice group.

To create a secure frame for the group, the group facilitator works with team leaders to establish a regular time and a confidential space for the team to meet. In the initial RPG sessions and when new members join, the primary task of the group is explained. Namely, to provide a regular, non-judgmental setting to explore clinical encounters with patients, team dynamics and organizational issues (Patrick *et al*, 2018). To help with this task, a supportive and empathic stance is taken by group members, led and modelled by ourselves as the facilitator. Clinical situations and encounters with patients are explored, with a constructively challenging and non-collusive stance from the facilitator where needed.

There is a confidentiality boundary, with appropriate limits to this, for the sessions, which helps participants to express their countertransference feelings so these can be thought about and processed. The edges of the boundary we usually hold are around issues to do with risk of harm to group participants, patients or others in their system. Everyone is invited to participate in discussion. Varying perspectives are encouraged as people will 'hold' different parts of an overall clinical situation.

We are all very clear that RPGs aren't therapy for staff. The facilitator keeps the focus on work situations and staff members' responses to these, as opposed to the personal exploration found in therapy. The facilitator will step in when needed to keep members feeling safe and also to ensure that no one individual is 'in the spotlight'.

Participants keep responsibility for their work (Hawkins & Shohet, 2007). The RPG is separate and distinct from other formal patient management meetings, such as ward rounds. In our experience, this allows staff to explore their responses to patients more easily and with less pressure to try and 'solve' problems too soon, which can foreclose the discussion.

Our view of the role and stance of facilitator

RPG facilitators are not part of the teams that they are helping to reflect. This 'outsider' status preserves facilitators' ability to hold a democratic, neutral stance in relation to the teams they work with. Furthermore, it will prevent them becoming part of the problems they are trying to assist with. It is important that the same RPG facilitator runs the sessions for a particular group, to allow a trusting relationship to develop and to provide consistency (Patrick *et al*, 2018).

The role and stance of the facilitator draws on relational therapy approaches, Balint group practice, group-work leadership skills, systemic approaches, and skills as an educator (Johnson *et al*, 2004; Johnston & Paley, 2013; Scanlon, 2012). Our main role is to facilitate and conduct the discussion and exploration by the group, as opposed to being overly didactic. This allows the clinical team to work things out at their own pace and provides time needed to name, reflect on and process feelings. An RPG is not primarily about gaining factual knowledge from an 'expert' facilitator about what is happening. Rather than coming in and giving a verdict on what is being said, the facilitator aims to tolerate and keep in play contradictory and multiple views as expressed by group members (Johnson *et al*, 2004). This helps generate and preserve a plurality of ideas, which is important as no one person can pick up on all aspects of the patient. This stance can also help teams to reflect on 'splitting' (Gabbard, 2010) within the team.

Drawing on psychodynamic and group leadership skills, I aim, as the facilitator, to keep the group thinking and exploring about what is being discussed, including looking for meaning and asking for feelings in relation to the clinical work. Without being overly didactic, the facilitator attends to keeping the group on task. In any group when difficult situations are being discussed there may emerge a 'flight from the group' phenomena whereby the group starts to discuss or criticise people who are outside the RPG. The role of the facilitator here is to steer the group back to task, perhaps using humour, observation, or empathy (eg noticing how hard it may be to talk about the work with the patient).

We have outlined elsewhere a suggested competency framework for RPG facilitators, which can be used to inform appropriate training for facilitators (Patrick *et al*, 2018).

Overview of a typical RPG session

Combining observation of RPGs with qualitative accounts from participants, McAvoy (2012) developed a model that conveys the course of a typical RPG:

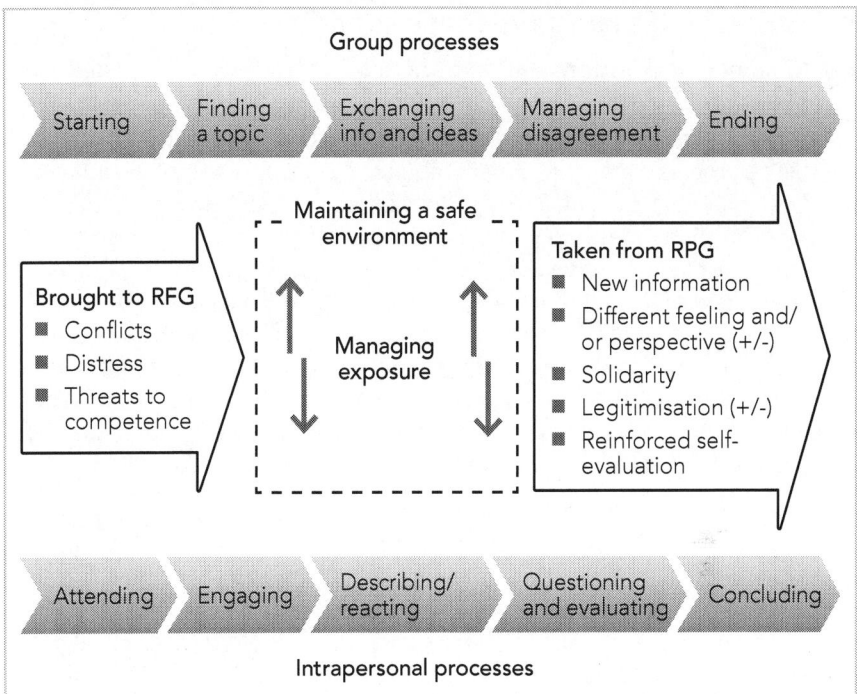

A reflective practice session usually starts with members introducing themselves as needed, and (restating) the key principles of the group for the benefit of new members and as a reminder for existing members. As the facilitator, we have all recognised that a key role at the start of the session (and potentially throughout) is setting and maintaining group frame and norms.

There then typically follows a phase where the group finds a topic. One or more group members then talk about a clinical situation, which may include conflicted feelings, perceived threats to competence, or complicated clinical situations. With the topic decided and some 'material' brought to the group there follows a phase of exchanging ideas as different group members respond to what they have heard or describe their own direct experience of the clinical situation. Understanding deepens as the group 'tries to digest' aspects of the clinical encounter 'that could not be seen before' (Rüth, 2009). There sometimes emerge differences in opinion or disagreements, and here our role is to help the group to make use of these divisions in the service of understanding the interpersonal situation better. From an individual participant's perspective, the various views and discussion put forward by the group often result in the participant re-evaluating their initial responses.

Processes underlying reflective practice groups (RPGs)

Containment of emotions and experiences

Containment refers to a fundamental process of finding understanding and managing our feelings through certain interactions with others (Gabbard, 2010). The process starts with us communicating with trusted others about our distressing or confusing feelings and experiences. All being well, the other person (or a group) notices what is being communicated, reflects on the impact on them, and then can hand something back (Bion, 1962) to us about our distress in a modified and acceptable form. This interaction leads us to feel more 'contained' about our original experience, ie we have a sense of being understood and that our experience is more bearable than we first felt. It is well recognised that a considerable element of patients improving in psychiatric hospitals is due to their distress and disturbance being 'contained' by interactions with steady, calm and receptive staff (Adshead, 1998).

RPGs can increase clinicians' capacity to act as a container for patients' experiences. The safe and supportive setting is conducive to staff noticing and exploring what is happening in the patient's mind and how the clinician feels in the patient's presence. The RPGs can then help clinicians to make sense of their feelings in relation to the patient, ie to explore what it is about the patient's sense of himself or others that ends up evoking certain feelings in others. Finding understanding and support in RPGs (Adlam, 2016) may increase clinicians' capacity to tolerate their experience, so that it may be more possible to sustain working with disturbing patients, without, for example, becoming as short-tempered or overwhelmed with a sense of hopelessness.

Clarifying clinicians' responses to patients

Even for the most experienced and skilled clinicians, our own perception of and responses to patients, may not always be clear to us (Rüth, 2009). Bringing a clinical encounter for discussion with other clinicians in the RPG allows for multiple perspectives to emerge, and for other group members to 'pick up' aspects of the patient-clinician interaction that the clinician was initially unaware of (but may have been affected by). One example could be in an RPG, a clinician realised he had been acting somewhat harshly towards a patient due to feelings of dislike towards the patient that he previously had only been dimly aware of.

Exploring responses in the wider system to working with patients

If staff members' feelings in relation to patients are not adequately named and processed, as well as having the risk of counterproductive responses to the patient, these feelings may, without realising it, be displaced onto other parts of the organization (Moore, 2012). It is also recognised (Moylan, 1994) that an institution can pick up difficulties and defenses of their particular client group. An institution or system can struggle to contain the distress and disturbance from working with many patients who may have similar kinds of difficulties. For example, a general ethos within staff in a forensic institution may be somewhat suspicious, or the staff ethos within an anorexia nervosa service may be to over-work and not take proper lunch-breaks. In RPGs, through observing and discussing these systemic responses, 'staff are more likely to be aware of when [these are] happening and to use feelings to tackle the problem in a direct and appropriate way' (Moylan, 1994).

Managing the level of emotional contact with patients

For clinicians who are overly emotionally disturbed by clinical work, RPGs can help provide perspective and objectivity; and for clinicians who have become more detached and inured to clinical work, the groups encourage closer awareness of the emotional aspects (Evans, 2016). We, as facilitators, have recognised a need to adapt according to the level of emotional contact of the clinician – taking a more exploratory stance that is attentive to the emotional aspects of the clinical work to help bring someone closer; and a more supportive or intellectual stance for someone overly emotionally connected to allow permission to step back and leave work at the door.

Working with the parallel process within the group itself

When discussing a disturbing or difficult staff-patient encounter in a group, sometimes a 'parallel process' can emerge in the group itself (Scanlon, 2012). Namely, one person (or more) becomes more identified with the patient's position and another (or others) with the staff member's position. A version of the situation that is being discussed by the group actually gets replayed within the group itself. If carefully managed, this may provide an opportunity for greater understanding of the situation under discussion as it becomes a real 'live' situation rather than something more abstract.

It is the facilitator's role to manage this situation, according the particular circumstances and level of sophistication and development of the group. With a reasonably secure and experienced RPG, it may be possible for the facilitator to sensitively draw attention to the parallel process, normalise this, and attempt to use it as a vehicle for understanding. In other situations, the facilitator may need to fairly quickly reduce the level of affect in the group, use supportive explanations, and perhaps steer the group onto less emotionally charged ways of exploring the topic in hand.

Journey's end?

We hope that this tour through one type of reflective setting has given you a sense of the 'whys', 'hows' and 'whats' of our perspective. We acknowledge that 'there is more than one way to skin a cat' and, at the risk of becoming overly metaphorical(!), we have all tried to keep people in the reflective tent rather than treating RPGs as some mysterious and exclusive club. You will hopefully have seen that there is still work to be done in demonstrating more concretely what we feel convinced about anecdotally, that RPGs are a way to help us, the patients and our organizations engage in the work of caring more effectively and safely.

Chapter 3: Cognitive Analytic Therapy – the model

Jenny Marshall and Jamie Kirkland

> *'CAT's richness as a model of the self, mind and emotion means there is much work to be done outside of the therapist's room.'*
> (Steve Potter, 1999)

Introduction

In this chapter, we introduce the CAT approach as an individual therapy, defining core features of the model, but specifically expand it as a model that is being applied more widely across teams and systems. The approach has been adapted for use beyond therapy and we explore some of these uses within indirect work, highlighting commonalities and differences within formulation, consultancy and specifically reflective practice.

What is the CAT approach?

CAT was developed by Anthony Ryle during the 1970s and 1980s (Ryle, 1990; Ryle & Kerr, 2020) as a collaborative time-limited psychotherapy firmly set within the UK's National Health Service (NHS). CAT was developed initially for working directly with adults in outpatient services but it has continued to develop and increasingly more has been written about its use within specialities, such as with young people (Jenaway & Mortlock, 2008; Barnes, 2016), people with learning disabilities (Lloyd, 2011), older adults (Hepple & Sutton, 2004) and with specific populations such as forensics (eg Pollock *et al*, 2006; Ramm, 2010). It is listed on the University College London's core competencies website as a distinct therapy[1] and there are organizations accrediting and supporting CAT therapists across the world.

Importantly, CAT is a transdiagnostic model not developed solely with one presentation in mind, and there is increasingly positive research demonstrating its efficacy for a range of presenting difficulties (eg Calvert & Kellett, 2014) and specifically a range of personality disorders (eg Clarke *et al*, 2013).

---

1   www.ucl.ac.uk/pals/research/clinical-educational-and-health-psychology/research-groups/core/competence-frameworks-15

Defining CAT

CAT is a relational approach (Ryle & Kerr, 2020). This model acknowledges that human beings are born primed to relate to each other. CAT believes that we learn relational patterns early in life which we continue to use later in life both with others and ourselves. This relational understanding can provide a powerful way of describing patterns of thinking, feeling and behaving that can lead to distress and conflict, both at a one-to-one and also at a broader level in society (see www.acat.me.uk).

Core features: Reciprocal roles

Central to the understanding of CAT is the concept of 'reciprocal roles'. Inspired in part by object relations theory (see Ryle, 1982) and further developed by Leiman (2002), it suggests that a person learns and internalises positions, or roles, when relating to others. These roles form the basis of interactions with others through behaviours that occur when moving from one role position to another. Simply put, we treat people in the way we anticipate they will treat us, and from the way others relate to us we learn how to relate to ourselves.

To demonstrate this I am going to use the reciprocal roles of loving to loved (Kirkland & Baron, 2015). A child who is loved by its parent experiences not only the role of 'being loved', but the child also observes what it is like to be the loving caregiver. This experience includes feelings, thoughts, actions, behaviours, indeed anything that being in that role leads the child to experience. As a result, both positions, the *doing to* loving role and the *done to* loved role, are therefore learned and internalised by the child; loving to loved, as shown in Figure 3.1. What is key to understanding the development of reciprocal roles is that the child can alternate between both positions, such as receiving love from a parent (other to self) and giving love to a doll (self to other). By experiencing both roles the child then internalises both (loving to loved). One may therefore consider internalising loving one's self as the basis of the development of self-worth.

Figure 3.1

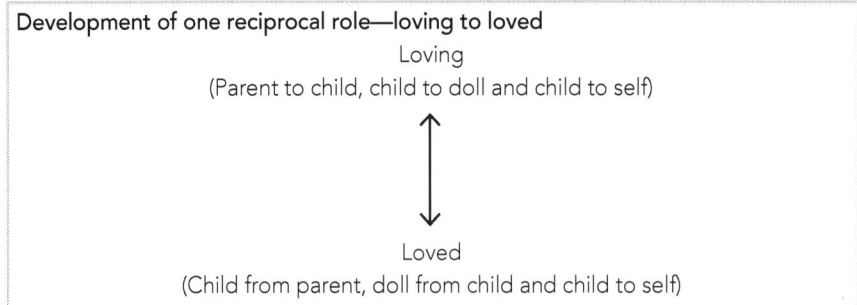

One role exists in relation to the other and so is termed 'reciprocal'. The development of a reciprocal role, therefore, is 'other to self', 'self to other' then 'self to self' – or, to put it simply, *'You do to me; I do to you; I do to myself'*. This is an extremely useful concept in CAT. It acknowledges that a person relates to others by taking up a role position which asks that other person to reciprocate the role. This in turn becomes known as a *reciprocal role enactment*. To make sense of this is extremely helpful when working with staff teams. It allows for different positions, or voices, to be acknowledged. Staff often will not all feel the same towards an offender. They will take up different positions. They will be invited into reciprocal role enactments by the position the offender takes up in relating to them. Understanding this can be invaluable in the reflective process. Too often, being unaware of these enactments can lead teams to feel 'split' or silenced simply because differing views are held. The strength of the CAT approach is that each position is valid and is acknowledged.

Healthy personality development allows for a range of these 'reciprocal roles', where a person can subtly shift between them depending upon need, circumstance, and so on. However, as an example, a person whose early experiences are predominately abusive and neglecting may develop a limited repertoire of roles to call upon and so they may get stuck in limited patterns of interaction. Considering the two positions 'abusing–abused' and 'neglecting–neglected': either they are the abuser (offender) forcing the other to take up the abused position (victim); or through internalising both the abusing–abused roles, they abuse themselves (through self-harm); or they enact the neglected position (fear of abandonment leading to no close relationships) so others neglect them; or internalise the neglecting to neglected position through lack of self-care.

Core features: Reciprocal role procedures (RRPs)

In order to maintain or escape from these roles, a series of thoughts, feelings and behaviours, called *reciprocal role procedures* (RRPs), are brought into play. These are described as *traps* (vicious circles), *dilemmas* (either/or thinking as the only solution) and *snags* ('I would if only...'). Examples of these procedures are set out in a self-report questionnaire used by CAT practitioners called The Psychotherapy File (2000). Traps are things we believe we cannot escape from; our solutions seemingly making things worse, confirming our failure. Dilemmas are decisions we make based upon a belief that there are limited options, with our answers not perfect but better than a perceived worse-case scenario. Snags are characterised by lines such as, 'I want to change my behaviour but...'. They can be seen as behaviours that hold a person back, stopping them from moving forward in their life.

It is these RRPs that can often become unhelpful and so cause difficulties for the person or the team. For example, in Figure 3.2, a person may feel themselves to be lonely and describe this as being in the 'neglected' role and so believe others are 'neglecting' them. In order to escape this, they may desperately seek out others, but they may do so in such a way as to appear to be neglecting the needs of that other person. They might describe this as a dilemma such as, *'Either I'm involved with someone and likely to get hurt or I don't get involved and stay in charge, but remain lonely'*.

Figure 3.2

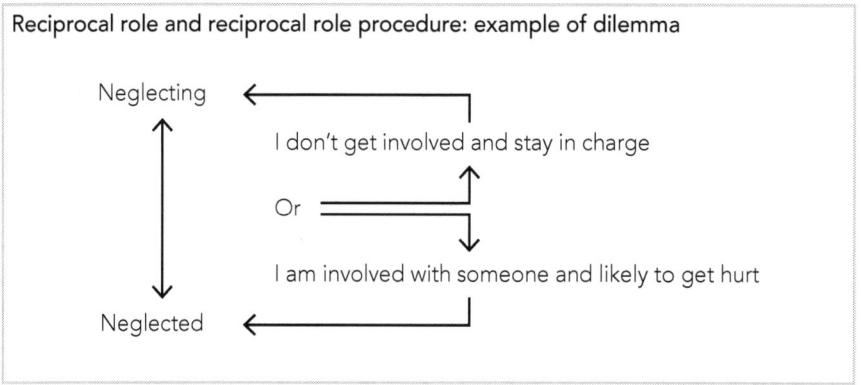

Reciprocal role and reciprocal role procedure: example of dilemma

Core features: reformulation, recognition and revision

It is with these concepts to guide that the clinician works alongside the client or patient or team in order to 'reformulate' the presenting problem, or target problem. After a relatively few number of sessions, a letter is written to the client containing a succinct, empathic and focused narrative of what has been learned in the early sessions, described as a re-formulation to acknowledge the client has already formulated their difficulties. The aim of the CAT approach is to acknowledge the inherent abilities that the person previously tried to use to survive, when faced with many challenges, but unhelpful procedures (traps, dilemmas and snags) have developed and contributed to a 'stuckness' in that person's life or repeating patterns of unhelpful behaviour. A fuller explanation of the development of prose reformulation can be found in Ryle and Kerr (2020).

Core features: Using a diagram or map

A central technique in the application of CAT is to use a diagram, known as a Sequential Diagrammatic Reformulation or SDR, but increasingly referred to as a 'CAT map', to illustrate the concepts of reciprocal roles and reciprocal role procedures. Such a map is worked on collaboratively with the client or team to enable the naming and recognising of unhelpful patterns. As work continues, the map develops new more helpful patterns of interacting or responding.

These are added to the map and called 'exits'. Therefore, a CAT map seeks to provide the client or staff with a shared and consistent language.

Potter (2010) has written about making CAT maps more accessible to staff not trained in CAT. His work focuses mainly upon co-creating with a client in the therapy room. He also describes how this approach to 'mapping' can teach all the staff of a team a 'relationally enhanced' approach to care and treatment. In his work, Potter discusses three approaches to the mapping process, each more complex. Briefly, these are 'sketches', 'life-maps' and 'therapy maps'. The most complex, a therapy map, is more akin to the traditional SDR used in CAT therapy. Of less complexity, he describes life-maps as trying to capture the 'bigger picture and key positions of someone's life experience as a whole'. These are built upon from a series of 'sketches'. 'Sketches' are described as early and impromptu sketches of patterns of interaction that can be drawn from the client's initial accounts of interacting with the self, the others and the world.

Cognitive analytic thinking with offenders

An excellent introduction into the application of CAT with offenders is provided by Pollock et al (2006). The book was key in pulling together developing work in the area of CAT for a range of forensic presentations such as homicide, domestic violence, stalking, psychopathic personality disorder across a range of settings (high secure hospitals and community-based services). Perhaps of interest to our project is that Pollock et al (2006) not only provided a road map for working with offenders using a CAT approach but they acknowledged how the approach can cast its net wider to include a formulation of risk (offender to society) alongside developing a framework to understand staff reactions to the offender in order to work through a CAT understanding of transference and counter-transference).

The aim of a CAT approach has always been to reach a co-constructed, collaboratively shared understanding with the client. Mitzman (2010) writes that forensic patients typically present with themes of early, severe deprivation, neglect and abuse, identity disturbance, emotional volatility, abandonment (both real and feared), substance abuse and chronic self-harming. This can be confusing and anxiety provoking for staff without an understanding of the offender. The strength of a CAT approach is also as a systemic formulation (Ryle & Kerr, 2002). Kerr (1999) describes how a CAT formulation can help provide the 'secure base' for staff to work with disturbed patients. CAT practitioners can utilise the formulation to communicate a detailed understanding of risk procedures to staff, statutory and criminal justice agencies, and agree on an informed, proportionate and collaboratively shared response.

The use of the CAT model and CAT principles has been explored in various service settings with different client groups, illustrating benefits for patients and their staff teams within psychosis services (Kerr *et al.* 2005), within adolescent inpatient services (Mulhall, 2015), within forensic services (Kirkland & Baron, 2015; Marshall *et al,* 2013; Annesley & Jones, 2016), within YMCA services (Shannon *et al,* 2016) and across mental health and learning disability teams (Freshwater & Kerr, 2006; Thompson, 2008). Across these studies, there have been reported improvements in clients, staff reflection and in team functioning.

Using CAT in teams

Lloyd (2011, p22) captures the values of working with staff to improve outcomes for patients succinctly, 'one hour a week at most with a psychologist for a limited number of sessions is a drop in the ocean compared with the many hours the client spends with staff teams'. Lloyd highlights that the lack of a consistent and coherent model which takes into account interpersonal dynamics, can impair the quality of work or could even create or collude with difficulties, thereby maintaining the problems. She goes on to describe how the shared experience of describing and mapping out typical patterns between staff and clients can be an example of promoting psychological awareness in an engaging and accessible way. Staff can then explore difficult moments which can be viewed as 'invitations from clients for staff to get entangled in the clients' (or colleagues') typical problematic interpersonal and intrapersonal patterns in going about their lives' with the potential for staff to reciprocate by going 'head-to-head', 'head off' (divert), 'head in' (rescue) or 'head down' (avoid). The risk of getting involved in an unhelpful collision could reinforce patterns and reduce the chances of more helpful possibilities, whereas self-awareness gained through reflective practice encourages a 'non-defensive certainty' of how we all tend to join the dance to some extent.

Only in recognising how we go 'head first' do we start to negotiate a more helpful position from our position of realistic humility and empathic validation of staff experiences. There is a cautionary note in relation to what are described as 'toxic teams' who do not want to work with psychologists and whereby, in describing or illuminating the problems the staff team have, the team may feel humiliated, exposed, defensive and dismissive and try to push the psychologist out. It is suggested therefore, that a more limited approach could be taken, neither 'joining the dance' nor 'leaving the floor' but trying to take a more 'side by side' position.

The potential value of a cognitive analytic formulation to support the management of individuals within staff teams was noted in a formulated care plan approach to caring for people with borderline personality disorder (Dunn & Parry, 1997). This was echoed by Kerr (1999) who described how CAT was only partially successful, critically due to the absence of a shared understanding by team members as well as other agencies involved, but also how an extended contextual reformulation can offer a means of understanding the difficulties encountered and provide conceptual containment for staff. As an example in subsequent years, Kirkland and Baron (2015) highlighted how explicit reformulation helped educate key multi-agency members not only about the offender but about the part they might play, as well as providing a framework to begin to understand and contain potential team splitting and the resultant anxieties.

Kerr *et al* (2007) concluded that relational models are 'a fundamental requirement for the successful function of such teams and their members'. Carradice (2004) similarly highlighted the value of using CAT to inform indirect working to increase staff empathy, and in being accessible and containing for clinicians, helping to prevent enactments of unhelpful patterns. This led to developing the five session CAT model (Carradice, 2013), an innovative way of working by integrating both staff and client into a here-and-now way of working with relational dynamics and difficulties.

Across service settings, Freshwater and Kerr (2006) conducted a small-scale service evaluation which indicated that the majority of staff expected to make use of CAT in their clinical practice. Qualitative feedback indicated a perceived improvement in understanding or communication with clients, better preventative work, better management and reflection, increased hope by considering exits for those who were stuck, staff having more understanding of their own feelings towards clients and where they might be on the map, and benefits for team functioning with a shared language, a consistent approach and closer communication. Similarly, Thompson *et al* (2008), following introductory training, reported staff had increased self-assessed therapeutic confidence and skill, fostered the development of a shared model and suggested that whole team-trainings may facilitate cohesion and a shared language.

Within forensic settings, Mitzman (2010) argues that contextual diagrammatic reformulation within multidisciplinary teams are 'essential practice', supporting the development of a consistent understanding of the patient's treatment needs. More specifically, contextual reformulation is described as not only highlighting factors related to offending but also to immediate difficulties such as ward dynamics or splits within the team, contributing to a greater risk understanding. Marshall *et al* (2013) described an overarching relational model based on CAT principles to give a common language and support reflective practice for frontline staff. Kirkland and Baron (2015) illustrated how using a relational model such as CAT, and particularly diagrammatic representations (CAT maps) of the formulation, could enable agencies working with individuals to share a common formulation and language. A more formal evaluation within a forensic setting (Doyle *et al*,

2019) indicated that following group reformulation sessions with staff there was increased cohesion between staff members.

The value of CAT has not only been articulated for individuals in therapy and in supporting teams, but for organizations. Shannon *et al* (2016) described the use of cognitive analytic concepts as a flexible, user friendly, valuable and effective relational way of enhancing and transforming working within organizations, teams and with clients. The benefits of this approach was described not only with clients, staff and managers but also throughout processes such as recruitment and human resources. Walsh (2019) describes how conceptual models are needed which explore the interaction between 'person factors' and 'environment factors' and highlights how the organizational response to stressed staff has been to provide counselling or stress management delivered through the occupational health model. She describes how woefully this fails to take into account the complex reasons for ill-health at work, suggesting that ill-health emerges as a result of the interface between the psychology of staff and the psychology of the organization. Walsh (2019) goes on to argue that there is a need to develop better understandings of the psychological relationship between organizational systems and staff minds, and that CAT-informed supervision may be particularly valuable in the context of ongoing change and lack of stability to services, constrained resources and high levels of staff anxiety. She describes CAT as a supervision tool for maintaining the capacity of staff for thinking when they are overwhelmed, professionally challenged by organizational change and threat, and describes CAT as taking the next step from the Hawkins and Shohut (2012) model in providing a meaningful way for staff to understand what is happening between them and their work system.

Carson and Bristow (2015) describe how the way that organizations behave under stress is an indicator of their health and capability just as it is for societies and individuals, and they go on to describe the various ways that a CAT-informed approach can help individuals, colleagues, leaders and teams, describing four key areas: using CAT to help individuals (eg with the example of feeling bullied), working with two people in a team having problems working together, working with teams on their internal and external relationships, and working with leaders to support them incorporating the CAT model into their practice as coaches. They argue that the CAT model describes the world and ourselves in relation to it as interacting systems, the same systems approach needed for understanding human organizations and the relationships in and between them.

CAT and reflective practice

Over recent years, it has become increasingly acknowledged that there is a need to both offer psychologically informed management and treatment to patients with complex presentations, and for structures to be in place to support reflective practice. This has been highlighted as of particular importance within forensic services where staff are likely to be working with offenders who may be resistant, difficult to engage or hostile. However, these recommendations are not just limited to understanding and locating difficulties within the 'complex' patient.

Instead, they highlight the need for team-focused training which explores issues related to team working and team functioning, including: hierarchy, rivalry, conflict resolution and collaboration, clearly indicating the importance of dynamics within the team which may impact on patient care. In addition, leaders having the requisite skills is also referenced, not only requiring leaders to have individual therapist skills but also the skills to be team leaders and political players within the organization.

It is important to briefly touch on concepts such as formulation, consultancy and reflective practice, as they are closely linked but have some core differences. Although there has been much written about formulation, this will only be touched upon briefly here for the purposes of highlighting its relationship with reflection. One definition of formulation has been developed as part of good practice guidelines:

> *'Formulation can be understood as both an event and a process and it summarises and integrates a broad range of biopsychosocial causal factors. It is based on personal meaning and constructed collaboratively with service users and teams.'*
> (Johnstone *et al*, 2011)

Whilst formulation with a service user would be developed collaboratively with personal meaning embedded within, team formulation or consultation with a team can be considered to have the team as the primary client, particularly when the request is due to the team struggling or feeling stuck and therefore drawing heavily on team perceptions and reactions.

Much has been written about reflective practice, from succinct definitions ('reflective practice is a form of in-depth thinking about work activity with the aim of developing as a practitioner') to descriptions emphasising the difficulties in defining such a 'loose term' but highlighting 'a kind of artistry that also involves intuition, flexibility and critical evaluation of one's experience' (Johnstone *et al*, 2011, p2). Regardless of the definition, reflectiveness is seen as an essential aspect of formulation, particularly as it encourages the practitioner to increase their awareness of collaboration, sensitivity, flexibility and their own assumptions.

As such, reflective practice has much in common with team formulation or consultancy in that the primary client in reflective practice is the staff member, team or service. Reflection allows staff to co-construct meaning about the issues brought to reflective practice. In the same way that formulation in therapy can assist the client to develop new insights which may guide changes they choose to make, staff can develop insights which allow them to change their practice should they choose to do this.

As an example, an offender detained in a secure unit had an index offence of attempted murder. On a particular day (related to an anniversary) staff were aware he needed some space and agreed to an unescorted pass for a short time in the local area. He returned late and clearly intoxicated. Upon challenging him he became aggressive, leading to a restraint. Staff reported later that they felt 'let down', angry, disappointed and unsure they had made the correct decision, leading to a tightening of restrictions placed upon him. Individual CAT work allowed the development of an understanding of how early trauma had left him with a strong need to avoid humiliation, to see life as a battle between being in control as the 'top dog' or in a shameful, worthless 'bottom' position. The work was able to understand how this came into play during the index offence and became a way to share with staff his 'pressure' points. In turn, case consultation was able, with permission, to introduce this to staff, who were able to consider how they might best manage risk, nurse him and maintain safety and boundaries through a care plan that attempted to avoid unhelpful enactments. Finally, reflective practice sessions were utilised to help staff think through what these strong enactments left them feeling, and how they were challenged in their professional judgments, how they felt they had lost compassion when they thought he had 'let them down'.

Although there are many different reflective practice models, the roots of reflective practice has predominantly been within the psychodynamic tradition, with Balint groups being the most well developed. Chapter 2 explores these approaches in more detail. In Chapter 4, Steve Potter presents an argument for a CAT approach to running reflective practice before, in Chapter 5, we consider the skills and competencies that may be called upon of facilitators running reflective practice.

Benefits of using the CAT model for reflective practice

The legend of Narcissus tells the story of a beautiful young man who falls in love with his own reflection and, in doing so, loses sight of the bigger picture of his own life. Bound up with the story is that of Echo, in love with Narcissus but herself cursed so she cannot tell him. Unable to both be in dialogue, they both eventually fade away. This is an interesting myth to bring to the theme of reflective practice. We cannot reflect solely on our own; if we do, we are at risk of falling in love with our own story and being unable to see outside perspectives. The CAT model is inherently relational and its value in reflective practice is having a common language for understanding our relational interactions, which are at the heart of providing healthcare on a day-to-day basis. It is ideally placed to be able to use the model to explore such dynamics with our service users, with our colleagues and teams, and with the wider organizational and political context.

Summary

The CAT model is primarily a relational model and, in viewing the self as socially constructed, understands the self in relation to others. As an individual therapy, it is fundamentally collaborative, advocating a side-by-side co-constructed narrative reformulation of difficulties. CAT is increasingly being used as a model for both team formulation, consultancy and reflective practice but research to date has been limited and more rigorous outcome studies are needed. Initial findings suggest that it brings with it benefits of collaboratively engaging teams with a narrative to tell; a story to be understood with the aim of increasing relational awareness of dynamics with reference to their self, team and organizational dynamics.

Chapter 4: Relational mapping – an alternative approach to reflective practice

Steve Potter

Introduction

Mapping out patterns of interaction as an aid to team reflection and discussion is an accessible and versatile alternative to traditional forms of reflective practice. It involves putting key words on big sheets of paper, or a white board, in front of a group such that all can be involved, see what is being said. The aim is to build the resource of reflective capacity of teams on a routine basis such that when there are crises or complex issues there is more goodwill to tolerate diversity and uncertainty of views and feelings.

Over the past 20 years facilitators from different professions, in the varied ways described in this book, have been using 'map and talk' to help mental health teams take a small step back and think about their working relationships with each other, the people in their care and the wider context of organization and society. On a personal note, this author has initiated two days of 'map and talk' training and follow up supervision with over 30 multidisciplinary teams along with many introductory talks about the 'map and talk' approach over the past 15 years.

This chapter describes how reflective mapping works and some of its benefits and limitations. It focuses on the qualities and dimensions of relational awareness that can be enabled. It explores the processes of engaging openly with words and stories and proposes that a distinctive purpose of mapping is to keep the story of a specific experience open long enough for new perspectives to be noticed, named and negotiated. The chapter concludes with a typical example of reflective mapping derived from work in forensic settings but applicable more widely as well. The example explores temporary feelings of helplessness in a team and the pattern of judging the feelings of helplessness as a sign of uselessness and the consequent pressure to appear to do something to demonstrate a capacity to fix things and be professionally useful. Reflective mapping can simultaneously locate this 'helpless means useless' pattern in our heads, in our interactions as colleagues and in the culture and society around us.

As is shown throughout this book, reflective mapping can be applied in different ways. It is versatile and adaptable to different mixes of professions and contexts. It is therefore best not to brand it as a distinctive model or package. The approach goes by various names such as process mapping, relational mapping or, in some contexts, as CAT mapping (indicating its derivation from Cognitive Analytic Therapy). For this chapter it is called 'reflective mapping' or '*map and talk*' for short.

The important debt to CAT concepts is apparent throughout this book but it is best to make clear that reflective mapping is not directly offering therapy, formulation or diagnosis, but simply an aid to shared thinking that subsequently might inform any, or all of these elements of professional practice in their appropriate context. In developing the CAT approach, Ryle's invitation to relational thinking was focused on individual therapy but it increasingly became clear, through working and reworking the ideas pragmatically, that the application of the model as a systemic and contextual approach was also of value (Ryle & Kerr, 2020; Kerr, 1999; Kemp *et al*, 2017).

Seeing and sorting what we are saying to each other

In the following section, four ideas are identified as the conceptual building blocks of reflective mapping. These are: externalising, triangulating, reciprocating and disentangling.

Externalising

Mapping key words as we talk helps us see what we are saying. Negotiating with the words on paper helps renegotiate with our thoughts and feelings and navigate between each other's points of view. Externalising our ideas and feelings on to paper or white board opens a visual gap between the words on our minds and the words produced by the pen. It is a process of doing a double take or having second thoughts. It helps us track, hold, guide and record the conversation. With the aid of what is externalised our inner thoughts can go deeper and/or reach more widely. We can more clearly handle our own and others' projections and associations. In the normal rough and tumble of group conversation it can be easy to doubt what has just been said or deny a link between two points of view, but with the map as an external and fresh recording, it is easier to review and recap and affirm who said or meant to say what. There is room for being in two minds and having mixed feelings. The externalising of thoughts and feelings on to paper and the process of validating different lines of reflection helps people feel they have a part in things and engage with each other.

Triangulating

At the same time, there is a triangulation between our interpersonal relationship as speakers and listeners, our inner reflections and the words on the map. It lessens the individual burden of ideas and makes them less intensely and individually opinionated. The significance of this three-way space of you, me and it (the ideas and feelings on paper) is in the group process that develops. It can be me, the group and the map. It can be me, one idea on the map and the whole map. It can be our work, my role and the pattern named on the map. It can be us, them and the map. The main point is that with triangulation there comes a space for shifting perspective and hovering between one corner of the triangle and the other two. The focus of the triangulation can move around. Through the triangulation there is more room for co-creative thinking and analogies and parallels to be drawn from the emerging discussion led by the mapping process.

Reciprocating

It is through mapping out our different reciprocations that we make our maps relational rather than simply cognitive or mind maps. An emphasis on the relational context to our reflections allows them to be both personal (this is part of me) and collective (this is what we are like) and organizational (this is what the system is like). We have the space through the map to see if our reciprocation is forced, chosen, embedded in a professional role or a fixed way of thinking. We can see how we are reciprocating the push and pull and the call and response of each other's views. The CAT concept of reciprocal role procedures is the working tool for mapping these patterns of interaction (see Chapter 3). Attention is focused on the links and gaps between us. Knowing how we reciprocate helps us see how a specific way of thinking or acting is co-created between us, and we have more chance to share the responsibility. There is more scope for tolerating differences or of finding consensus. Reflective mapping tends to bring into focus familiar patterns between us to reflect on.

These have informally been called dances as in the 'Helper's dance list' (Potter, 2014, see Appendix 1) to emphasise the interactive and reciprocal focus. The idea of mapping out reciprocal role responses as patterns of interaction is to get to know the steps to some of these familiar dances we do as colleagues with each other and with patients. It offers the possibility of changing the steps to the dance and knowing when and why to step out of the dance. One such dance is mapped out and discussed as an example at the end of this chapter.

Disentangling

The fourth conceptual tool is taken from Karen Horney, writing in the middle of the last century (1945) as one of the first to take a relational and interpersonal view and make it accessible. She described her therapeutic work as an inter-subjective process of getting entangled and then disentangling the entanglements (see also Jeremy Safran's similar term of *disembedding*, 2000). It is an apt way of describing the push and pull of the triangulation of patterns of reciprocation. We get caught in each other's feelings and ideas and through mapping them out on paper and the processes of externalising, triangulating and mediating there is greater scope for disentangling.

Empathy is central to effective work, but empathy is a close relative of projection and over identification. We can lose ourselves to another, to a role or to an ideal with too much empathy and then recoil to an excess of detachment and distance. Working intensely with others with deeply troubled and damaged lives requires empathy and we will need to be open to inevitable entanglement but to have the reflective capacity in ourselves and from our colleagues to disentangle ourselves and others. Working relationally and empathically is a continuous process of entangling and disentangling self from others, work roles from personal roles.

In summary, reflective and relational mapping involves externalising our various ideas and feelings about a specific experience and seeing a triangulation between them, us, and the words on paper. In the process we can map out the reciprocal patterns or interactions as the work and personal 'dances we do' and this gives us a greater possibility of disentangling ourselves from the inevitable entanglements of self, system, role, purpose and need. As we sift and sort our points of view, go head-to-head with each other and work side-by-side, we develop a process of greater reflective capacity and relational awareness.

Then and now

The idea of the 'map and talk' process so far is one of creating a shared space which is external and negotiable. If space is the first relational feature of the mapping process, then time is the second. Often in this reflective work we are mapping a local moment in time. The mapping activity helps make transferable and general what is local and specific. To explore our memories of one incident we need to make comparison with similar or contrasting experiences. We are by analogy getting our library of mental maps out as we are mapping a new experience. Our questions are:

- Is what we are seeking to recall and describe in this moment also one of a run of events, something familiar or more out of the ordinary?

- Does it have a parallel with the past?
- Do I know this pattern? Is it deeply woven into me?

As we map out a pattern it is likely that the pattern will invite connection with other stories and memories of other events. For participants in relational mapping, it is this process of contrasting and comparing one time with another that invites a larger picture. One useful side of mapping with different times in mind is to map a future map. This can be one way of introducing a team to reflective practice. Mapping our hopes and fears brings time past, present, and future into play.

Links and gaps

The reflective mapping session is a process of the facilitator and the participants looking at the words on paper and seeing links or spotting gaps. Different people will see different patterns. Some will make links that seem self-evident to them. Others will be aware of gaps or areas on the paper or white board that are unmarked and alarmingly or enticingly blank. The emerging map is an invitation to sustained curiosity. As teams share and give voice to their reflections there are likely to be contrasting points of view and shifts in perspective between small detail and big picture. The process of mapping can do something, and often very little is enough, to validate and hold these contrasting views and reflection. We want to make links but where there are links there are also gaps. It could be argued that lists on flipchart paper or the more common mind maps will do just as good a job at holding court to multiple opinions, but the special contribution of map and talk is its relational or multi-relational approach and its emphasis on the process of shared discovery. Increased capacity for relational awareness within a team or group comes out of this open discussion of links and gaps in search of patterns. There is no such thing as a correct map, only a valued, open and productive conversation arising from the process of making the map by making links, tracing out patterns and seeing gaps.

Between us and them

After a day of training in reflective mapping for all staff involved on one ward, one of the healthcare assistants said, 'I get it, it's not about [the patients], it is about us'. We discussed this view and decided it was about us and them and our awareness of the interactions within and between groups, whether groups of patients or different professional groups. It is easier to talk about them than talk about us. The process of mapping is seeking to open a space between us and them, self and others, the roles I take, or am given and the person I am. The reciprocation is social as much as it is psychological. In the later section entitled Developing relational awareness, this multi-layered and multi-directional process is explored further. One aim of reflective mapping is to generate a sense of our map of our conversation and the patterns of interaction that any one of us could be pulled into or be pushing on to others. The psychoanalytic language and dynamics of transference, projection, defense and identification are very relevant to this interactive process. The emerging map can be a space where possible projections, transfers and identifications can be more easily named, noticed and negotiated. Within any and every reflective practice group there are power dynamics and differences of role and awareness. These psychosocial dynamics of status, personal and professional prejudice and group-think get entangled with institutional and societal forces of racism, ethnic and gender inequalities. The mapping process is helping to recognise and work with these differences by bringing them into helpful dialogue.

An open story method

One part of reflective mapping comes from holding the story of an experience open for long enough for new ideas and feelings to be noticed, named and negotiated. The diagram below illustrates the 'Reflective and relational awareness through mapping and talking together'. In the map shown, this process starts with box 1 and the reciprocal relationship between talking over the details of an incident or event and the shared experience of listening to more than one point of view.

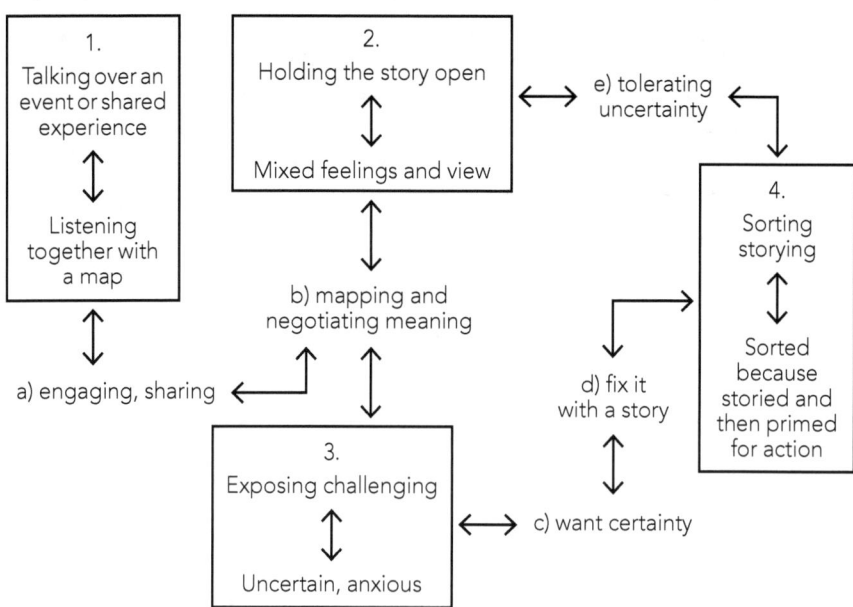

Point a) on the map indicates the way in which 'map and talk' is containing and engaging and offers a scaffolding for further exploration without getting lost on the way. The combination of working with ideas on our minds and words on paper heightens a sense of negotiating meaning. This creates two contrasting experiences with varying degrees of intensity and division. On the one hand there is space (as in box 2) to hold the process open and alive of giving a narrative account or 'storying' the experience. On the other hand, it means tolerating uncertainty (e) and inviting the ability to hover over contrasting points of view, ideas and positions. It involves tolerating ambivalence and mixed feelings.

Such a process of staying open and in dialogue brings with it a very human and understandable experience of challenge, exposure and anxiety, as in box 3. A response is to seek certainty to reduce anxiety. The longing for certainty is partly fulfilled by getting closure around a **fixed story** that shows things are sorted. Evocatively, this can be called sorting by storying the story to meet a need for narrative coherence. The process of diagnosis, the choice of treatment, the pressure between professions to come up with an action are all part of the drive for closure and resolution. Sometimes, it can be passed from one profession to the next.

The psychiatrist says, 'Let's get the psychologist to do a reformulation'.

The nurse says, 'Let's get the psychiatrist to change the medication'.

The social worker says, 'Let's change the care plan, or get the family involved again.'

All or any of these actions may be wise on their own or in combination but the point here, in the middle of reflective practice, is how they push the story on to a premature closure.

Holding the story open is partly to bring people on board with a sense that their views are heard and held in mind and everyone's anxious uncertainty can be tolerated. This helps develop a sense of shared ownership over the course of action that is ultimately proposed. It helps work with the preceding topics in this chapter. It helps see what we are saying, then and now. It offers a framework for depth and perspective and making links and seeing gaps between us and them, self and others, one team and another. It helps build the central equation of reflective mapping in developing relational awareness as highlighted in the next section.

Developing relational awareness

The preceding descriptions have been building up to one conclusion: that map and talk = reflective practice = relational awareness. What is relational awareness? Our relational awareness varies depending on how richly and variously we can hold in mind and make links across three worlds.

A table of three dimensions of relational awareness and qualities that help in its development and orchestration		Dimensions of relational awareness		
		Within us (internal self)	Between us (interpersonal)	Around us (contextually)
Qualities of relational awareness	**Hover and think** Making links or finding gaps between thoughts and ideas, perspective and detail. Curiosity about memories and stories, past, present or future	1. Curiosity and self understanding	2. Dialogue and shared perspectives	3. Roles, systems and social identities
	Shimmer and feel Tolerating the anxiety of mixed emotions, uncertainty and ambivalence; with empathy, sincerity, commitment, courage and sensitivity	4. Ambivalence and authenticity	5. Empathy and involvement	6. Sensitivity to diversity, power and difference
	Participate and do By choosing to do things together sharing responsibility and leadership with self-control and expression that is in role and enabling	7. Self-control and assertive expression	8. Co-creative work and activity	9. Leading, helping and organizing

Firstly, the internal world within us with its different self-states, levels of awareness and authenticity and control. Secondly, the world between us interpersonally with its push and pull of inter-subjective experience through roles, through projection and identification and through meeting whole person to whole person. Thirdly, the impinging, enabling and restricting social systems and cultures that are the context for our lives alone and together. These three dimensions are itemised in detail in the nine-item grid in the table above. Our capacity to be relationally aware depends on others. It is a shared activity and experience. It is a mix of emotional and social intelligence (Goleman, 1995; 2006). It is the awareness that is needed in teams and organizations with complex needs in complicated societies. It counters the desire to simplify and reduce meaning to one dimension or one source.

There are three qualities with which to engage the three dimensions of relational awareness.

These are:

- hovering between ideas and thoughts
- shimmering between emotions and feelings

- moving between participation and observation.

In the table above, the quality of hovering implies the ability to hold in mind contrasting ideas. It varies in focus with each dimension of relational awareness. Similarly, the quality of shimmering in and out of contrasting feelings gives rise to a capacity to tolerate and work with ambivalence and mixed feelings on the one hand, and empathy for and risk of involvement with others and sensitivity to social differences of power on the other. The third quality is that of taking action in a relationally aware way and in the process being able to work with others in a way that shares the give and take of authority and leadership. A fuller account of relational awareness and an introduction to the relational awareness measure is available at www.mapandtalk.com/ram.

The qualities, dimensions and nine items that make up this grid are not all that is needed to describe the many dimensions and qualities to developing relational awareness, but they are sufficient to enter the way of thinking it seeks to evoke.

A key to the relational awareness grid

The following short descriptions largely follow those found in *Therapy With a Map* (Potter, 2020) with some adaptions to fit the focus on relational awareness as part of reflective practice.

Hovering

1. Reflection and self-understanding:
   - Being able to independently hold in one's own mind the push and pull, and orchestration of different ideas, values and narratives with compassion and curiosity
   - Seeing links between past, present and future beliefs, and the interplay between picture and detail in exercising personal judgement
2. Dialogue and debate in sharing ideas:
   - A capacity to negotiate and navigate each other's views and beliefs and reach an understanding that fits mutual tasks and creates space and perspective for more than one story, strategy, or truth
3. Curiosity about values, systems and societies:
   - The resources and the ability to keep making sense of the complex world around in the context of diverse lives, cultures and systems of social power
   - The ability to discern ideology and propaganda from thought and theory and see self and others in and out of roles in society

Shimmering

1. Ambivalence and authenticity:
    - A capacity to accept, assert and value truths within us whilst tolerating ambivalence and the simultaneous presence of contrasting and conflicting feelings
    - A sensitivity to the push and pull of feelings with others through their resonance within us
2. Empathy and involvement:
    - The capacity to share involvement and interact appropriately with each other's feelings without being swayed into one state of mind for long unless it is jointly and sensitively chosen
    - A feeling for changes in mood and moment, harmony, and disorder. A curiosity about the retelling and the re-orchestration of each other's personal and professional experience at work. An ability to see when we are identifying strongly with someone at the risk of loss of perspective on ourselves or others.
3. Feel the diversity and power of us and them:
    - A feeling for, and openness to, cultures and society in a global context wherein multi-local and universal forces and themes interact
    - Compassion and curiosity for what is felt to be fair and not fair based on the ability to put oneself in the shoes of others in the world without losing a personal identity or depriving others of a freedom of identity
    - A capacity to name and negotiate patterns of prejudice within and between work groups

Participating

1. Taking part in role with self-control and expression:
    - The ability to choose and act, to do things with a mix of self-restraint and expression in a way that orchestrates the parts, the roles and the whole sense of self as a person
    - Knowing when and when not to hide or protect self behind a role by living with a divided sense of self and managing by appearances for the sake of a specific task or context.
2. Co-creative work and activity:
    - Being flexible and inventive and able to act together in a focused and sustained way to make things or provide services whether practical or artistic, personal or collective
    - Recognising and valuing the processes and procedures of this shared labour and productivity
    - Delighting in seeing something jointly achieved and mutually owned and attributed. Respect and gratitude for these qualities in others

3. Consenting to ways of leading and being led:
   - Situated knowledge in practice of leadership and organizational roles, and how to participate as leader or follower in and out of role, formally or informally
   - A capacity for a thinking and living with a democracy of ideas and feelings in co-operation with others and systems in society
   - A culture of mutual aid in helping each other contribute

The central assumption is that I cannot know and act upon my ideas and feelings without taking yours into account and those of the people around us. For example: item 8 (*co-creative work and activity*) is dependent for its quality, direction and intensity on the surrounding organizational culture and the variations in individual capacity and willingness for self-control on the one hand and assertion and expression on the other hand. Or item 4 (*ambivalence and authenticity*) is dependent on movement in box 5 (*empathy and engagement*) back and forth between self and others. At the same time this depends on awareness of differences of power and authority as depicted in item 6 (*feel the diversity and power of us and them*).

The grid highlights the qualities and values involved in using mapping to facilitate reflective awareness across the three dimensions. The items in the grid are like instruments in an orchestra, and to extend the analogy the quality of reflective music that is orchestrated will involve a harmony and a movement among all the items on the grid. What we are mapping are the lots of little disruptions of or breakthroughs in our working lives. To do this well we need a framework of values and qualities and the relational awareness is one such framework that is multidisciplinary and works across different models and theories. Thinking along these lines gave rise to the simplifying idea of the *one-thirds rule*: that one third of what is going on as the subject of our reflections is coming from me, one third from others and one third from the system, culture or context around us. The idea of the thirds rule has been a useful catchphrase in reflective practice for teams to double check where the power behind a pattern of interaction is being located.

Feeling helpless does not mean we are useless

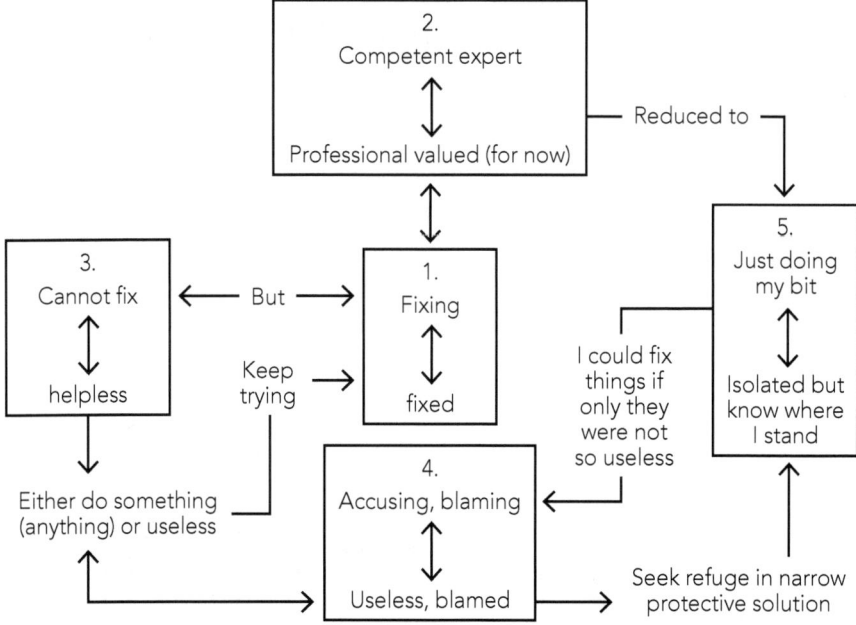

The following example of mapping was first developed to help teams of doctors, psychologists, nurses and allied mental health professionals reflect on the pressures to come up with a diagnosis and respond to the demands from the patient or from management to get things fixed. It seems to capture a recurring pattern in any work with complex needs and systems working under pressure. At the time of writing, it applies to the current crisis in management arising from the coronavirus pandemic. As an example, it highlights the many ways mapping can draw out patterns we pull each other into. The diagram starts at point 1 in the middle of the map with the pressure to fix things. It is voiced like this:

> 'If I can fix things for others, I am competent and feel valued by others.'

The healthy pay off takes us to box 2 on the map and a feeling of doing things as a competent expert valued by colleagues and society. Feeling professionally valued in this way re-enforces pride in fixing things to the point where it may be overvalued, and it becomes a source of shame or blame when things and people for many reasons cannot be fixed. There can be a pattern of relating both within us and in the team and wider society that goes something like this:

> 'If I am fixing things then I am competent and therefore valued which biases me to want to fix things more. We become addicted to fixing things and rush into action too quickly and risk missing out on shared thinking time. This can make us feel like action man or woman, but it

ends up being a fragile and exposed position with us worrying whether we have got things wrong or failed to take people along.'

In such a pattern we feel helpless (box 3 on the map) when we cannot fix things. Feeling helpless about something can shift under the pressure of organizational, professional, or political scrutiny to feeling useless. It might be voiced like this:

'I, or we as a team, will do anything to avoid the painful mix of feeling of point 4 (of self-accusing and blaming or expecting others to be accusing or blaming).'

The pressure to do something becomes strong and risky. Time for reflection is swept away. Position 4 on the map is a dreaded place that can easily be merged with feelings of helplessness. Not knowing what to do now is confused with never knowing what to do. Not 'taking action' is seen as 'weak' or 'neglectful'. The pattern seems to invite a response to do anything rather than feel useless. We will push others to do things. The nurse will prompt action from the doctor, the manager to the team, the politician to the people, the social worker to the psychologist and so on. Or vice versa. The politicians will promise or pretend to do something rather than feel useless for being helpless. Supplementary patterns to this are:

'I could fix things if only the other lot were not so useless. If we are feeling helpless, someone, somewhere else must take the blame and be accused of being useless.'

In the face of this there is a place of retreat in 'just doing my bit'. It is the 'solo-in the-silo' solution. This position (point 5 on the map) is reassuring in part: at least I know where I stand with myself and my small part of the job or professional orbit. It allows some self-esteem and it may result in good quality work but in a fragmented system. With limited awareness of the relationships of the parts to the whole the individual good work may be isolated or swept away. From within the silo/solo position there is the risk of a voice saying:

'I could fix things if only others would work with me or were not so useless or rigid.'

Mapping this 'helpless is not useless' pattern should offer an increase in relational awareness. But it can also point out ways to a better solution. One key response is to tolerate helplessness and not so quickly convert it to uselessness. Finally, a simple example may help highlight this.

I am cycling and have a flat tyre. I have one problem – the flat tyre. I try and fix it but cannot. I feel helpless. Now I have two problems, one with the tyre and one with me feeling helpless. At this point I could seek help and share the problem or tolerate my helplessness. Or I can add a third problem in judging myself as useless. Ultimately, the flat tyre can be fixed with help. The feeling of being helpless can be sorted with self-acceptance, trust in others, or skills training. However, the merger of feelings of helplessness and uselessness create a punctured sense of self (personally or professionally, individually or collectively) wherein I feel I have become the flat tyre. This is a more difficult repair job.

What skills are needed for reflective mapping?

The different ways of establishing relational awareness mapping in forensic settings are described throughout this book. A step-by-step guide to 'map and talk' is in Chapter 6 of this book and its roots in therapy and in cognitive analytic therapy can be found in Potter (2020). However, this chapter concludes with comments on what attitudes and resources both facilitators and participants need.

Facilitators need support both in time, funding, and training. It is essential for one or more members of the organization to have training in CAT. A partnership between external trainer and supervisor and internal facilitator works well. Facilitators need a relational mind set as depicted by the section on relational awareness, skills in group facilitation of experiential learning. Not going one-on-one with participants keeping safe by keeping to themselves knowing the other forums and places where difficult issues can be discussed or processed. The space for reflective mapping will need protecting so that its distinctive contribution can be seen within the wider range of activities.

Participants in reflective practice can go a lot further in participating if they know the basic skills and concepts. Hands on practice in the ideas and methods of reflective mapping for a day is a valuable training experience in itself and whets the appetite for using reflective practice and shows how to join in.

What are the limits of this approach?

The clearest frustration for any approach to reflective practice is that it is not solution-focused. It opens a negotiation of what an experience or interaction means and does not go down the line to decide on a course of action. As in the description of the open story method, it is biased towards careful and accurate description of interactions before discussion to revise or resolve them. However, there is every likelihood that awareness enabled by reflective mapping will lead to changes in behaviour and there are plenty of other kinds of meetings where lessons drawn from reflective practice can be applied to care planning and treatment choices. Reflective mapping is not a replacement for meetings where decisions are needed, and action must be agreed.

Another limitation, which is indicative of the unconscious bias and institutional dynamics of organizations, is that whilst reflective mapping lends itself very well to mapping the social and historical dynamics of personal experience (especially in individual or group therapy), it is challenging for teams to talk about differences of ethnicity and status directly. It may be that by more self-conscious mapping of these dynamics a better understanding of the change process and resistance to change can be worked out.

Concluding comments

Working in an organization is personal. It is a professional role-bound activity, but personally engaging and exposing. Working in teams is emotionally demanding and the roles we occupy have an impact upon our own (and colleagues) whole sense of self. The help we give each other to manage the personal impact of work is largely informal and off the record. Or the help is given at a distance after a crisis or breakdown. The personal and the organizational are much more entangled than our HR policies and systems of management and support acknowledge. We keep boundaries and understand where to be reserved or hold back and when to reach out. The dilemma of being authentic and then vulnerable or withholding and then safe is captured by item 5 in the *Helper's Dance List* (www.mapandtalk.com/helpers-dance-list).

> *Genuine and vulnerable or safe but less real: either (a) I show feelings and feel genuine but somewhat vulnerable or (b) I safely hide feelings, appear professional but less the real me*

Nowhere is this truer in mental health work than in forensic or criminal justice settings. Role distance and the defensive coping procedures are important but so is a sense of our personal involvement and capacity to tolerate exposure. It is a dilemma that shows up in reflective practice mapping sessions. The current and protracted pandemic highlights this dilemma even more so.

Reflective mapping is not an end in itself. It is a medium for experiencing and developing a shared relational awareness – a shared thinking space that is personal as well as organizational. There is a great pressure for organizations to manage by appearances which is to manage by minimizing the exposure of the self behind the roles. 'Don't take it personally' the organization seems to be saying. But we do and we must take it personally. It is personal as much as it is professional and organizational.

Role-bound interaction is fine on the football pitch when what is being passed between players is a ball, but when what is being passed is a vulnerable adult with physical and mental health problems, the interaction is between persons negotiating roles, navigating self-insight and interpersonal sensitivity and organizational understanding. It requires space to reflect in a semi-structured personal and professional way. The 'map and talk' approach offers one aid to such a process.

PART 2: Facilitating reflective practice – considerations and practical steps

Chapter 5: What are the core competencies needed to deliver reflective practice?

Jamie Kirkland

> 'After a while you could get used to anything'
> (Camus, 1942, p77)

> 'The worker should know what he is doing, be sure about group objectives, his authority, have planned the session thoroughly, and be able to convey to group members that he can be relied on'
> (Benson, 2019, p54)

Introduction

No experience required?

Have you heard that there is no experience like experience itself? Is that how we 'hope' to become as practitioners. We start with some theory and 'hope' that over time we just get better at things. Training courses assure trainees that they are going through stages and will one day get to 'unconscious competence', a dangerous notion if there ever was one if it is translated to mean you can do it with your eyes closed now, no more training or reflection needed!

I am not suggesting that an existential crisis of Camus should develop when seeking to deliver reflective practice. A kind of detached 'whatever will be'. Nor am I avoiding the need for a considered and professional level of competence, as argued by Benson. But surely we, as practitioners, can start somewhere between the two?

There are numerous papers and books describing how to run reflective practice groups (RPGs) or sessions. However, there are less areas of guidance indicating the skills or competencies required to deliver these sessions or what skills the facilitators need. Much of this chapter draws upon the work of a Scottish group of forensic practitioners who produced a position statement on running reflective practice in forensic settings (Forensic Network, 2018). This chapter concentrates upon the competencies this group considered essential to run RPGs and the tables are referenced from that work. I aim to consider, in this chapter, how utilising a Cognitive Analytic Therapy (CAT) approach is compatible with this position statement.

Many of the groups run tend to follow psychodynamic approaches, as described earlier in Chapter 2, and it would not be without merit to believe that as a forensic practitioner you would not be able to even begin to contemplate facilitating such groups without years of group analytic training, and certainly not by being a CAT practitioner.

But this is not the remit of CAT. As a transdiagnostic model, it is not just that we apply this theoretical thinking across human distress on an individual one to one level, but also across teams, and systems (and even nations!). After all, not all analytically trained clinicians are necessarily suited to facilitating RP groups, just as being a CAT practitioner does not preclude you either. The aim of this chapter is to both suggest core competencies one may need to deliver reflective practice generally, but also to argue that using a CAT approach is ideally suited to delivering this.

In order to promote some confidence that we can apply our skills, as CAT practitioners, to reflective practice perhaps the thinking should be:

What are the skills you do need to deliver this type of support?

Then you could consider, as a clinician, what you need to work on in order to develop these competencies. There has been some work in traditional psychodynamic literature considering both the role and stance of the facilitator as well as how to set up and maintain group principles. I shall both illustrate this and also relate the ideas to a CAT-informed approach.

The group set-up: role and stance of the facilitator

The role and stance of the facilitator of RPGs draws on ideas and skills from several domains (Johnson *et al*, 2004; Scanlon, 2012) namely relational, in the main psychodynamic/analytic and group dynamic/analytic therapy approaches. Alongside this theoretical underpinning, it is assumed that facilitators require group-work leadership skills, awareness of systemic approaches and skills as an educator. The role of a RPG facilitator should be one that is voluntarily applied for or taken on. It will be unhelpful for professionals to be made to take this role on as it will be likely to cause difficulties in maintaining a helpful frame for RPGs.

Key aspects of the role and stance of the facilitator (Johnson *et al*, 2004; Johnston & Paley, 2013; Scanlon, 2012) have been suggested to include:

- Conducting and facilitating discussion and exploration by the group, as opposed to being overly didactic. This allows the clinical team to work things out at their own pace
- Keeping the group exploring and thinking about what is being discussed, including looking for meaning, and asking for feelings (in relation to the clinical work)
- To tolerate and keep in play contradictory and multiple views as expressed by group members, rather than coming in and giving a verdict on what is being said (Johnson et al, 2004).

The group set-up: setting and maintaining group principles

Reflective practice groups are not therapy for staff. The facilitator keeps the focus on work situations and staff members' responses to these, as opposed to personal exploration as found in therapy. The facilitator will step in when needed to keep members feeling safe and also to ensure that no one individual is 'in the spotlight' and by doing so keeps the group on task.

In addition, most settings require that facilitators are not part of the teams that they are helping to reflect. This 'outsider' status, it is argued, preserves facilitators' ability to hold a democratic, neutral stance in relation to the teams they work with. Furthermore, it will prevent them being part of the problems they are trying to assist with. In CAT terms we may consider it to be alongside the team rather than being outside of the team. There may be a subtle difference here. An oft quoted criticism of psychodynamic facilitators are that they can appear 'aloof'. The CAT approach promote being 'with' the person not 'apart' from them. Steve Potter has called this 'joining the dance'.

Intrinsic to the role of the facilitator is to have knowledge and experience of the RPG processes, and to be able to direct the group to employ these productively. Additionally, the facilitator must be able to distinguish between working in an RPG and working in other clinical/therapeutic situations. With this in mind, it may be of merit to provide some definitions outlining the difference between RPGs, Clinical Supervision, Case-Consultation and Therapy. These have been suggested in the table below (Forensic Network, 2018).

Table 1. Differentiating between RPGs, supervision, case-consultation and therapy

Factor	Reflective Practice	Clinical Supervision	Case-Consultation	Therapy
Definition	Reflective practice sessions seek to develop the capacity to reflect on actions so as to engage in a process of continuous learning. It involves paying critical attention to the practical values and theories which inform everyday actions, by examining practice reflectively and reflexively. This leads to developmental insight. (Kirkland, 2016).	Supervision (Roth and Pilling, 2009) is a formal but collaborative relationship which takes place in an organizational context, which is part of the overall training of practitioners, and which is guided by some form of contract between the facilitator and the participants. The expectation is that the participants offer an honest and open account of their work, and that the facilitator offers feedback and guidance which has the primary aim of facilitating the development of the participant's therapeutic competences, but also ensures that they practice in a manner which conforms to current ethical and professional standards.	These sessions are a theoretically-based explanation or conceptualisation of the information obtained from a clinical assessment. The sessions seek to offer a hypothesis about the cause and nature of the presenting problems and are considered an adjunct or alternative approach to the more categorical approach of psychiatric diagnosis. In case consultation sessions, formulations are used to communicate a hypothesis and provide framework for developing the most suitable treatment approach.	Therapy offers a safe, confidential place to talk about a person's life and anything that may be confusing, painful or uncomfortable. It allows you to talk with someone who is trained to listen attentively and to help you improve things. (BACP, 2018)
Set agenda?	Free flowing	Goal directed	Model dependent and will be about a particular case.	May be free flowing or goal directed – model dependent
Facilitator Stance	Facilitator activity dependent on group dynamic	Facilitator active	Facilitator active	Model dependent
Collaborative?	Facilitator encourages group to do the thinking	Facilitator collaborates with supervisee in thinking about the patient	Facilitator collaborates with group in applying the psychological model about the patient	Model dependent

Chapter 5: What are the core competencies needed to deliver reflective practice?

	Reflective Practice Group	Supervision	Case Consultation	Therapy
Reflective Stance?	Facilitator supports reflection	Supervisor supports reflection but also educates around model and ensures fidelity	Consultant supports reflection but also educates around model and ensures fidelity	Model dependent
Group Focus?	One of the primary foci is on group dynamics	Some focus on group dynamics	More focused on patient/client/presenting dilemma but model may determine this	Model dependent
Link to patient management?	Ideas about patient management may emerge from group but not explicitly on the agenda	Explicit link to patient management	Explicit link to patient management	Not applicable
Goal directed?	Less emphasis on defined goals beyond enhancing reflection	Clear goal at maintaining fidelity to treatment model, enhancing patient outcome, ensuring quality of care	Emphasis on achieving outcomes in direct relation to patient care	Direct emphasis on improving patient/s outcome
Facilitator Knowledge?	Facilitator has expert knowledge of RPG processes but maintains non-expert view of situation	Facilitator has expert role in model and supervision	Facilitator has expert role in model and case-consultation	Therapist has expert knowledge and skills in model and may maintain non-expert view of situation depending on model
Educational Component?	Less emphasis on imparting theoretical and technical knowledge	Emphasis on imparting theoretical and technical knowledge	Emphasis on imparting theoretical and technical knowledge	Less emphasis on imparting theoretical and technical knowledge
Confidentiality	Boundary of confidentiality within the group (but also held in professional registration frameworks so can be breached if risk to patients or worker)	Boundary of confidentiality within the group (but also held in professional registration frameworks so can be breached if risk to patients or worker)	Boundary of confidentiality may be held within the group but will be negotiated depending on task (but also held in professional registration frameworks so can be breached if risk to patients or worker)	Boundary of confidentiality within the group (unless serious, imminent risk to patient/s or others)
Group affect focus	Emphasis on identifying and then containing/processing affect of the group	Emphasis on identifying affect for goal directed outcome	Emphasis on identifying affect for goal directed outcome	Emphasis on identifying affect for goal directed outcome

Competencies required to run the group

Once we establish the broad aims of the group, we can then focus on guidance for those who facilitate reflective groups in forensic settings. Why are competencies necessary? Competencies are necessary because often facilitator training is at a post-graduate level, meaning that facilitators tend to have attained a level of training before they feel able to run groups. In addition, clinical practice (in the UK) takes place within the NHS and Criminal Justice services and so requirements for clinical governance (ensuring quality of delivery and patient safety) need to be met.

Once these pre-requisites have been met we might want to think about the skills a person would want to have, or develop, in order to facilitate a group. In an attempt to begin to think about what competencies are required, the 'Forensic Matrix' working group set about to attempt to define this for forensic mental health and criminal justice settings (Patrick *et al*, 2018).

Below is a list of what were previously the core competencies that the working group agreed RPG facilitators required to run groups.

1. To be able to facilitate reflection within relational contexts
2. To understand and be able to work with affect in the RPGs
3. To be able to tolerate disturbing narratives
4. To be able to manage interpersonal conflict within the RPG
5. To be able to provide a safe space for RPGs including manage intra- and inter-group boundaries

Each of these areas will be discussed below. They are broken into both the knowledge and skills the group felt were important in 'having' the skill. The group also provided reasons as to, 'why is this important?'. Although the document was seeking to not be model specific, for the purpose of this book, I will consider the implication for those wishing to provide CAT-informed reflective practice. As such it may provide a reference point when beginning to think about the skills one may wish to develop in order to facilitate a reflective group or indeed a service may wish to utilise as a framework in supporting staff development.

1. To be able to facilitate reflection within relational contexts

We may consider it important to have significant experience of working in forensics directly or having an appreciation of issues in forensic issues through further education. A core mental health professional qualification (eg nursing, psychiatry, psychology, OT, social work etc) with at least two years post qualification experience in a forensic service may be considered essential.

For people who are seeking to develop their practice as reflective practice facilitators there may need to be evidence of an academic ability to complete reflective practice training. Facilitators would normally be required to have completed previous courses of a similar academic level such as a post-graduate diploma or above, which have included having prepared and written essays or similar academic texts. Clearly, the two-year CAT practitioner diploma would meet this criteria.

Adequate knowledge and experience of psychotherapy or counselling would be assumed. This would include elements of both theoretical input and clinical experience in which the professional would have treated patients in a formal therapy or counselling structure under regular expert clinical supervision. Such a training course will usually have been of at least one year's duration. This it could be argued would provide a grounding in relational understanding on an individual level.

Added to this previous experience of being in RPGs for at least one year is suggested by the group and that they also have an appropriate supervisor and demonstrate ongoing attendance at their own supervision for RPGs. Such an idea extends the facilitator's experience from the individual to the team.

CAT is a relational model. It integrates theories, including object relations theories. In CAT terms known as dialogism (Bahktin, 1929/1984; Hermans, 2001) where the internal 'voice' (self) and external 'voice' (others) creates a dialogue. Many of these occur thus creating a 'multiplicity of voices' (Leiman, 2002). It has therefore, at its heart, an understanding of human relations both 'self to other' and 'self to self' with the concept of reciprocal roles. Using these ideas allows for an exploration of differing positions and multiple voices within a reflective practice group.

Table 2 Core competency 1 – facilitate reflection (Potter, 2013)

Knowledge	Skills	Why are these important
Understand the concepts and experience of transference and countertransference	Be able to focus on the relationship and the push and pull of transference and counter-transference feelings from the staff member and elsewhere so as to be explored and processed in the room – keeping a consistent and interested stance in the patients	Reflecting on the process of care and treatment is not something that we can easily do on our own. Even the most experienced practitioner needs a bit of help in terms of understanding their work with complex forensic patients – as well as a setting that can help them understand and make use of their relationships with staff and patients
Understand an interpersonal approach to focus upon creating a collaborative and reflective relationship	Be a skilled communicator, sensitively creating collaboration and reflection	
Understand psychoanalytic concepts that relate to individuals	Be able to draw upon and potentially teach RPG members about basic psychoanalytic concepts such as projection projective identification in a readily understandable way – as well as help them reflect on the relevance of these concepts to their everyday work	
Understand psychoanalytic concepts that relate to groups		
Understand psychoanalytic concepts that relate to organizations		
	Be able to hold and maintain a genuine, curious and empathic stance towards RPG members and material	
	Be able to reflect upon their own associations to material discussed in RPGs and share these when appropriate and in an affectively modulated way	

2. To understand and be able to work with affect in the reflective practice group

To bring a group of people together, to share and reflect upon one's reactions to their work is to open up thoughts, feelings, emotional reactions. Frustration, despair, hope, anger and joy are among the emotions we all display and the reflective group will be no different. Groups can both serve to nullify emotion and thinking as well as amplify it, eg, the concept of 'Groupthink' (Janis, 1972). The facilitator needs to be able to subtly shift and hold this emotion and use techniques to shine a light upon the emotion without letting it destroy the group.

CAT has a tradition of acknowledging the core pain or the 'gut' responses. The clinician is not required to deny transference and counter-transference reactions. In CAT terms it is understood as 'reciprocal role enactments' – the invitation to take up the reciprocating role inhabited by the individual or team. The model is, therefore, not overly cognitive at the expense of emotion. Emotion can overwhelm if there is no structure to help the facilitator, a criticism of an overly cognitive approach is that it disconnects the facilitator. We are touched by our work and forensics can be difficult in relation to the 'macho' culture but reflective practice groups can support the acknowledgement of the emotional and relational impact that the work has on us.

Table 3 Core competency 2 – understand and be able to work with affect

Knowledge	Skills	Why are these important
Understand that participants may find it more challenging to take part in groups where the expectations are that they discuss the emotional impact of the work – this may be seen in a lack of affect brought	Help group to notice, identify, safely manage, process and then aim to contain each other's affects. Do not avoid the affect in the group	The purpose of RPGs is to help health professionals further understand themselves and their motives, perceptions, attitudes, values and feelings associated with patient care (Price, 2004)
Group members will bring different affective response that you will see when running the groups, facilitators will need to be aware of the impact of this upon themselves	Manage facilitator's own affect in relation to the group and try to avoid over- or under-engaging with the group's affect. This would include understanding that facilitators need their own supervision and reflective practice. This would include using supervision effectively for your RPG work	
The importance of being supportive at times to staff struggling with difficult situations	Engage in an explicitly supportive and constructive dialogue themselves with staff and staff with each other during difficult situations	To help staff manage the day-to-day complexities and strain of forensic environments
The importance of acknowledging positive interactions and outcomes both in and out of RPGs	Engage in an explicitly supportive and constructive dialogue themselves with staff and them with each other when things have gone well	To help staff recognise when things have gone well and build on these experiences and processes
Understand the importance and necessity for having supervision of facilitators' RPG work		

3. To be able to tolerate disturbing narratives

Mitzman (2010) writes that forensic patients typically present with themes of early, severe deprivation, neglect and abuse, identity disturbance, emotional volatility, abandonment (both real and feared), substance abuse and chronic self-harming. However, the narrative is not only about being a victim but also of being an abuser. The forensic practitioner will be forced to confront, at times, terrible deeds done to others, by those they work with. As a facilitator you are being asked to hear, tolerate and help to manage these narratives of the group. But perhaps even harder is that not being the clinician working with the individual you have no direct ability to affect change, the emotion is felt 'second-hand'.

CAT is a transdiagnostic model and can frame these differing reactions. The CAT community trains and has experience of working with a range of challenges and trauma. The expertise is there to support clinicians who want to run reflective practice groups because these areas have already been worked in with CAT trained clinicians.

Table 4 Core competency 3 – tolerating disturbing narratives

Knowledge	Skills	Why are these important
Understand that facilitators will sometimes hear difficult, challenging, grim, violent and perverse material	Be able to listen non-judgmentally, listen and tolerate the difficult material brought	Forensics presents a particularly high demand on clinicians' skills. Patients and clients in forensic services pose significant management challenges, often presenting with violent or aggressive outbursts and with complex histories of serious offending and trauma, which can be difficult and distressing for staff and RPG facilitators to deal with
Understand that facilitators will sometimes hear hopelessness and despair from staff	Be able to provide a safe space for staff to feel heard, held in mind, empathised with, understood and contained	
Understand that facilitators will sometimes hear hatred and guilt from staff	Be able to not react to this, not judge staff feelings expressed, work with this to build reflective capacity	
Understand that facilitators will sometimes hear anxiety and anger from staff	Be able to make sense of this in relation to the staff's work and context – then help them make sense of it and process it	

4. To be able to manage interpersonal conflict within the RPG

With such disturbing materials staff will respond on many levels. At times they may be repulsed, angry, numb, depressed, anxious. They may 'split' – a term often used to blame different positions within terms. This may manifest itself through conflict within the group both overt (shouting at another member) and covert (turning up late). The technique of CAT mapping explicitly acknowledges differing positions and that staff may subtly shift their positions. It can serve to legitimise differing opinions and begin to help negotiate a way through conflict (illustrated in Chapter 8).

Table 5 Core competency 4 – managing interpersonal conflict in RPGs

Knowledge	Skills	Why are these important
Understand that there may be conflict within the RPG because of the material RPGs are working with	Facilitators need to be able to form a neutral though empathic and understanding relationship that is sufficient to evoke within the team an increased interest in them in understanding themselves, colleagues, other disciplines and, especially, their patients	"Relationships are crucial to successful RP groups. You will have to form a relationship with up to 30 people depending on the size of the ward team. Relationships are with each individual member of the team, with 'the team' as a whole and with the 'group' who turn up for sessions each week…" (Johnstone and Paley, 2013) It is important to hold in mind that teams will not always 'get along' even with the provision of containing spaces such as RPGs and, in fact, some disagreements may be important to be held in teams to ensure different perspectives can be held
Understand that not all staff will hold similar views about each other or their work, there will sometimes be differences of perspective and conflicts within teams	Hold in mind that facilitators need to be available to anyone working in the team, with equal attention available to all. Facilitators will need to be able to accept and integrate differences, manage conflict ensuring that all are heard	
Understand that forensic mental health work can push and pull staff in extreme ways. Staff may seek containment of their fears, challenges and difficulties by wishing to gain the 'support' of you to the detriment of opposing views/staff	Facilitators need to keep a high level of self-awareness to try to notice when, even inadvertently, they get split off into supporting any sub-groups. And to be able to reflect on groups when the facilitator gets deflected from their neutral stance	

5. To be able to provide a safe space for the reflective practice group including managing intra- and inter-group boundaries

To provide a safe space the facilitator needs to be able to be relied upon. This is demonstrated in time keeping, confidentiality, providing a structure to the meeting, and using a similar working space. It allows participants to arrive at a 'moment in time' where their concern is to be able to reflect because they are being 'held'. But CAT also has 'tools' that aid this. The use of letters to teams and maps can help scaffold those attending the groups. It is central to the CAT approach to acknowledge Vygotsky's (1978) notion of zone of proximal development (ZPD). Not all staff have experienced reflective practice in their training, CAT is an approach that can help to nurture and contain this experience.

Table 6 Core competency 5 – provide a safe space for RPGs including manage intra- and inter-group boundaries

Knowledge	Skills	Why are these important
Understand the need for consistency, coherence and regularity for RPGs to create 'safe spaces'	Ensure the groups run regularly; that facilitators and groups are predictable and remain consistent and coherent with their model	RP groups focus more on the patient and professional relationship. The emphasis is on the experience of the professionals, their feelings about the patient and the situation evoking a dilemma that not infrequently has a moral dimension as in judging the patient, or themselves, sometimes excessively critically or uncritically
Understand the need for and limits of confidentiality in RPGs	Hold in mind that forensic environments deal with risk and can be risky contexts. Understand the need to hold confidentiality but also when to breach it if necessary	
Understand the difference between reflective practice and therapy	Manage facilitators own and others' self-disclosures. Not delve into staff's personal histories nor intervene therapeutically during RPGs. Tactfully redirect where appropriate	Staff need to be able to feel safe within groups and know that their boundaries will be acknowledged and respected
Understand the importance of distinguishing between information that should stay in the group and useful information that might leave it – such as concerns about risk of harm	Help the group respond in different, more productive ways to patients whilst preserving the boundary of the RPG and its members	→

Knowledge	Skills	Why are these important
	RPG facilitators should be capable of running groups that contain professionals who may be of a higher grade and/or level of clinical experience than themselves	

Summary

The purpose of the reflective practice competencies framework was to help practitioners focus on knowledge and skills they already possess and then identify areas that will need development. The latter will allow staff to demonstrate the competencies they already have and support them to build others to allow them to be confident to be an RPG facilitator. The framework was not designed to be either an exclusionary set of 'tick boxes' to stop people delivering RPGs nor to direct them to many years of psychoanalytic training. However, I would argue that CAT is ideally placed to provide reflective practice to groups and CAT practitioners have many of the competencies required to deliver.

There is 'more than one way to skin a cat' to reach and demonstrate the competencies required. For example, being able to 'demonstrate an understating of psychoanalytic concepts that relate to individuals' may be attainable via different routes, different backgrounds or different trainings, be they therapeutic or professional. As such, the working group are not asking for practitioners to demonstrate qualifications but rather to establish their RPG facilitator competencies.

The purpose is also to help managers to identify suitable clinicians for training in RPG facilitation and for clinicians attending RPGs to feel confident that their RPG facilitator has the relevant training, skills and experience to deliver a creative, well-boundaried and helpful group. This was a description of an attempt to describe competencies that might be considered to deliver RP in forensic settings. It may be of value to those services wishing to consider training needs, benchmark standards and apply good governance. However, perhaps more importantly it should be the beginning of a conversation within the service and across all staff groups as to whether these can be achieved from the skill set already existing in that service.

Chapter 6: Steps to reflective mapping

Steve Potter

Introduction

This chapter offers a step-by-step guide to reflective mapping. It details a method of learning from experience about the push and pull of roles and relationships involved in working together. The goal is a more relationally aware and reflective group and organizational culture. As each step is described the associated concepts are briefly reflected upon though the concepts are also explored in Chapter 4. The chapter concludes with tips for facilitators and participants who try out making maps in reflective mapping sessions. There is a more detailed description of the use of mapping to develop relational awareness in *Therapy with a Map* (Potter, 2020) and workshops and video material can be found at www.mapandtalk.com

Starting a reflective mapping group

The first step is to encourage a few colleagues to meet to sample the approach. This might be accompanied by introductory days of training and some informal one-to-one demonstrations of how mapping develops shared thinking. Most of the initiatives in reflective mapping have been led by someone who is inside the organization – most typically a psychologist who has trained in Cognitive Analytic Therapy. As with any approach to learning from experience, it needs a mix of 'bottom-up' and 'top-down' initiative. The 'top-down' need for reflective practice is often born out of a crisis, a challenging inspection or a realisation that not enough time is spent talking about how teams are working together regardless of the pressure to get on with what they are doing. The 'bottom-up' initiative is a sign that frontline staff are being valued and involved.

The 'map and talk' approach to reflective practice has immediate appeal. It is transparent and involves people with different professions and status working equally and side-by-side at the activity of making a map of what they see going on. Modest expectations are an essential first step with the aim of establishing a small group meeting regularly. It might promote interest to show mapping as a means of highlighting the key elements of a case formulation or of talking through a common kind of interaction between patients and different groups of staff. It can be enough for people to give it a more sustained try if moments of seeing how mapping helps sustain a conversation without jumping to conclusions. Any informal start needs to be followed by a suggested pilot programme with one or more multi-disciplinary teams.

Set the stage

Once the idea of meeting has been agreed the second step is to establish a routine of meeting. The tools are pen and paper (big sheets) table or flipchart or white board. How to arrange the group will depend upon its size. Up to six is best around a table with flipchart paper. Up to 12 people gathered around a flipchart stand or white board works well. Encouraging everyone to come and stand around the flipchart gets people up and moving and improves participation. Sitting down after the mapping process is a visual and mildly dramatic way of marking the change in focus and tone of the discussion to something more reflective. A bigger group than 12 needs some idea of groups within groups and it may be that a small group of three or four people (who were most involved in an event to be mapped) need to come forward and gather close to the white board or flipchart stand.

A routine way to start the meeting is to check in with everyone by listing on the flipchart incidents, topics or themes that might be suitable for mapping in more detail. The choosing of one initial item is part of the scene setting for the session. The list can be referred to at the end of the session to see if, on balance, the right topic was chosen or if in working on one issue others on the list are seen in a new more reflective light. There may be parallels drawn from the incident chosen to be mapped onto the others on the list. The group may be very aware it is choosing a safe topic, or a risky one, or letting one or two members of the group run the show. When reviewing how the session went at the end it is important to go back to the list and wonder what lessons can be drawn about naming and choosing topics for next time.

The facilitator needs initial success in showing how mapping works and it is always possible to work with an example that has been discussed a little in advance of the meeting in the early days of such meetings. The focus can vary from something very specific or a more general theme. It is also important that the focus of discussion is not an event whose main participants are absent. If it is a theme, it is important to keep linking to instances and specific examples. The test is that the event discussed and mapped draws upon the direct experience of the people present. It is best not talking in the manner of a debrief about something that has just happened as the feelings may still be strongly in the air and it is too close in time and too personal to get a perspective on. An unsettling experience needs digesting or processing individually before it can be reconsidered through reflective practice.

Words here and there

Mapping is a way of tracking a conversation as it develops. Words spread out on paper help ask the question: Is this what we are saying? Is this where the conversation is going? The map allows 'here and there' thinking. Some of us are here in our thinking (pointing at some words on the map) and others of us are there (pointing at other words on the map). Pointing here and there gives equal validity to both positions and invites thinking about the links and gaps between them. Our eyes are looking for patterns in what our ears are hearing. There is an element of free association. We can all see the main contours of what is being said. Mapping the key words of an experience of an event begins to give it the qualities of a story. There is a plot or pattern here. Mapping centres on teasing out patterns. As will be considered shortly and elsewhere in this book the conceptual tools and conventions of CAT mapping helps organise these patterns into relational templates for thinking reflectively.

Using relational mapping templates

The mapper might get the conversation going using words spread out here and there but as skill and confidence grows, she or he will have in mind several mapping templates that act as a loose and flexible scaffold for drawing out patterns. These templates are close to our everyday thinking and are designed to help the mapper shape and hold the discussion without intruding on it or steering it.

The first template looks at our interactions in terms of roles and the push and pull of reciprocation through various patterns of coping and response. The reader familiar with the language of cognitive analytic therapy will recognise this as the description of a reciprocal role procedure. It is called the action, impact and response (Potter, 2020, p44).

The second template looks at the interaction between several roles and how our feelings and responses within a role are shaped by our appraisal of options to respond in one way or another. The template is known informally as the hopes and fears (Potter, 2020, p76). Most of the events in our lives are experienced with hoped for outcomes set against feared ones.

Most maps, with practice and familiarity, have combinations of these two templates and invite a third which is concerned with the judgements we make about the patterns we have internalised as part of our lifelong roles and identities and their enactment within the workplace. Our judgements may be deeply woven into our identity, or way of life, or be central assumptions of the organization. Reflective mapping seeks to make our judgements and their origins and ownership more visible and negotiable.

Action, impact and response

The cognitive analytic framework builds its relational thinking about patterns of interaction by using the idea of roles and how they are reciprocated or not within and between us. Roles make up our sense of self and our personal and social identities at home and work. Role is a versatile and loose social science concept pointing inwards to an orchestration of roles within that are also expressed interpersonally with others and interactively with organization and society. The following steps show how events, patterns and themes are linked by the process of mapping. Roles in CAT terms are made up of reciprocations and procedures which are the steps and elements of how we respond to each other at work.

When using relational mapping in therapy, a key interest is in the relationship between one role and another (for example role as wife and mother) and the array of life roles and the whole sense of self and personal identity. In contrast, when using relational mapping with teams, the focus is more on roles within and between groups and professions and the positioning of power and influence formally and informally through role reciprocations.

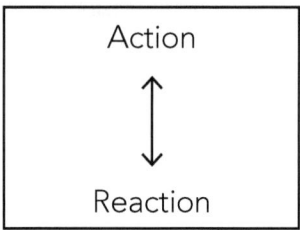

When reflecting on an event we may talk first of our feelings and what we did to manage them. It may be that several words are put in the bottom end of the diagram above. We may or may not be able to describe the actions that led to our reactions, but the template is inviting us to think in terms of a fast, unprocessed response. We are interested in moments of reflection which might be called second thoughts. We can remember the actions and put the words down for them. We can link to the impact those actions had on us and in turn think about the way of coping as a form of response to those feelings.

As we map out the shared pattern, we are asking how common it was? It is a process of teasing out, or untying the knots of fast unprocessed reactions to actions. What might get mapped are words for an action and an immediate reaction. For example: I was pushed, I pushed back. Someone looked happily at me, I smiled back. Mapping is opening these immediate reciprocations to self-exploration on the one hand and interaction with others on the other hand. It is hoping to show how the two are linked. Here,

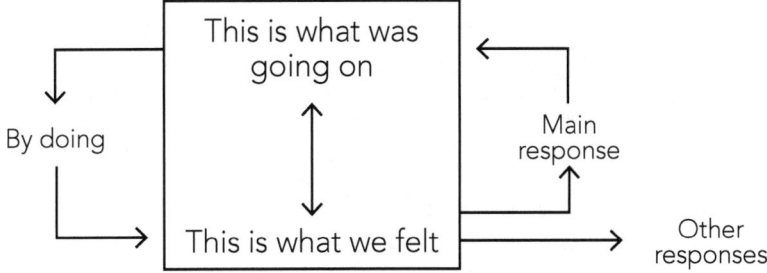

what someone was felt to be doing (the action) is put in words at the top end of the box and the emotional impact – the subjectively felt experience is put into words at the bottom end of the box. This is the impact of the action. There is an arrow linking them to indicate the push and pull between them. Did you smile at me because I looked happy or do I look happy because you smiled at me? As shown in the diagram above we turn the action and its automatic reaction of the first diagram into a three-way negotiation between action, impact and response. The impact is usually a feeling and the response is a negotiation that weighs this feeling against the action and imagined or rehearsed ways of coping. The response is understood as an appraisal of what we did, or could have done, given those feelings in relation to what was going on.

Much of what we are mapping are the details of habitual and automatic role responses. Mapping them out is a way of compassionately raising awareness and sustaining curiosity. When trying to fully understand our patterns of interaction we need to link together what the cognitive psychologists call our appraisal of the situation including the feelings, memories and choices of behaviour and their imagined or anticipated consequences.

Mapping the response step by step

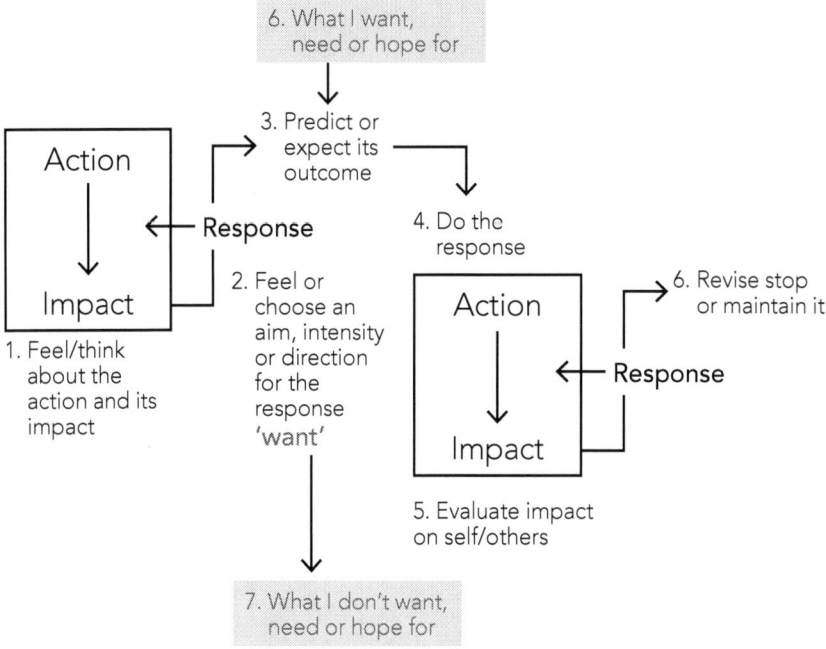

The above map gives the full detail of the concepts and methods of mapping. No map is ever as tidy as this but the sequence and layout is for the mapper to have in mind as a template. It begins with what the group feel or think about the action and its impact on them as in box 1. The response is in most cases automatic but in promoting group reflection we are wondering at point 2 on the map what was the intention, intensity and direction of the response. And how much was it possible to predict an expected or intended outcome as in point 3. The outcome is in turn another reciprocal role box of action-impact and response as in box 4. There is the possibility then in the process of reflective practice to wonder at point 5 in what ways could the pattern be revised, softened or made worse in some way. This whole reciprocal role sequence is the basic formulation of cognitive analytic ideas with a map. It may track both individual experience and group or subgroup experience. The process of mapping is a form of awareness raising.

With a greater shared awareness, we might then have one level of understanding about how a group pattern works. We can then reflect on the circumstances that might give rise to such a pattern. We might see the direction it goes back into; increasing the impact; or reverse the roles by taking over the action; or going elsewhere with the response. We might know something more about the intensity of the response, or the enduring or temporary nature of the response. We might be asking how typical is it? Is it just like us to do this or not at all like us?

Hopes and fears

At the heart of mapping and talking is a common process of seeing something hopeful, facing a challenge and fearing something harmful.

Basic map for any moment or story: hide and seek with hopes and fears

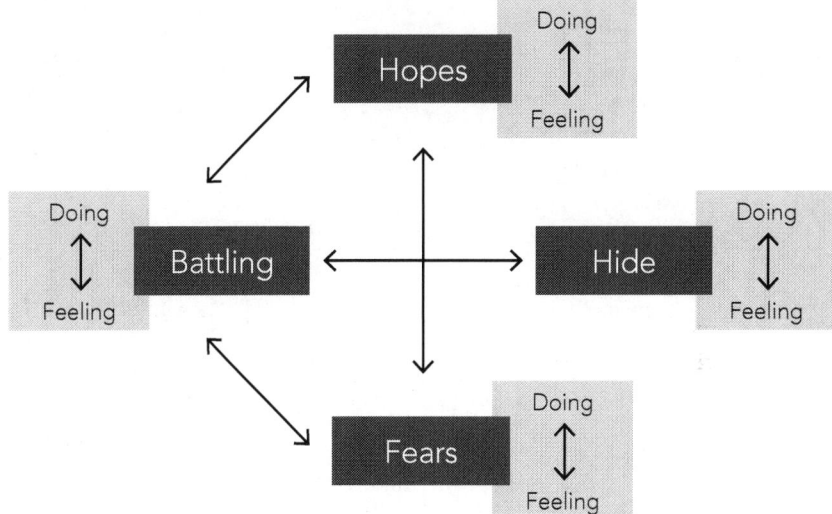

We often find ourselves in a struggle against our best intentions, within ourselves or with others to achieve a desired or hoped for place and avoid a feared or hopeless place. In the process we have a fourth place to which we can retreat in search of safety but often at the cost of cutting off or hiding from the up and down experience of the struggle to achieve something good and avoid something bad.

In other words, moment by moment, we can play hide and seek with our hopes and fears. On occasion, from within a hiding place we can overvalue the things we want to achieve, and they become our dreams and can be untested and unreal. Similarly, if we routinely hide from our feared places things that might once have been scary or disturbing and which have been coped with by avoidance, if tested in the present circumstance, are not so scary or no longer a source of active danger. Our challenge is to map and talk about the swing between our hopes and fears and the seesaw between hiding away and joining and battling for our best intentions.

A warm-up map for introducing relational mapping with a team

```
                    2. What would we              3. What would we
                       be doing?                      be doing?
                          ↑↓                             ↑↓
                      If things were                 If we were the
                      going well…?                   dream team?

  1. What are we doing
  to manage ourselves                ↖    ↗
      as a team?          →      Risky response choice
         ↑↓                          ↙    ↘
   How do we feel
      about…?
                    4. What would we              5. What would we
                       be doing?                      be doing?
                          ↑↓                             ↑↓
                      If things were                 If we were a
                      going badly…?                  nightmare team?
```

The above variation on the hopes and fears template is one that can work as a good warm-up mapping experience for a team new to the approach. It is a way of guiding a team to map their current state of play. It starts with box 1 and the question to be answered is, what are we doing to manage ourselves as a team? This triggers the response question at the bottom of box 1 which is how we do feel about ourselves? In response to those feelings there are two routes (and no doubt a thousand variations inbetween). The upward route is to consider the dynamic between being in box 2 or 3. Or aspiring to be there. The first box 2 asks if things were going well for the team what would we be doing.

This is a great starter question for a team on its first mapping outing. It can help bond the team and give them a positive experience of mapping together. Seeing the tension between box 2 and 3 is also an engaging discussion topic. All teams, like all individuals have some notion of what being a dream team would be like, if only for the moment. Posing the question can help think in terms of future expectation. Teams can be overly controlled by their own, or the organization's (or the patient's) idealised version of what service provision should be like. There are risks in going for our dreams and missing what might be good enough. And equally there are risks in being either over idealistic and making it achieve dream team or be nothing and facing the risk of things going badly. It can however be helpful for a team to look at the reciprocal relationship between things going badly and what would they or others be doing (box 4).

Similarly, a team can get stuck in the groove of things going badly for fear of a return to a nightmare time as described in box 5. There may be comparisons with other teams and other organizations where the team has been through a nightmare time of disorganization.

Confidence in mapping and talking derived from this simple template can help build confidence and curiosity to map out more specific experiences. Mapping like this is a series of baby steps in developing reflective capacity. Accepting the shared ownership of one pattern can help take responsibility for other patterns. Similarly, a key concept of mapping is established if a team can become familiar with the idea of a reciprocal relationship between what we are feeling as a team and what we, or others are doing to establish and maintain that feeling.

Another level of reflection

We can only navigate our thinking around what we notice. We can only negotiate with each other what we name. We use the mapping process to help notice links and patterns, but we also need to be open to what we don't notice, or where there are gaps in our memory, or in the voices willing to speak up. The qualities of hovering and shimmering, of joining in and stepping back are helped by seeing the mapping process as an aid to navigating our way around complex ideas and feelings.

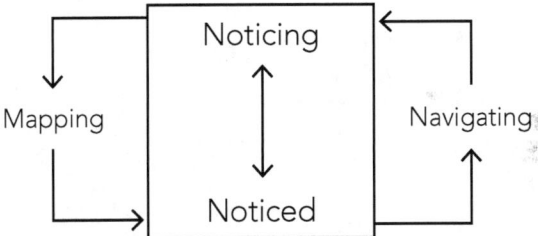

When we put words on paper, we are naming what is on our minds and what we hear each other thinking and feeling. The gap between naming something and it being named is a gap we can open further. Holding the process open is done with the pen and a capacity on the part of the mapper to constructively dither and not rush things. If at any time the mapping becomes an obstacle, it can be put aside, and talk continues in the normal way. However, in such situations it can help to wonder what processes might be involved in making the mapping an obstacle as they may be symptomatic of other factors restricting reflective capacity in the team. Mapping should never be an imposition or a runaway machine. It is a gentle, tentative background process that comes to the foreground to recap and review the reflective conversation.

Chapter 6: Steps to reflective mapping

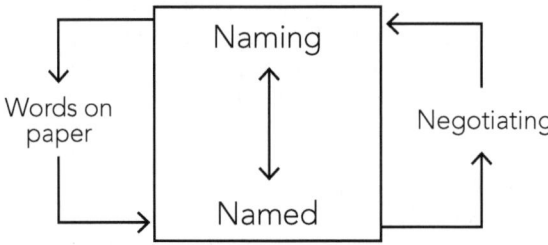

As we map out a pattern, we are not just remembering what happened but evaluating and passing judgement. In the process of navigating and negotiating our understanding with and through the map, we are affirming, validating, dismissing, accusing, commiserating. As in the map below what I want and don't want in response to a feeling depends on how I appraise what I can do and where I can go with it. This is a matter of judgement and calculation which may be driven by values and judgements woven into my identity and role.

Our response to what we feel is a kind of negotiation (open or closed)

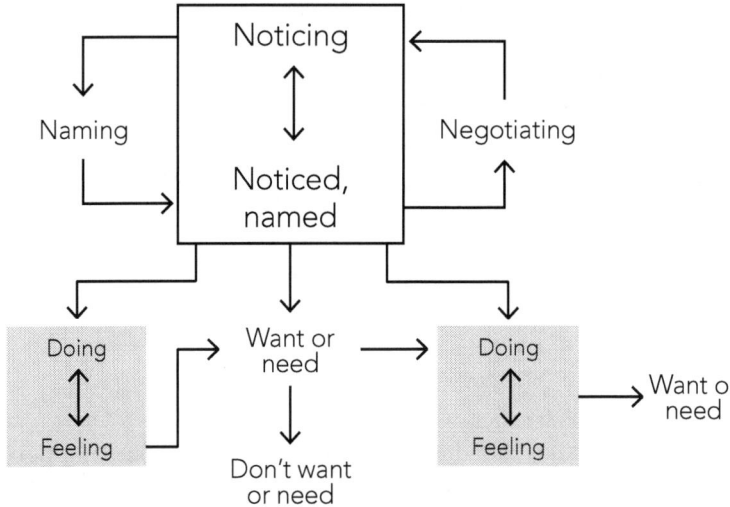

In the figure above there is in green a meta-level or second level of mapping which explores the tone and intensity in which I notice what I am doing. If this second level of judging and evaluating can be introduced to the map and marked out as such it extends our capacity to learn from the map.

Recapping is key

Recapping every few minutes with the map as a means of tracking the conversation as it develops is a way to involve people, get an accurate map and have a dialogue with yourself and your co-facilitator about what you are creating. Recapping brings the map alive as an aid to listening and gives rise to opportunities to add second thoughts or new mixes of feelings to what is already sketched out on the map. Recapping may bring new people in to participate who have held back during the first run of the discussion. It is also a means of discovery and self-scrutiny for the mapper. Some of the mapper's 'thinking' behind the emerging map can be shared. He or she may discover something new for themselves in the process of recapping and wonder out loud about adding it to the map. Don't hesitate to start afresh or indicate the intention to make a tidier map. One simple option in the early stages of learning to map is to invite participants to add to or rework the map.

Part of the training in mapping is learning to use the mapping process to manage the limits of what feels safe and helpful to explore. Mapping as a process comes alive when it is in the potential reach[1] of both person mapping and the person or people bringing the stories or events to be mapped. It is hovering and shimmering in a space which is not too far from safe and not too far from risky. The mapper holds and leads the conversation with the process of mapping which with its externalisation of thoughts and feelings can be a catalyst as much as a brake. The map allows all those involved to negotiate pace, direction, intensity and control of explorations. Reflecting on what has just happened to a team is too soon to process in a reflective way. People need help, things need doing, first reactions need processing and digesting. However, sometimes there is no choice but to map and talk about a serious moment of risk to self and others. Such moments are more likely to be negotiated safely with a map than without one. Mapping can make it easier to discuss difficult things and it is less likely to lead to enacting a blaming or shaming conversation.

From messy to tidy maps

After some time of mapping there is likely to be a lot of words and phrases on the sheet of paper and circles, lines and arrows everywhere. If working on a white board this can be tidied up and the main patterns can be more neatly portrayed. It is useful to photograph the messy map on the white board before reshaping it even so. If working on paper which is more normally the case, then the process of making a tidier map is an important shared experience of clarifying and lifting from the paper patterns from the discussions and stories represented by the map so far.

---

1 Zone of proximal development, L. Vygotsky, 1978

Writing or audio-video from the map

In Cognitive Analytic Therapy the transfer of reflections from one medium to another such as writing from a map or making a map of what has been written are key mechanisms of change. Jenny Marshall (*Chapter 12, Leadership and Cognitive Analytic Therapy: part one: relational dynamics and culture*) for example has made powerful use of letters to a ward team or group of managers where they have gone through an important process of thinking with the map. The letter consolidates and clarifies what has been shared through the map. Reading out loud from the letter is similar to the process of recapping already mentioned but has a greater quality of giving voice to key feelings and ideas. If it is not written it can be delivered as an audio-video report using a phone. In the context of reflective mapping, it can help a lot to be ready to write a short sentence or paragraph about the pattern that has been identified and the changes that might be taken on because of it.

Equally, as a map becomes established and there is a partnership feeling of working side-by-side together, and after there is an established pattern of recapping and reworking or revising the map, then it may help to do a special recap by audio or video recording the recap around the map. Most phones now have a video or an audio function. The recording process involves talking through (the mapper or the talker can lead but probably one is the main voice). The person recapping needs to be clearly addressing the mike or phone and to be mindful of clearly naming where the audio recording is referring to on the map.

Mapping the moment in the room

Every reflective mapping session should have a readiness to give attention to the patterns of interaction between people and ideas in the room in the here and now. It can be a helpful way of reviewing progress towards the end of a meeting or a way of making a link between what is being discussed and how it is discussed. The 'hopes and fears' template (Potter, 2020) is a useful template for any such reflections but also opening one or more reciprocations on paper as a focus for attention. For example, how did one group feel as a reaction to what the other group were doing. And how did they cope? A good reason for working at a table with plenty of paper is so-as-to be able to stop and say: 'I wonder if we could just map out where we are going together.'

Top tips for facilitators

Here are ten top tips for facilitators that help them establish and maintain reflective and relational mapping:

1. Take charge through the map

Any form of meeting needs some good authority to keep focus and avoid harmful banter or unwanted individual exposure. The facilitator's authority will vary with his or her status and the clarity of the task of the meeting, but one resource is to give the mapping process authority. What we are making together is a map. It functions as a symbol and agent of structure and co-operation. The content of the conversation arising from mapping together is all important but the map a bit like the agenda in a business meeting can be a source of reference and a guide to how the content is shared and developed. Reflective conversational mapping is a democratic process and the aim is to build consensus on the one hand but also give space for the diversity of views.

2. Be modest in aim

Be modest about how you think the mapping might help. It is a success and a contribution to reflective practice if the conversation flows and doesn't 'yoyo' between banter and silence. If several contrasting points of view are built upon and associated mixed feelings are shared. And if this has happened with the mapping process as the relatively unobtrusive assistant then it is more than enough. It does not matter if the words on the paper are a mess, or if no one can remember what the map was about a week later. More memorable and tidy maps can be made with practice, skill and familiarity with mapping in the group.

3. Show don't tell

The golden rule of fictional and creative writing applies also to reflective mapping. It is: *show, don't tell*. Which is to say use the map and the mapping activity of real examples as the way you introduce the methods and skills of mapping. Don't give a lecture about the art of mapping. Demonstrate it. Whilst you may well want to present a finished map to introduce the idea of mapping the real lesson comes from making a map live about a specific moment there and then with the group being introduced to mapping.

4. Do not go head-to-head

The challenge is to work side-by-side with the group when you are standing at the front of a room full of people and you have the magic marker with the top off and a dauntingly blank sheet of paper, and the group is in a hurry to get to the next task and full of feelings about the meeting they have just finished with management. It is at such moments that there is the risk of going head-to-head. There is a pull to do the mapping for the group. Or worse, doing the mapping to the group in the form of a confrontation or form of going head-to-head with members of the group. Those who are excessively interpretive or fixed in their method of formulation can end up doing a map to the group against the democratic spirit of mapping side-by-side. So practically, don't get into an argument, or one-on-one conversation about what to put on the map. Invite dialogue through the words on the map.

5. Use the map to help you

Those taking part in reflective mapping won't make friends with the mapping process if the mapper is not doing so. The mapper as facilitator needs to always be working through the map and be inviting others to help him or her get a workable and accessible shape to the map.

6. Don't overlook the quieter words

There can be times when mapping and tracking a conversation that the loudest voices and strongest opinions dominate. Don't miss putting the strongly held views on paper but listen out also for the quieter words. The facilitator is modelling the listening function of the mapping process. It stands or falls as evidence of listening and the mapper's job is to use the map to show that someone is listening.

7. Trust someone else to make the links and see the gaps

The mapper and facilitator are often too close to the process of mapping to see the emerging patterns. There are times to constructively dither with the pen in hand and let the group make the links and find the gaps on the map. Our brain's need for coherence is such that we will see a pattern out of a mess of words and arrows.

8. Work with allies

Being able to get a conversation going with a map is something some will have more of a knack for than others. In many cases it has been an occupational therapist, a healthcare assistant who has got the relational and dynamic idea of reflective mapping quickest and in the latter case a front-line view of what is going on. Mapping together develops a relational mindset but some people by virtue of temperament, status or professional role will not see patterns on paper or see the push and pull between people and events. Reflective mapping allows a subtle change process to be nurtured where authority in that moment of reflection is distributed and there is an opportunity for open dialogue. In this context an ally is not someone who agrees with your view or the view emerging on the map but the person who can hover and shimmer between different feelings and ideas and bring another perspective.

9. Make friends with mapper anxiety

Just as there are first time nerves in learning to ski or play the guitar or be a parent there is what we have dubbed *'mapper anxiety'*. This anxiety may be more than an anxiety about being a good mapper or getting the map right. It may also be a signal anxiety between those taking part that something important or troublesome may be touched upon. The mapper needs to befriend and tolerate his or her anxiety because it may be the key to being able to hover and shimmer with the uncertain process of working with feelings in the moment or feelings that are being transferred onto the activity of mapping. If the anxiety can be tolerated and such traps as perfectionism, doing the mapping for the person, or putting the mapping off or dismissing it as a conversational aid can be avoided then anxiety can be an acceptable and integrated part of the process of reflective discovery.

10. Practise on your own with small groups
A great way to gain confidence in the informal process of mapping is to practise with small groups of four or five around a table with a big sheet of paper that all can see, touch and add to; or practise mapping on your own as a way of reflecting on your working day and little incidents that come to mind. Mapping alone can be a major resource for self-reflection, self-talk and supervision. Relational mapping skills can be developed by practising with a colleague or friend. If you are professionally involved in helping people, mapping with simple goals such as helping track the conversation or spot a pattern can be done well without risk of harm or embarrassment.

Concluding comments
There is much more that could be said about the steps to reflective mapping. Many of the answers will be found in the other chapters and pages of this book. In summary, the mapping facilitator or consultant needs to use the process of putting words on paper to help a reflective conversation develop. Moments of hesitation, checking and wondering about the right words with those present are moments inviting another level of reflection. It enables ideas and feelings to be discussed without loading the ownership of the ideas and feelings onto one person or pointing fingers at each other along the accusatory lines of you said this when I did that. It is more possible to help build a relationally aware and reflective culture in the organization or team by talking with and through the map about what we are doing and how we are party to this or that pattern of interaction.

Chapter 7: Reflective practice – case studies from forensic settings

Jenny Marshall, Louise Yorke, Alison Bickerdike, Clare Bingham, Nicola Kemp, Vicky Millar and Mark Ramm

Introduction

Many forensic services have adopted CAT as a model for reflective practice but interestingly the different services have implemented these in different ways. This chapter aims to demonstrate the versatility of the model and is by no means an exhaustive list of examples of how the model can be implemented. In true CAT style, this chapter is a collection of voices from the forensic CAT community sharing their experiences.

The first voice sharing their experiences is Louise Yorke. Louise developed a model for a whole systems approach to reflective culture which incorporates a relational philosophy, an operational model and clear methods for translating these into practice to improve routine care. This is a clear example of building a reflective culture simultaneously from the 'top-down' (philosophy and operational model) and 'bottom-up' (systems for improving clinical practice).

First voice: Building a whole systems reflective culture – relational discovery the model and practice – Louise Yorke

Reflective practice is a core element of personal and professional development. However, it is often implemented as a stand-alone function within the workplace. Deemed as necessary for wellbeing and ethical practice, but often poorly misunderstood and implemented, reflective practice can become an intended or poorly valued and poorly attended element of a service, with negative implications for practice. Integrating reflective practice and developing a reflective culture may be one answer to the eternal question, how do we improve reflective practice for the individual and the organization.

Environments that support emotional and physical wellbeing make good personal and professional sense for individuals as well as organizations. Internationally, as described by organizational and clinical literatures, relational approaches have demonstrated the capacity to revolutionize environments, whether these relate to the person, group or associated system. Talked about in recent years using the term wellbeing, it is recognised that when the strategic focus is relational the culture of the workplace improves. Benefits of a relationally informed environment include improved recruitment and retention, lower stress, bullying and sickness absence, fewer complaints, increased motivation and improved productivity.

Inspired by this knowledge, in 2016 a novel model, Relational Discovery, was developed. Relational Discovery is a service framework with a tripartite function, described as:

1. A philosophy of care that can shape relational culture
2. A six-element operational model that supports the implementation and sustainability of the approach
3. A relational means to enhance and inform routine clinical practice.

Informed by relational theory and the Cognitive Analytic Therapy (CAT) model, and consistent with trauma informed ways of working, psychologically-informed environment approaches, and the extension of recovery frameworks to the more curious and egalitarian, Relational Discovery was designed to be used flexibly in healthcare settings, across both the clinical and operational elements of an organization. However, the model is equally applicable to non-health contexts. The model aims to support and sustain the dynamic process of development and change that is equally applicable for management, the employee, patient or customer.

By developing a model to support cultural change and promote the wellbeing and development of staff as well as patients so that they can continuously improve delivery of excellent care, Relational Discovery aims to foster a therapeutic learning culture to nourish and improve the quality of life of all people working within or using services, their families and friends. Named as a model of good practice in healthcare (Royal College of Psychiatrists, 2016–2018), whether implemented in part or fully, Relational Discovery is designed to support financial and organizational wellbeing and stability.

The three elements of Relational Discovery are identified as:

1. Relational culture
- Develop and publicise a statement of relational intent with an associated relational vision
- Recognise that culture is what we do every day and that every action affects relationships and culture

- Acknowledge that relationships can make, maintain and positively or negatively change problems or challenges that we experience
- Understand that past, present and future relationships affect us all in our relationship with self or other across the lifetime, which means that staff as well as patients, the employer as well as the employee, the vendor as well as the purchaser are involved in a dynamic relationship of reciprocation

2. Six operational elements – embedding a relational focus to:
- **Human resources policies and procedures;** including recruitment, line management, capability and disciplinary procedures
- **Teaching and training:** embedding a relational focus to induction and having a modular training programme from awareness to clinical training in cognitive analytic therapy, relationally informed reflective practice, supervision and consultation
- **Reflective practice:** ensuring that reflective practice and supervision is informed by the understanding of reciprocation and how self, other and society are linked in relationship. Developing an understanding of importance of and the multiple elements of reflective practice
- **Risk:** embedding relational understanding to consideration of risk to the person, the environment and the organization, including financial stability and sustainability
- **Pathways approach:** a relationally-informed pathways approach improves access to services, for example in a healthcare environment it improves access to therapies, provides a modular template for patient care pathways and staff development/careers. Pathways approaches are designed to improve flexibility and creativity and avoid duplication rather than to restrict or constrict
- **Governance and marketing:** governance is required in all organizations to ensure safe working, good practice and relevant monitoring and measurement required for operational stability and growth. Communication of strategy and associated processes is a vital element of the Relational Discovery model.

3. Clinical practice

As Relational Discovery is informed by clinical theory and specifically Cognitive Analytic Therapy (CAT), it is helpful to have service elements that are explicitly informed by CAT including therapy and visual relational mapping, as well as implicitly by relational and dialogical approaches. CAT can be used as a stand-alone therapy or provide a relational framework or understanding that compliments formulation and other therapies.

Implementation and sustainability

In order to implement and sustain this we continue to ask the 10 key questions:

1. Have we embedded or could we benefit from a Relational Discovery or Relational Discovery informed approach?
2. Does our approach consider the three elements of:
   - Relational culture?
   - Operational model?
   - Clinical practice?
3. Do we understand what it means to be in a relationship (with a thought, feeling, sensation, behaviour, with an object or another, with history, now or in the future)?
4. Have we considered the relational impact upon or from the self, other and society?
5. Have we involved all stakeholders? including, service users and carers, as well as administrative, clinical and operational managers.
6. Relational culture change needs to be understood, valued, and actively and financially supported by service managers and embedded within strategy and operational procedures. Have we taken this approach?
7. How are we implementing this? Are we using an iterative approach and responding to need?
8. Are we monitoring the impact of relational discovery?
9. Are we aware that relational culture change is not always easy?
10. Do we remember that culture change is a long-term process?

By continuing to ask these questions the invitation for a reflective practice using Relational Discovery is made.

The second voice comes from Jenny Marshall. In a similar way this describes the development of an overarching reflective model which was developed using both a 'top-down' and 'bottom-up' approach to develop a model for clinical practice. The model was clearly embedded and sustained for a period of time before being expanded beyond frontline culture to influence a relationally informed culture at a managerial and leadership level.

Second voice: building the scaffolding for reflective practice – Jenny Marshall

Forensic services are often working with the most complex issues and there can be a tendency to request reflective practice when there has been a major incident or crisis situation. However, the nature of these situations evoke strong feelings in staff which can compromise their ability to think and reflect. Instead, staff can be overwhelmed with fear of being scrutinised or criticised and judged as inadequate. At such times, the reflective space cannot be used effectively.

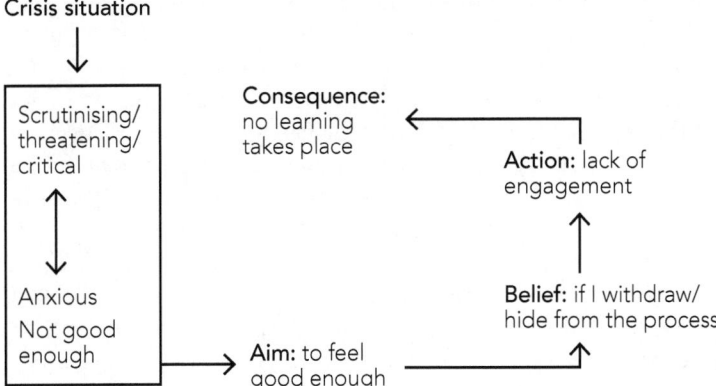

In therapy, clients do not access therapy sessions as stand-alone sessions in response to a crisis situation. The therapy framework provides a 'scaffolding' in which to build a therapeutic relationship, foster trust and safety and a secure base from which to explore difficult and often painful issues. It can be argued that reflective practice requires the same level of 'scaffolding'.

The initial 'scaffolding' was started with the senior leadership team which could be likened to gaining planning permission. It was necessary to enlist their support and backing in the development of an overarching reflective model to be developed across the service. Individual ward teams would receive two days training covering key components of the relational model including:

- the impact of early experiences and the development of reciprocal roles
- the impact of trauma on relationships and emotion regulation, relational patterns through the life span
- the development of mapping skills, applied to self-reflection, service users and teams.

The plan was to follow this up with regular reflective practice and for the model to be rolled out across the wards over an initial period of five years. Once planning permission had been gained, the actual building of the 'scaffolding' could start and this required support from key members of the nursing management structure, in order to develop processes for staff to be released from the wards to attend training and to cover the wards for reflective practice.

In the early days, there were numerous examples where staff changed their practice as a result of the reflective space. There were times when staff became more aware of how they were interacting and how they were being experienced by others. One staff member experienced a 'lightbulb moment' when an assault which had been previously thought of as happening out of the blue, was seen in a different light, 'I was humiliating him'. In another example, a significant shift in empathy was observed when staff discussed a service user who presented with ongoing psychotic symptoms and aggression. The space to reflect allowed them to notice brief interludes with him when he would discuss his interest in Shakespeare from his school days and they were able to remember him as a teenager who had hopes just like anyone else. Staff were able to reflect on the pulls to go head-to-head, reflecting in one case about how they seemed to have the same conflict at the same time of day each day and just noticing this seemed to free them up to consider how they could choose to do something different. The group format allowed for reflection on team dynamics and the pull to be controlling in order to achieve safety. Themes of power and control are often present in forensic services and reflection on them can allow staff to consider *'Is it necessary control and restrictions?'* which is important in a culture where we are trying to reduce restrictive practice.

Over time, it became apparent that holding the space for reflective practice was in a similar way to therapy, fostering trusting relationships and safety between facilitators and staff attending. An example of this was being approached by a member of staff who had been experiencing difficulty feeling compassion for a service user and wanted to develop some understanding of why this was happening. In a caring profession, it can be incredibly difficult to acknowledge struggling with empathy when it is at the heart of what we do, and this highlighted both the trust in this being safe to acknowledge, but also the belief that reflective practice would help.

It was also observed that the reflective practice was predominantly being attended by frontline staff and not managers who would often selflessly man the wards to release their team to attend. This led to the development of an adapted training for managers covering:

- reflection on their early experiences and relational patterns
- relational patterns within their work role as managers
- the relational dynamics within their managerial team and the wider organization.

Surprisingly, within these sessions, it was apparent that although the managers had not been attending reflective practice, they felt that they still spoke the language of the reflective model; that somehow, it was in the culture and they felt it gave them a voice. A testament to this was the service going through an integration and organizational change shortly after; the managers requested to increase their reflective space to support them through this transition suggesting that they trusted reflective practice as a safe space.

A further development followed with training for the leadership team. This was a significant investment of time for the senior leaders to dedicate and commit to two full days. Themes explored related to the self as a leader, management of organizational change and the leadership relational dynamics.

As with any building work or scaffolding, cracks may appear and repairs may be needed; maintenance is essential to any structure and this has been the case with reflective practice. In healthcare the workforce is only human and as such we will always be on the map but with ongoing attention to both the scaffolding of reflective practice and space, we can try to do this knowingly.

Our third group of voices comes from Alison Bickerdike, Clare Bingham and Nicola Kemp on behalf of a team of practitioners from different professional backgrounds. Uniquely, this example illustrates how reflective practice can be embraced within multidisciplinary teams in a collaborative manner and the importance of a robust supervision structure for reflective practice facilitators.

Third voice: 'Doing with not to': the map and talk approach – CAT-informed multidisciplinary reflective practice – Alison Bickerdike, Clare Bingham, Nicola Kemp

In 2013, there was increasing recognition at a national level of the need for effective reflective practice (RP) spaces. Both the Francis (Mid Staffordshire NHS Foundation Trust Public Inquiry, 2013) and Winterbourne (Department of Health, 2012) inquiries emphasised the abuses that can occur when compassionate care is absent or lost. Within our own service (a large Forensic Directorate in East London, comprised of 16 wards across low and medium secure services), the psychology department had historically been tasked with providing RP to some wards, on a 'case by case' basis. This often took the form of a psychologist delivering a session to often a very small group of more junior nursing staff. This sometimes left the nursing team feeling like reflective practice was being 'done' to them while the psychologists felt like they wanted to help but did not have enough training, supervision or any governance structure to safely facilitate these spaces. The different disciplines across the service started a dialogue about how reflective practice could be different. We decided that we wanted to train a *multidisciplinary team* of RP facilitators rather than the role being held by one discipline alone, and three RP project leads started a project to deliver RP across the whole Forensic Directorate.

At the same time, the three RP project leads (two of whom had become CAT practitioners) had begun liaising with Steve Potter about the application of the CAT model in Reflective Practice. The accessibility and transparency of a CAT-informed mapping approach lent itself to our aims of training a number of staff across disciplines with the focus on 'using CAT' and not 'doing 'CAT'.

We called our project 'Map and talk'.

Approach

In 2014, the Project Leads and Steve Potter ran an initial 5-day training attended by 34 facilitators across the disciplines. Training was based on the 'Map and Talk' model (Kemp *et al*, 2017). The training included teaching key concepts and 'tools' of CAT, within a structure for delivering RP 'Map and talk' sessions, and of 'using CAT' rather than 'doing CAT'. The main concepts covered were: the CAT model; reciprocal roles; the helpers dance, and the rule of thirds (applying this learning to the interactions between staff, service users and the wider system, and considering the roles we are recruited into as RP facilitators); and a Map 'template' to facilitate the mapping of reciprocal role procedures.

We allocated a multidisciplinary pair of facilitators to each ward across the medium and low secure services. As well as discipline we considered a range of factors when pairing co-facilitators including breadth of experience, gender, ethnicity, culture, aiming for diversity over uniformity within the pairs. Although all facilitators work within the Forensic Service, they were not allocated to wards on which they had clinical duties. Each ward now has a monthly RP 'Map and talk' session at their away day for the whole multidisciplinary team. Another ward covers the nursing rota for this time, enabling as many people from the team to attend as possible.

The training is embedded, supported and updated through a robust supervision structure. Each pair of facilitators attend one of three monthly supervision groups, five or six pairs attending each group. Each group has a pair of supervisors, multidisciplinary whenever possible, mirroring what happens in the ward-based groups. Supervision groups provide an opportunity for skills practice, sharing the experience of delivering 'map and talk' sessions, mapping the process of the 'map and talk' sessions and therefore reiteratively engaging in a reflective process about the process of reflective practice. Three of the supervisors are also the project leads and responsible for development of the project structure, maintenance and governance. The supervisors/project leads have monthly external supervision with Steve Potter.

In this way the supervision structure helps maintain competencies, supports an iterative process of reflection taking place with an increasingly wider lens on the Forensic Directorate, and maintains emotional support for facilitators, supervisors and groups. This supervision structure is described in more detail and discussed in Chapter 10.

Reflections

At the time of writing, 'Map and talk' has been delivered across the East London Forensic Directorate for over six years. We have successfully established a safe, inclusive, multidisciplinary facilitated CAT-informed relational approach, training over 60 multidisciplinary team (MDT) members of staff to date continue to deliver monthly MDT reflective practice sessions at monthly team away days.

One of the unique features of our approach seems to be in the MDT focus across the structure of the project mirroring the structure of the teams and wards. The inclusiveness of our approach encourages side-by-side collaborative reflection, as an antidote to the task focused, hierarchical dynamics often re-enacted in forensic structures. The Map and talk model enables those very structures to also be named and reflected upon, thereby increasing access to alternative relational positions, and helping to combat the repetition of unhelpful relationships and procedures. The ethos of 'name the dance not the dancer' is also crucial as an antidote to what can be a pervasive culture of blame in forensic systems geared up to assess and manage risk.

Working in pairs has also been a unique feature of our model, and important in maintaining the 'doing with' aspect. This brings the benefit of modelling multidisciplinary working, enables both parts of the pair to wear 'different hats' and name these different perspectives in a helpful way; and enables disentanglement of roles and greater opportunity for reflection when, as a facilitator, our own third is activated and we too are 'in the dance'. It allows us to explore and reflect on other dimensions of difference such as gender, culture, age, power and how this might impact on the roles we, staff and service users are recruited into. In addition to bringing the experience of delivering a session to the supervision group, pairs often map in dialogue to debrief afterwards.

The CAT model lends itself to multidisciplinary working, it is not owned by psychology or psychologists, as we sought to replicate with the 'Map and talk' model, creating a 'common language' to reflect together on the interpersonal dynamics of the service.

As well as the positives, this approach has also raised challenges, such as ensuring competencies of all facilitators. The impact of our supervision structure, multidisciplinary working on our experience of this model of Reflective Practice, is further outlined in Chapter 10.

Summary

We have found 'Map and talk' an approach which works well with and reflects some very positive aspects of our culture which is synchronous with origins of CAT. We think it fits particularly well with the wider East London community setting, in the ability to name and acknowledge social, cultural and other inequalities bearing on our Forensic setting.

The fourth voice comes from Mark Ramm who describes a longer-term and more organic development of CAT within a medium secure unit with CAT Practitioners exploring and developing various applications of CAT in a forensic setting, including the use of CAT in the provision of reflective practice.

Fourth voice: contextual Cognitive Analytic Therapy in a forensic setting – Mark Ramm

Having completed my CAT Practitioner training in 1999, I was appointed as the Head of Psychological Services for NHS Lothian which included a new regional medium secure unit (the Orchard Clinic) serving both male and female forensic inpatients which fully opened in 2001.

Like many others I saw that in addition to 'doing' CAT as an individual therapy, we could be 'using' CAT understandings to underpin many other aspects of forensic work. Over the years various colleagues including Laura Black, Jamie Kirkland, Vicky Millar, Shauneen Porter and Louise Tansey have helped me to explore the application of CAT to formulation driven teamwork, the systemic operation of organizations, risk assessment and risk management (Ramm, 2010).

Within the Orchard Clinic a particular focus has always been understanding and managing the relationship between staff and the patients since this was identified as being a primary mechanism for therapeutic change. The importance of what was initially referred to as the Therapeutic Milieu has increasingly been recognised and this term now overlaps with concepts such as Structured Clinical Care. Livesley (2012) describes this as something that is required to support the change process and any structured interventions to address personality disorder.

However, how did things start? Initially, I was in a situation where I was the only CAT practitioner in forensic services in Scotland, and no one that I was working with knew anything about CAT. In addition to providing some initial trainings I began doing CAT therapy with patients and talking about this and sharing my general CAT understandings with Clinical Team members. Trainees and the staff who I appointed to the Psychology Department also became enthusiastic about CAT. As interest grew, a crisis situation in relation to the management of a particular patient provided one catalyst for CAT to further develop.

A CAT framework was used to structure a series of multidisciplinary meetings with a confused and troubled clinical team during which staff could express their feelings, explore the traumatic development and psychological functioning of the patient, and examine the dynamics which took place between themselves and the patient. Since this process arrived at a successful conclusion that included effective but compassionate methods for moving forward this experience had a transformative effect.

In spite of the lack of outcome research, the success of this contextual application of CAT meant other senior managers backed the development of CAT within the unit, in particular by agreeing that the limited training budget would be spent on continuing to provide an annual five-day CAT training. This introductory training had been written by myself in conjunction with Ian Kerr and was originally co-delivered with him. It has been repeated at least once every year since then and is attended by all disciplines and all levels of staff from nursing assistants to Consultant Psychiatrists. It has also been delivered to various other forensic services across Scotland.

However, although this CAT training has consistently been valued by staff, and appears to provide a clear model and common therapeutic language for guiding the general approach of the Orchard Clinic (particularly in relation to complex trauma, personality disorder problems and offending behaviour), an ongoing challenge has always been to find better ways to support staff and to link CAT understandings more directly to actual service delivery and specific interventions.

Over the years different clinicians have explored the facilitation of contextual work with staff at the unit in different ways. The most common format has been via staff meetings which became known as 'CAT chats'. These have generally involved a CAT practitioner from the psychology department facilitating ward-based meetings with the staff there once a week. They usually involve use of the 'Map and talk' approach which Steve Potter helped us to further expand at the Orchard Clinic.

In providing CAT chats, facilitators have generally taken the approach of responding to what the staff need at any particular time. Therefore, the format has often been flexible rather than prescriptive. This means that, sometimes, staff have wanted to discuss a single incident or to express their feelings about the organization or a patient. Sometimes, a series of interactions with a patient have been considered and patterns identified. Sometimes, an examination of a patient's life history or a fuller CAT formulation has been developed from the staff's point of view, and so on.

It should be noted that in recent years all staff at the Orchard Clinic also have access to completely separate, closed, monthly supervision groups run by a psychodynamic psychotherapist who is completely independent from the unit. However, a central and recurring question in development of CAT chats has been whether they should simply be a confidential reflective space for staff or whether they should (at least in some cases) more directly inform clinical interventions. Both ways of conducting the meetings have occurred in the Orchard Clinic at different times. Clearly staff feeling safe to express themselves at the meetings must be the priority, but frequently it has been the staff attending CAT chats who want to share their newly gained insights in order to improve clinical care beyond their own practice.

Therefore, it has generally seemed better to think about a structured way of doing this as opposed to insisting that nothing which is expressed at the CAT chat should be shared outside the meeting. However, as those expressing personal views need to be protected and clinical decision making should only take place at full clinical team meetings careful measures need to be put in place. It is noted that those attending CAT chats must always agree to what (if anything) is fed back from the meeting that may be used in the formal decision-making process. Although this is not an expected or even routine outcome from CAT chats, CAT understandings are now one of the agenda items at CPA meetings.

Although there are currently 8 CAT practitioners at the Orchard Clinic including a music therapist and a psychiatrist, job plans have meant it is clinical psychologists who have generally facilitated the CAT chats. At one point an ACAT CAT skills level training was run in-house to empower more nursing and other staff to take on the role and this definitely enhanced the general process. However, perhaps because the complex CAT chat facilitator role is not clearly defined, it has generally reverted to clinicians who have experience of delivering individual therapy. This therefore places an additional requirement on them to remain inclusive and collaborative in the way that they conduct the role and avoid taking on the position of 'expert'.

In addition, it should be noted that the CAT chat facilitators also tend to know the staff and the patients who are involved in the process. A downside is clearly that they may be too close to the issues that arise and perhaps lack sufficient objectivity. But on the other hand, they are better placed to fully understand whatever is being raised. Also, by being part of the team that is struggling with an issue they are clearly seen as trusted group members rather than external experts who have been deployed to 'judge' and 'direct'.

Clearly, whenever a CAT Chat is allowed to have several functions (sometimes simultaneously) this has the potential to cause various complications and problems. In addition, the complexity and judgement required by this way of working has meant that the CAT Chat facilitators have needed to be experienced clinicians. However, to date it seems that this innovative approach within the general background of a CAT-informed culture at the Orchard Clinic has provided many more benefits than difficulties. It is encouraging that a research study of a CAT Chat meeting using a Repertory Grid analysis reported positive effects from this approach (Doyle, Tansey & Kirkland, 2019). However, exploring what works best is an ongoing process and continuing research and evaluation should be central to the evolution of practice.

The final voice in this chapter comes from Vicky Millar. This very personal example illustrates some of the key principles involved in reflective practice, keeping a dialogue going, fostering connection between staff, holding high emotion and mapping to enable different ways of thinking/feeling including empathy.

Fifth voice: contextual Cognitive Analytic Therapy in a forensic setting: personal reflections – Victoria Millar

Contextual CAT was already embedded in the culture of the Orchard Clinic when I arrived. Contextual CAT allows a shared inter-psychological space (Leiman, 1994) to allow staff to come together with the aim of creating a safe enough space to explore their experiences.

There was a four-day introductory CAT training that took place a couple of times a year for all staff to attend in order to give a basic grounding in CAT. I found this training hugely helpful and wondered about keeping the dialogue going between trainings. As a department we evolved the 'CAT chat', essentially providing a shared inter-psychological space for all staff to tap into. At this stage I was able to hold a basic CAT frame and to use some of the CAT concepts, such as reciprocal roles (RRs), reciprocal role procedures (RRPs), and target problem procedures (TPPs) to begin to develop with staff a contextual sequential diagrammatic reformulation (SDR) or map. I was then able to, with supervision, map in the room with staff (generally nurses) in relation to discussions around the service user, to help create a shared understanding (Kerr, 1999).

CAT embraces a clinical stance of (pro)active participation and collaboration (Carradice, 2004). However, in reflecting back now I realise I held a simple frame, but initially I struggled to hold the theory behind the frame, and it has been challenging to integrate this frame with the, at times, complex theory. Also, contextual CAT, due to the emphasis in my work place, was the beginning of my CAT journey. Therefore, rather than adapting individual therapy I was learning contextual CAT 'on the job', which has felt quite demanding in this complex environment.

Personal therapy and supervision has helped me to become aware of my own RRs and RRPs. Personal therapy in particular helped CAT come alive for me where I could feel myself within the maps we were co-creating, holding in mind my wish to care and fix, essentially to contain. Part of the importance of my CAT journey has been to integrate the frame and theory while sitting with the struggle. This concept of sitting with the struggle is hugely relevant within contextual CAT. My hope is that via CAT chats we are able to create a shared inter-psychological space where staff are able to think about countertransference and to learn to sit with the struggle of working in a complex environment. Personally, I also found the concept of holding the observing eye useful, which allows you to hold a broader view and perspective when you can feel overwhelmed while caught up in a RR enactment. Contextually, the observing eye can also be helpful in holding in mind the many addressees.

At the core of the shared inter-psychological space in CAT chats were maps. Mapping is a useful tool that enables sign-mediated activity, as a transitional object, to aid internalisation. Leiman (1992) notes the mediating role of signs in the construction of mental activity. Leiman (2002) goes on to state that '*signs do not exist in the abstract… signs emerge only as part of human activity*'. Thinking of an example of a violent offender whom one member of staff described as a 'psychopath' after meeting him once, in mapping we were all also able to identify (and identify with) the 'frightened wee boy'. Another service user had a limited number of dominant RRs (abusing-abused, neglecting-neglected). This in itself was a powerful sign regarding the despair and sparseness in this man's life, which was felt in the room when we were mapping. The maps therefore enable staff to perhaps see the same RR enactments that they can be caught up in, from another perspective that can then be felt and internalised.

In continuing my CAT journey and more specifically my contextual CAT journey, as I continue to integrate the CAT frame with theory, I have felt how complex contextual work is. I am now very aware of the role of zone of proximal development (ZPD) (my own and staff attending the CAT chats) and how complex it can be to hold in mind and attend to the ranges of ZPD in the room, when the room is an ever-changing landscape (due to open attendance and differing levels of professional and CAT training). I wonder if I may have been more in a 'doing to' role, due to inexperience and anxiety to get it right and my (now known) wish to contain or fix. This 'fixing' role was highlighted by Steve Potter in the 'Helper's dance' (Staunton, Lloyd & Potter, 2015). The 'Helper's dance' resonated with me and helped to validate my experience in terms of at times feeling overwhelmed when working contextually, while again reinforcing the aim of sitting with and tolerating the struggle, a concept that can be mirrored throughout the culture of secure care.

CAT chats were developed in the clinic as a means of reflective practice, I can now reflect, by accident. Originally the aim was to contribute to the CAT environment within the clinic by keeping a CAT-informed dialogue going between trainings. The initial thought was to use a protected space and time as an opportunity for multidisciplinary team members to get together and talk about patients, using a CAT frame. Staff members generally picked 'tricky' patients that they were struggling with. In time there was consultation with charge nurses regarding the patient we talked about and the staff that attended, which allowed the space and time to be protected as staff were allocated to attend. It also allowed oversight regarding the dynamics on the ward, which was helpful and could be the focus of more discussion in terms of how the CAT chats were set up and to think further regarding their purpose.

Once together I wanted staff to feel heard, validated and increasingly I am aware it was an opportunity for staff to feel connected. Connected with each other in the room, but also to reflect on their connections with patients, colleagues and management. The CAT frame was invaluable in terms of giving a structure to the sometimes, high emotion in the room. Mapping was a central tool employed to be alongside one another and to co-construct and reflect an understanding of what was being said, in a CAT frame. I hoped that the map would allow those attending the CAT chats an opportunity to step back, to perhaps hold the observing eye and to begin to put together the experiences of patients in terms of their early life experiences and the reciprocal roles that we identified. At this point an additional aim was to elicit a degree of empathic concern to allow staff to perhaps see the patients in a different light, even just momentarily.

Attempting to hold the zone of proximal development (ZPD) for all participants in mind, it was then sometimes possible for staff to reflect on their practice in terms of perhaps seeing how some of the interactions they have with patients are re-enactments that they are pulled into, or begin to identify that they react to specific patients as they may 'press buttons' due to aspects of their own personality.

Since CAT chats were not specifically designed at the Orchard Clinic to deliver reflective practice, but instead have evolved over time in a way that generally incorporates most aspects of reflective practice, they raise some interesting possibilities in applying CAT thinking to reflective practice.

Summary

This chapter contains the voices of CAT practitioners using CAT as a relational model within forensic services. There is much to be learnt from hearing the voices of experience. The examples have illustrated how reflective practice may develop serendipitously, on a micro level through 'CAT chats'. When this happens, it is not to be underestimated, at best it may create 'buy in' once the service has seen the value, at worst it may still create glimmers of understanding, or compassion in otherwise perplexing situations. In other examples reflective practice may develop as part of a strategic or organizational plan to create a more reflective, compassionate and relational culture. These voices have been brought together to share practice but this is by no means an exhaustive list of ways that the model can be implemented. Instead, what has been illustrated is the versatile nature of the model. One of the underpinning principles of the model is that it is a collaboration. Our recommendation in any service looking to develop reflective practice would be to work in collaboration to find the model which bests fits the service 'push where it moves'. In true reflective style, one service could not claim to have 'got it right' or to have a 'finished product'. Organizationally, there is much that can still be learnt from these experiences and we hope as authors that this can be the start of a dialogue and reflection on the ways in which CAT can be used to enrich services, organizations and culture.

Chapter 8: Crossing and uncrossing the line – using CAT reflective practice to think about the reciprocal role enactments encountered in critical forensic situations

Jason Hepple

Introduction

Over the last few years I have developed a way of conducting CAT reflective practice in groups that is a development of the traditional Balint-style group (Hepple, 2019). CAT has always been an active and collaborative therapy, where the therapist formulates and maps out reciprocal role procedures that describe enactments both between the client and others in the outside world and also those occurring in the therapy room between client and therapist.

The more psychoanalytic style of a traditional Balint group involves a less active facilitator with more peer-led reflection and processing of material. My experience of running CAT reflective practice groups, particularly for junior doctors, showed the need for the facilitator to intervene quite actively in some situations when risk or safeguarding concerns emerged. This need for active containment, advice and supervision will clearly occur more often when staff are less experienced and the clinical setting is acute or forensic.

What has evolved is a flexible format that still begins with one of the participants presenting a case or work-related 'situation' followed by the opportunity for others to question and reflect. The facilitator will then draw together the threads into some form of formulation using the CAT principles of reciprocal roles and procedures. Sometimes, a simple map will be drawn. Material may be compared and contrasted with other cases and larger themes may emerge. The clinical work is always thought about in its organizational and social context and the emotional impact of professionals being drawn into enactments can be reflected upon. Any risk or safeguarding issues that have emerged will be named by the facilitator and a plan agreed for taking the next steps to manage these. All in all, this style of CAT reflective practice group is more of a hybrid of reflective practice and supervision based on CAT principles. Feedback suggests that it is helpful and containing and provides both a chance to process some of the emotional baggage accumulated in a busy mental health role as well as offering a learning experience.

Crossing and uncrossing the line

I will now offer a reflective formulation of a particular sort of critical situation that can occur in acute and forensic settings in mental health work. These ideas have evolved following a number of reflective practice groups and workshops where participants have brought this sort of material. The situations I am talking about can be thought of as ones in which the client has 'crossed a line' and the possibilities of returning back seem difficult to think about. The commonest situation of this kind is a hostage situation, so I will use that as an example, but there are other situations where the map may be helpful, for example when children have been kidnapped from an ex-partner or a person is holed up and threatening suicide and the situation becomes protracted. Professionals working in forensic settings will sometimes be caring for clients who have been involved in these situations in the past so I hope this formulation may be helpful in reflecting with and on these clients after the event.

The situations I am alluding to with this example are not motivated by terrorist or political ideologies, but are times when a client, who has often had a background of severely adverse childhood experience, finds that they have just been pushed too far; 'a straw that breaks the camel's back' allowing feelings of hurt, grief, helplessness and rage to motivate the person to lose their normal inhibitory mechanisms and take action that 'crosses the line'. Below is a brief fictional vignette I have used in workshops to set the scene:

Darren

28 years old. Lone, armed hostage-taker

Darren's background: Darren has no knowledge of his father. His mother had a heroin addiction and was unable to care for him. Darren was severely bullied at school as he was small for his age and then groomed and sexually abused by a teacher whilst in care. He was convicted of violent offences as he grew into adolescence. He has been barred from seeing his ex-partner due to perpetrating domestic abuse. She is mother of his two girls (8 and 5 years).

He has arrived at their bungalow uninvited and forced entry. He has now taken the three of them hostage. He has a hand gun. The police have arrived with an armed response. Darren is demanding a helicopter to 'take my family to Ireland' and is stating that he is 'not going back to prison.'

At first sight there seems no way back for Darren. He has already committed a number of offences including taking hostages and being in possession of a firearm. The first concern of the police will rightly be the safety of the ex-partner and the children. Darren may get shot and killed if he doesn't surrender to the police. He may kill himself or harm the hostages if the pressure builds on him. The reciprocal role 'annihilating to annihilated' must be one of the roles that occupies the territory above the line on the CAT map.

The reflective task is now to build the CAT map to describe the reciprocal roles below the line (the antecedents from Darren's relational past) and to describe the powerful role plays being enacted above the line; now in reality rather than just in fantasy. With the reciprocal roles mapped out it may be clearer to see how this situation evolved but, most importantly, it may be possible to reflect on the re-enactment of these roles in the present between Darren and the hostages, the police, the negotiators and any mental health staff that may become involved.

One of the first principles of CAT when dealing with harmful reciprocal role enactments is, as Tony Ryle (1998, p307) stated: *'The therapist's job here is straightforward – not to join the dance.'*

This seems a tough ask in such a critical situation, but maybe there are ways for, say, a mental health professional or negotiator involved to relate to Darren without re-enacting the harmful role plays from his past. The first task is thus to build up the map to get an overview of the situation.

Below the line

From what we know of Darren's past there is the combination of neglect and rejection leading on to abuse. A mother with a heroin addiction may, to the child, often be self-absorbed, neglecting and uncontaining, leaving it hard to name and process unmanageable feelings. The fact that Darren has no knowledge of his father may feel like a rejection as is the fact that he was taken into care because his mother could not look after him. The bullying introduced physical abuse, contempt and humiliation. As Darren grew up he may have learned to 'turn the tables' and become physically abusive of others to protect himself. When, in care, he also suffered sexual abuse after being groomed by a teacher, he may have seen this teacher as someone who did not reject him and offered him care and whom he allowed into his trust. It turned out that he was in fact deceived and that this man did not care about Darren but was only interested in his own gratification.

The predominant unmanageable feeling may be described as 'rage'. By this I mean feelings of great anger and helplessness that cannot be directed at an appropriate person and so are either projected out onto 'the world', 'people', 'the universe' or against the self in the form of self-contempt and shame. King Lear rages against the storm when he gradually becomes aware of his own destructiveness towards his daughters. I sometimes use a metaphor of the 'can of rage'. Fuelled by fires of hurt from the past it feels as if the pressure is building and will soon destroy the self and others. It causes fear of the self and the destructiveness it seems to contain. This can sometimes be called 'the monster in me'. It is rage, in my understanding, that can cause some people to 'cross the line' when under extreme stress.

So, I would put the reciprocal roles under the line into two groups:

neglecting / rejecting to neglected / rejected / worthless

abusing / contemptuous / deceiving to abused / humiliated / deceived

Above the line

When thinking about the reciprocal roles above the line I am influenced by a formulation of 'aggressive men' that extends the CAT understanding of narcissism rather than the more 'borderline' formulation of abusing to abused and the compensatory ideally caring or rescuing self-state (Shannon *et al*, 2006). The compensatory state to the reciprocal roles I have described below the line is one with admiring to admired as its basis. The only source of admiration for Darren, for example, may be to be feared and to be feared he needs to be in a position of omnipotence and control.

This is essentially a grandiose compensatory fantasy state. It is often the denouement of 'superhero' stories and films, where the arch-villain finally gains omnipotent control over the good guy superhero. The omnipotent self gains transcendent, perhaps godlike, powers of life and death over those under its omnipotent control. The other is helpless and in awe.

It is easy to see how this may be a successful fantasy self-state. Darren is perhaps imagining a time when people finally look up to him and maybe he can take revenge on those who have hurt him. The worm has turned. This has similarities with Erikson's 'shamelessness' (Erikson, 1963) where a person is so shamed and ostracised that they may feel they have nothing to lose in fighting back without thought of the consequences.

The difference here between fantasy and reality is that, in fantasy, the line has not been crossed. It is the crossing of the line in reality that brings with it the real prospect of life never being the same again and death being a real and immediate concern. Here we introduce the reciprocal role 'annihilating to annihilated'.

So, above the line we have:

omnipotently controlling / admired to omnipotently controlled / in awe

annihilating to annihilated

The problem with crossing the line in reality is that the omnipotence is often very short-lived. In Darren's case the police are already outside. The surge of power associated with finally crossing the line must, in my imagination, be tempered all the time by the alternative reality of death or incarceration. Others are in seeming awe of the omnipotent self but the flip side of this, of course, is that others also hold Darren in fear and contempt as he has finally proven what a 'monster' he actually is. The 'monster in me' is on the loose and Darren will likely be afraid of himself in this regard and feel shame for this part of him. So, we have a critical situation above the line that soon starts to resonate with the reciprocal roles below the line. This seems a general truth about narcissism, in that narcissistic, sycophantic admiration is always delivered with a simultaneous dose of contempt.

Putting all this together, we have the following map:

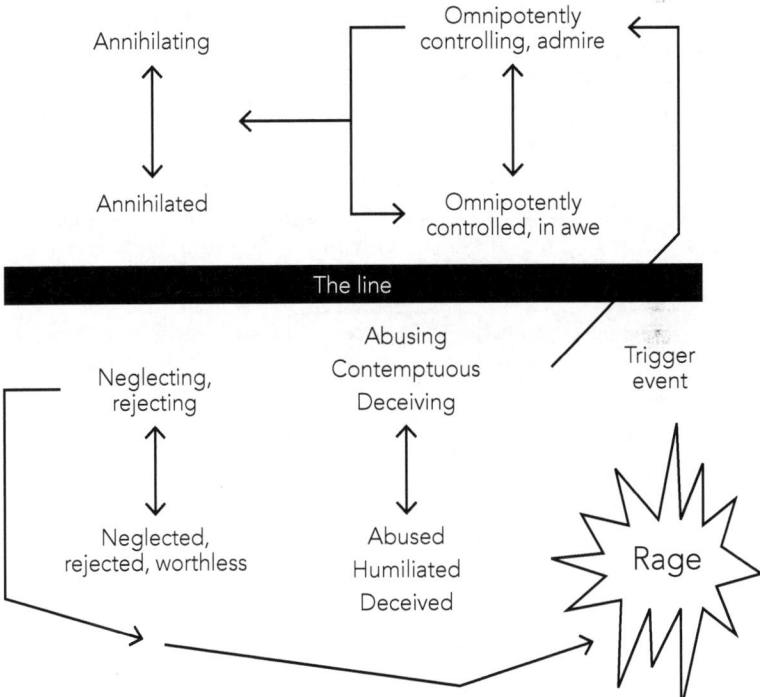

The map

The unmanageable feelings deriving from the bottom's roles of neglect abuse and humiliation fuel a desire to 'turn the tables' and assume the powerful top role positions (neglecting, abusing). Behaving in these positions does harm to others and then leaves the self full of self-contempt with possible self-abuse and self-neglect. In the face of some form of trigger event the controls that keep action below the line fail to operate and the line is crossed. Omnipotence may be experienced as if to prove that the reason this procedure did not work previously was because it 'did not go far enough'. Soon comes the realisation that this is reality and not fantasy and there is no easy way back. When the police armed response arrives, Darren is left in awe and terrified. There may be an oscillation between awe and terror and trying to regain omnipotent control by making threats and demands. Time passes and annihilation looks in through the window. Staring up from below the line are the unmanageable feelings of humiliation, shame and worthlessness.

Exercise: How to get off the Map?

This is the exercise I have used to help people think about how they might get into dialogue with Darren without enacting the reciprocal roles on the map.

> Imagine yourself at the scene in some professional role. It would be easy to be on the map. The situation is terrifying and presents a real risk to those on the scene of getting shot or injured. It would be easy to be in fear/awe of Darren in this proximity to annihilation. It would also be easy to neglect the fact that Darren is a person with inherent value, in favour of the pressing need to weigh up his welfare and that of the hostages. As time passes it may be easy to feel contempt for Darren and blame him for the pain and suffering he is inflicting on everyone. It might feel OK to deceive him; promise him something that is never going to materialise. Play him along until he makes a mistake and force can be used. All of this is on the map.

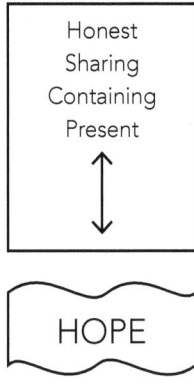

You have Darren on the phone? What can you say to him?

Some ideas

Here are some ideas that have evolved from people thinking about this exercise.

The present

The first approach is to concentrate on the present. It is clearly not the time for psychotherapy and asking questions that bring up material from Darren's past, as this could lead to unmanageable arousal and escalation. The present is something that the two of you share. It may be possible to be authentic and honest (not deceiving) while sharing some of the thoughts and feelings you are having in this situation. We are trying to enact the reciprocal role:

- In order to try to offer some containment it may be good to concentrate on the immediate environment that you and Darren find yourself in. It will be important for you to feel safe and to convey that to Darren. How safe does Darren feel? Maybe he could change his position, for example, by moving away from the windows and having his back to a solid wall. Once some immediate safety has been achieved it may be possible to help Darren ground himself in his body; to think about his posture and breathing.

- In order to maintain an honest position with Darren it will be important to establish the boundaries between your role and that of the police present and to share this with Darren. In the way of a mediator it may be possible for you to be alongside the conflict and not directly part of it. You can be honest in sharing perhaps that you do not have control over the police operation but that you are prepared to pass questions on and feed back the answers to Darren. If Darren is frustrated by the police response you can empathise with this. Will they actually order a helicopter? You can say that you honestly don't know. Does Darren actually think they will do this?

- Once there is some containment then it may be possible to share some of the feelings that you are both experiencing in this situation. How is Darren feeling? Is the situation as scary for you as you imagine it is for Darren? There will clearly be fear and Darren may well express a lot of anger. Can this be honestly and empathically brought into dialogue? Through the anger may come some of the child-derived bottom role feelings of hurt, grief and shame. If you 'feel' for Darren when these are exposed (and this has to be authentic), can you share this empathic counter-transference? 'I can feel that there is a lot of hurt here going back a long time.' 'That makes me feel sad when you talk about what has happened to you.' The presence of annihilation can be brought into dialogue in an empathic way by sharing your concerns for Darren: 'I am really worried for your safety if we don't find a way out of all this'.

- If there has been a containing dialogue it may be possible to move on to introduce the concept of hope. This line crossing situation feels hopeless, but it is clearly possible to de-escalate it and have a good outcome from where you both are now. Using the concept of hope starts a future orientated discussion.

The future

Listening
Creative
Hopeful

Both of you are alive and both of you have a potential future. It may be good to ask Darren about who is going to be important to him in his future. Clearly his family are important and so their safety is paramount. Can you both reflect on how the children are feeling in this situation? How would they like it to end? Is there anyone else important in Darren's future who is not here (maybe his parents, or siblings, or friends)? What would they want to happen now if they were here to ask? What would they say?

To maintain an honest position it will be important not to collude with the idea that Darren can just walk away from this situation without getting arrested and charged. But clearly, the sooner the situation is de-escalated the better the outcome for everyone. If a future orientated dialogue is possible, then the big question is: 'How are we going to get out of this situation?' If Darren is prepared to enter into this dialogue then your mediator role may be very useful at this point. What is Darren worried about happening if he were to hand over his weapon? What are the police suggesting as a way of uncrossing the line?

These ideas are simply ways of thinking about the situation without re-enacting harmful reciprocal roles. Clearly, Darren may be too omnipotent and angry to enter into any of this at the present time. It may be possible even in this scenario to remain honest and hopeful and to empathically connect with Darren's feelings. 'I can feel how angry and upset you are about the way things have turned out – look Darren – I am going to stay around and if you want to talk to me again I will be here on the phone for you.'

Looking back at a crossing of the line

This has come up a few times in reflective practice groups and is worth exploring a little as the same principles apply from the map presented earlier. Professionals in acute and forensic services may often work with people who have crossed the line in the past and engaged in serious crime that has harmed other people and themselves. If the person in the future is able to express remorse and share the child-derived feelings that fuelled the crossing then it is quite possible to stay off the map and engage empathically and authentically in meaningful exploration of the earlier experiences that led up to that point using CAT or another model of psychotherapy.

Sometimes, however, the crossing is looked back on from the 'above the line' position and the person takes an omnipotent stance with the aim of putting the listener in fear and awe. I have known this to be the case with some people whose offences have been notorious. There is a certain amount of 'bragging' designed to shock and an invitation to become voyeuristically drawn in to learn more of the detail of 'secrets' about the crime that have not so far come to light. Some of the public have a fascination with all this and, as you will know, some notorious criminals attract an admiring even adoring fan base. This is a re-enactment of a reciprocal role I have heard Steve Potter and Karen Shannon describe as:

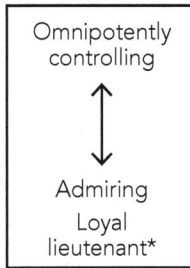

The invitation to the dance for the professional is to behave 'as if' admiring, mainly by not challenging the omnipotently told account. It may be that the professional does not wish to appear vulnerable to the person by expressing their own feelings and presents as cut off or withholding. This is likely to be playing out the deceitful top role as the professional is not expressing their empathic connection with the victims or with the person who crossed the line, and this may result in feelings of contempt and dismissal for the person and their crimes that are only expressed in supervision or reflective practice. It is as if a judgement has been made that the person is beyond or incapable of an empathic encounter. This is when words like 'psychopath' and 'evil' can be present in the conversation. This amounts to a contemptuous dismissal of the person who crossed the line and does not allow a reformulation of their story that remains empathic without failing to judge acts of abuse and neglect as wrong and harmful (Shannon *et al*, 2006).

The exit in this post-hoc encounter with the line is the same as in the critical situation. It may be possible to be honest, authentic and hopeful without dismissing or colluding with the person. Staying with the feelings to do with the empathic counter-transference is a good place to start. This may well be with the victims of the crimes to start with. 'When you tell me things like that, I can't help feeling for the people who were hurt that day. They must have been terrified, I know I would have been.' There will always be the person's story that led up to the crossing of the line and it may be possible to empathise with this and share this with the person. 'I am aware that a lot of awful things happened to you in the past that may have led up to that day. I am interested in hearing about that if you would like to share some of that with me.'

Finally, there are some people who relate a future fantasy of crossing the line in the same omnipotent way, even though they may never have engaged in any actual crime and may not, objectively, present significant risk of doing so. It is easier to see the hurt child speaking here and avoid being drawn into a contemptuous mocking of their threats and promises. In these cases it may still be important to empathically identify with imagined victims and then with the hurt in the person's own story.

Concluding thoughts

I hope that this has been a useful exploration of material which, in my experience, is regularly brought to reflective practice and supervision. It presents a way of looking at the re-enactment of harmful reciprocal roles that professionals may be easily drawn into due to the high emotional charge of the events themselves and also the power of the disavowed abuse and neglect at the heart of the person's story.

Chapter 9: Helping the helpers – the experiences of reflective practice from the perspective of facilitators

Jamie Kirkland, Heather Tolland, Emma Drysdale and Steve Jefferis

Introduction

In earlier chapters we have considered what a relational approach to delivering reflective practice (RP) might look like. We also explored what skills and competencies we feel would help those delivering RP and how a Cognitive Analytic Therapy (CAT) informed approach can be used. If we acknowledge that CAT, as a relational approach, works both inter- and intra-personally, and we do, then can we apply such thinking to helping those who deliver RP? What might developments in CAT approaches offer in the ongoing support to those that deliver RP? We are going to call this 'helping the helpers'.

We are going to focus upon a service response to delivering RP, describe the remit of this service and some of the challenges. We will describe a qualitative evaluation of the service through asking the helpers how they feel about the help they offer; through a relational tool called the 'Helpers dance list' (Potter, 2013, provided here as Appendix 1). We will also go on to consider developments in this area in a rapidly changing environment with reference to the COVID-19 pandemic through the development of the 'Covid Struggles List' (Jeffries, 2020, provided here as Appendix 2).

Setting the scene

Our identity is often shaped by the work that we do, and it is common to experience challenging and powerful emotions in our workplace, particularly in helping roles (Staunton *et al*, 2015). When things are going well, people can feel valued, however when they experience challenges, this can lead to feeling unappreciated and worthless. People employ coping strategies in response to difficulties they face at work, which can have an impact on their emotional wellbeing (Aitken & Schloss, 1994). This has led to an increased focus on helping staff to reflect on these difficulties and challenges using a relationally informed (psychological) model.

We are seeking to demonstrate in this book that the benefits of reflective practice in criminal justice and forensic environments are argued to be compassionate care, staff resilience, and an improved workplace environment. In forensic and criminal justice services, the challenges posed by patients with complex histories of offending and trauma, such as aggressive or violent outbursts can be distressing for staff. In addition, the secure environment presents barriers to person-centred care. Reflective practice is one way of supporting staff to deal with these challenges. But it is important to remember that those supporting staff and delivering reflective practice are also subject to the same challenges and pressures. The same stories, the same human reactions, the same difficult solutions or in CAT terms 'traps, dilemmas and snags', leading hopefully to more helpful 'exits'.

One might anticipate that for professionals' working in this area delivering reflective practice may lead to striving to provide the ideal caring role. This may mirror such a striving role throughout the services. We could see this 'striving to be caring' as both connecting with the offender through their trauma background or mental health distress, just as we might see the 'striving to be caring' as a professional's response to protect the public through ensuring offender treatment, rehabilitation and risk management. In turn these goals could be frustrated by barriers such as complex systems and a lack of resources. With this in mind, the political context of public services (such as the health or criminal justice setting) are likely to be of importance and in turn perhaps be reflected in the experiences of reflective practice facilitators.

In order to illustrate we will go on to present an example of a service where we used a CAT-informed tool, the 'Helpers' dance list' (Potter, 2010, provided here as Appendix 1), to begin to understand facilitator experiences of delivering reflective practice across community, low and medium secure forensic settings. This is in the context of a service where the model for delivering reflective practice is not exclusively CAT. We will go on to identify the main reciprocal roles and procedures held by staff delivering reflective practice in these settings and use the findings to develop a shared language with the facilitators to begin to enhance relational awareness.

CAT for staff approaches to working in challenging environments – developing a shared language

Cognitive analytic therapy (CAT) (Ryle & Kerr, 2020) as a psychotherapeutic approach, has a primary focus on relational difficulties. CAT takes a position that there are patterns of interpersonal interactions that people engage in that can become problematic and so the model seeks to develop a shared understanding of these patterns. The importance of a shared language was written about by Ryle (1978) in the paper *'A common language for the psychotherapies'*.

As a process this is achieved through (client or team) reformulation, in a letter, and by a diagrammatic representation of the patterns of interpersonal, behavioural, cognitive and affective patterns, termed a 'sequential diagrammatic reformulation' (SDR). The SDR can provide a shared language and be the basis for a consistent approach between staff teams and the patient or offender (Kirkland & Baron, 2014). In the evolving nature of CAT there have been developments in the use of SDRs. Potter (2010) explained three levels of 'mapping':

1. *sketches* (early and impromptu sketches of patterns of interaction drawn from the client's initial accounts of interacting with the self, others and the world)
2. *life maps* (trying to capture the bigger picture and key positions of someone's life experience as a whole)
3. *early SDR's* (a more complex therapy map akin to a full SDR).

There is a growing body of literature that explores the application of CAT-informed approaches to teamwork and this has been explored in earlier chapters. The premise of this book is that a cognitive analytic informed approach can help those who work in forensic and criminal justice services. CAT can help to understand the offending behaviour, help to understand the repeating patterns an offender may get into but most importantly help those working alongside to understand what they are pulled into and what enactments may be occurring. Having a model to understand this can help us all to make sense of the challenges we face. However, not all practitioners use CAT approaches; nor do all facilitators use a CAT model in reflective practice. It is in this challenge that we wondered if we can still use CAT tools to help the helpers.

CAT and reflective practice in a specific service example – Glasgow, UK

With a growing evidence base for CAT approaches, and the model increasingly being used across staff groups and teams the focus in the book is upon utilising CAT as a method to deliver RP. On a local level, reflective practice is a key component of staff learning and practice within the Directorate of Forensic Mental Health and Learning Disabilities (DFMH & LD) in Glasgow. Within the Directorate, reflective practice sessions take place across community, low and medium secure settings approximately every 4–6 weeks and are facilitated by the clinical psychologist on the ward, or working within the community. The format of the reflective practice sessions is flexible depending on the group and the style of the facilitator.

For example, it may involve discussing specific behaviours or situations on the ward/community, or it may be around a more general topic area.

Previous local service evaluations of reflective practice focused upon the experience of staff receiving reflective practice but little work has explored the experiences of the facilitators of the reflective practice. As a starting point, and informed by research indicating the value of staff being trained in CAT-informed approaches, members of the psychology department attended a four-day training in CAT applied to forensic settings. An accredited CAT practitioner and supervisor (first author) provided support and supervision to these staff. However, not all staff chose to utilise a CAT approach to the reflective practice they provide.

In essence the 'shared language' was beginning to be developed in the service but not everyone necessarily spoke it! In order to support relational awareness amongst those delivering reflective practice it was felt important to ask them how they felt about their practice: how they were pushed, challenged or held back; and, how they related to the task in hand. The aim was to see if using a CAT-informed tool could provide a means of providing a reflective space to the helpers.

CAT and reciprocal role's through the Helper's Dance list

The *Helper's Dance List* (Potter, 2013; see Appendix 1) was selected as an appropriate measure to provide insight into how facilitators perceive team interaction in reflective practice sessions. The list is a tool that consists of a checklist of 18 interactions that are typical of helping relationships, including caring, therapeutic and supervisory relationships. 'Dance' is used to describe these interactions to reflect that the helping relationship is a joint activity and it can work in various ways. The Helper's Dance List has been developed as an aid to reflective practice, in that it identifies the interactions or 'dances' typical of that specific team and raises topics for discussion. It can be used to identify 'unhelpful' dances that staff might be involved in and presents an opportunity to discuss how reflective practice may be improved thus providing discussion around potential 'exits' from these unhelpful patterns.

In using the list the respondents are asked to indicate the extent to which they agree with each statement, on a 5-point Likert scale. The checklist has similarities in function to the Psychotherapy File (Ryle & Kerr, 2020), except that it is specific for people in a helper's role. As the approach to delivering reflective practice sessions can vary, the beginning of the survey also asked participants to indicate which description most closely reflected a description of the approach to their own reflective practice sessions.

The data was to be analysed using descriptive statistics, showing the frequencies for each type of interaction/dance. It was then used to identify any particularly 'unhelpful' dances that are common among teams during reflective practice through the development of a CAT 'map' in a group exercise. As such the primary aim was to use this tool to help shape a conversation between the 'helpers', and provide 'reflection on reflection'.

What are you delivering?

One challenge we all face may be summed up as 'are we delivering what we think we are delivering?' In terms of a description of reflective practice, of the nine teams invited to take part in the study, six selected the description that defined reflective practice according to the local Directorate policy definition of reflective practice, which was:

> *Reflective practice sessions seek to develop the capacity to reflect on actions so as to engage in a process of continuous learning. It involves paying critical attention to the practical values and theories which inform everyday actions, by examining practice reflectively and reflexively. This leads to developmental insight.*

However, of those responding, three teams selected the description of their approach that defined *case consultation* as follows:

> *Reflective practice sessions are a theoretically-based explanation or conceptualisation of the information obtained from a clinical assessment. The sessions seek to offer a hypothesis about the cause and nature of the presenting problems and are considered an adjunct or alternative approach to the more categorical approach of psychiatric diagnosis. In reflective practice sessions, formulations are used to communicate a hypothesis and provide framework for developing the most suitable treatment approach.*

This was an interesting starting point. These self-reports suggested that the delivery of reflective practice for some was more structured, even safer perhaps, if following a case consultation route, rather than reflective practice. This may well be akin to the Balint type groups described earlier but it also challenges us to consider if already the helpers are perhaps taking up a position of 'doing to' rather than 'being with'.

Name your dance

In terms of the items scored as '*often*' or '*always*' on the Helper's Dance list, the frequently Danced 'Dances' are detailed in Table 1:

Table 1: List of 'dances' scored as 'often' or 'always' by participants on The Helper's Dance List

Name of dance scored as OFTEN or ALWAYS	Dance description
Bantering or reserved	There is a lot of friendly banter between us.
Never good enough	We have high expectations of ourselves which makes us think our help won't be good enough, others will be disappointed and we will cope by trying even harder.
Either it's our way or the wrong way	If we think we are helping in the right way we can stick to it stubbornly and find it hard hearing it could be done another way.
Lose perspective	We can get so involved in the detail we forget the bigger picture.
Switch off	When we are upset we keep our feelings hidden and switch off.
Not here, not now	We see the need to talk about what is happening between us but because it feels difficult we tend to put it off.
Tell us what to do	When we are not sure what to do we prefer to be told by someone rather than figure it out.
Bad guys	When things go wrong it is usually something that people other than us have failed to do.
If we don't help no one will	Other teams won't see the need, or have the know-how to help so it is left up to us to provide the care that someone needs.
Lack of resources frustrates us	We know what needs doing and how to help but when the money, the treatment or support is not available we feel frustrated, angry or helpless.
Looking after others means neglecting ourselves	We put so much into looking after others that their needs take over and we forget to look after ourselves enough.

Many participants described how their workload has been steadily increasing and becoming less relevant as they felt they were 'controlled' from orders above. These were captured by items such as: 'When the person or the team we are helping is too demanding: we feel put upon and suffer in silence but won't complain for fear of upsetting them and causing trouble.' Other items included: 'Lose perspective: We can get so involved in the detail we forget the bigger picture'. Comments relating to this included 'an NHS culture that is policy driven.' Perhaps this has led to feelings of helplessness with items such as: *'Our hands are tied: With a freer hand we could be more helpful but we must follow the rules.'*

The helpers then attempt to take the rescuing role and feel highly responsible and obliged to meet such demands for the benefit of the people they help. Of note was the comment: *'However, this is not always possible due to various barriers, such as lack of resources, which can lead to becoming overwhelmed, frustrated and helpless.'* Not a position to experience that makes the helper want to repeat the experience!

If there was an overwhelming sense from the responses that staff were striving to meet demands, a procedure labelled in Jones and Childs (2007), then it was also of note that those dances named as 'rarely' or 'not at all' were those that did not allow time to pause, reflect and just 'be'. Items not identified included 'let it be and wait and see' and are shown in Table 2.

Table 2: The items on the checklist for which the majority of respondents selected 'rarely' or 'not at all' were:

Name of dance scored as 'RARELY'	Dance description
Let it be and wait and see	When we are not sure what to do we tend to do nothing and wait and see.
Busy or bored	Either we are busy and feel needed or we are not busy and feel bored and restless.
Where were we?	We can get so involved in each other's feelings we lose sight of the task in hand or the purpose of the meeting.

Mapping the responses and looking for exits

These responses formed a starting point for a team discussion and a mapping exercise as can be seen in the figure below. Participants described a range of positions (reciprocal roles) they feel they take up in relation to those receiving the groups they facilitate. One theme was described as 'striving in relation to being helped'. The position of striving was at times feeling like a 'good guy' by helping a grateful and helped staff group through a shared, open banter, but it also elicited a set of roles being critical to criticised and judging to judged. These feelings being that the helpers were 'not good enough', that they must try harder and that 'if we don't help who will?'. Some of the literature (see eg, Lloyd & Clayton, 2013) has described this as shimmering between two positions of being heroic (I must try harder and rescue) or stoic (I need to save the team who are dealing with more than I have to deal with such as 13 hour inpatient shifts).

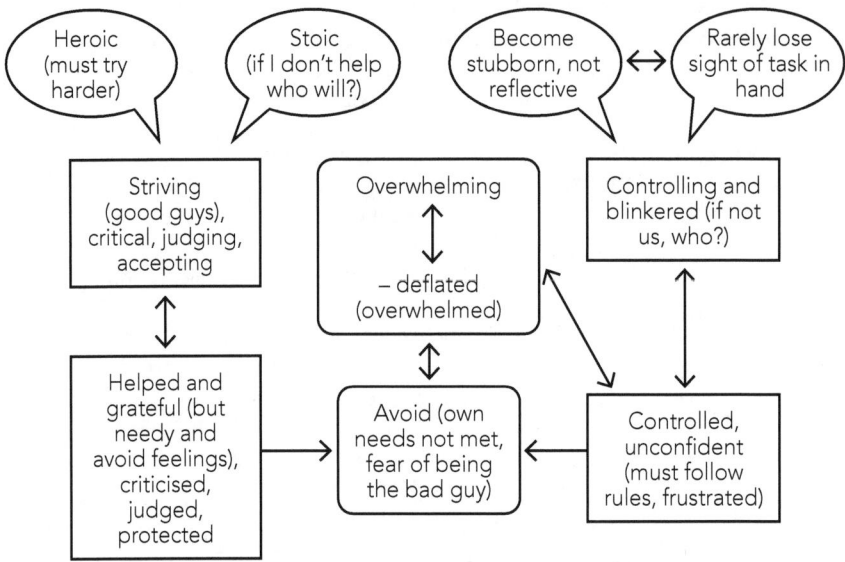

Whilst these positions can cycle at points the facilitator can feel deflated (overwhelming to overwhelmed). One exit is to seek out and enable the staff positions of being helped, grateful and heard. This may be the value of reflective sessions about reflective sessions (reflection on reflection) as well as regular update training. However, there was also evidence of avoidance. Participants described their own needs not being met, of neglecting oneself but also not addressing with the group difficult issues for fear of being the 'bad guy'. The desire to enact an accepting/protecting to accepted/protected role often meant that 'we put off what goes on between us'. This is a valid point because in this specific service it can make it harder for the facilitators to stand outside of the team because they are part of the team (psychologists deliver RP to their own team). Practically the helper is more available (being part of the team) and in such a varied service (community, low secure and medium secure settings) it can be logistically difficult to sustain external helpers. However, we do believe that using CAT mapping can allow some mitigation to this. The use of CAT mapping allows the helper to also be placed on the map.

From the mapping exercise it emerged that one alternative exit from feeling deflated can be to blame. This was demonstrated in the controlling/blinkered to controlled positions described by some. In the controlling role helpers discussed how in order to 'save' the team (the striving position) they would flip into blinkered controlling, become stubborn, really lose sight of the task in hand and keep tight control. In this position they are less reflective and perhaps too task focused. It is of note that facilitators 'rarely' scored that they would 'wait and see', something that one might consider an important skill in reflection! The reciprocal role is of being controlled. They described that a requirement to deliver reflective practice and follow rules (perhaps policy) can elicit feelings of being judged, but also frustrated. This then leads to lack of confidence.

From the dances that scored highly, many of the related comments appeared to overlap and so the 'striving to meet demands' trap has been suggested as a common combination of dances. Most commonly the procedure leads to helpers feeling overwhelmed, and participants often described feeling frustrated and helpless. However, for some the feeling of being overwhelmed is taken as a personal failure and leads to self-criticism and feelings of judgement from others. The trap is also likely to lead to low morale and many comments are suggestive of unhappiness.

What came out of the group mapping exercise was that there were many positive aspects to the responses. Participants often put forward their own exits to traps. For the 'striving to meet demands' trap exits included:

- choosing battles wisely
- accepting one's own limits
- seeking support from others
- redefining how success and failure is viewed
- building and maintaining a healthy home and work life balance.

In addition, the feedback for the Helper's Dance task was overwhelmingly positive. There was a shared realisation that similar themes were emerging – that it can feel like a lonely experience being the helper and that feeling of being pulled in many directions can mean one loses a sense of feeling grounded, from where space for reflection can flourish.

If the aim of this approach is to support, by scaffolding conversations, those that are delivering reflective practice, it also reasserts that creating a space to think allows us to creatively and sensitively respond to challenges in the workplace. Global events and political upheaval can dominate the discourse and crowd the thinking space. In the UK events such as leaving the European Union (Brexit) and the Black Lives Matter movement are two recent examples. The year of 2020 was dominated by the COVID-19 pandemic.

CAT reflective practice and Covid – the Covid Struggles List - Steve Jefferis

As the 2020 Covid pandemic took hold, healthcare staff found themselves dealing with enormous uncertainty, change and threat at short notice. Psychological services were in many cases invited to provide resources to support staff wellbeing. However, early evidence from China (Chen *et al*, 2020) sounded a note of caution: services' ideas about what psychological support should be provided were often quite different from what staff wanted themselves. At the Newcastle CAT Service (part of a large mental health and disability trust), when invited to make a contribution to staff support early in the pandemic, we wanted to avoid this trap by asking staff what they would find helpful. In two early online consultation sessions, particularly aimed at team leaders in our sister services, staff gave vivid descriptions of the challenges and stresses they faced. Rather than requesting advice on coping strategies, or direct psychological intervention, they said that what helped was space to air these experiences, and the mutual recognition that others were having similar experiences. This shared validation appeared to be, on top of practical matters of sufficient rest, PPE and resources for remote working, the main factor in supporting their own staff's wellbeing.

How, then, could this recognition of the value of reflection on the shared struggles be used more widely? Inspired by the Helpers Dance List, we drew up The Covid Struggles List – a two-page list of summary descriptions of the common struggles we had heard staff report (The list is freely available at http://tinyurl.com/CovidStrugglesMay2020).

The struggles loosely followed the pattern of CAT procedural sequences (especially dilemmas), and were written in accessible, everyday language. Our aim was to frame the struggles in general enough terms that they could be recognisable across a range of settings, with enough range to speak to staff members' diversity of personal circumstances and personal responses.

Examples of the struggles

If I put myself first I feel guilty. I might know I need to put myself first e.g. by having downtime, or protecting myself better from risks, but it's a crisis and if I do that I will feel guilty (or the organization might make me feel like that).

The 'overwhelmed' dilemma

The volume of information and instructions changes so quickly, and different sources conflict. It is too much. Sometimes I don't know what to do or what to believe. I either cut off from the flow of information (but something important might get missed) or immerse myself in it (and get exhausted again – perhaps I have trouble switching off).

The 'boundaries' dilemma

The world has changed so maybe we need to be flexible. But it can seem like either I stick to what I would normally do (but someone's needs don't get met) or I change the boundaries but then it doesn't feel OK.

Are YOU a hero? I may be invited to be a hero: by the world around us (clapping for the NHS), by my organization, by myself. That can feel good, exciting, special. But:

1. *If not a hero, I may feel overlooked, left out, even resentful*
2. *If I can't be a hero (for instance if I need to stay out of things for my own health) I may feel guilty*
3. *No one can be a hero all the time. What happens then? It may feel like we are never allowed to make mistakes, to not know the answers, or not to be firing on all cylinders.*

Work or home?

Home is topsy-turvy because of money, children, people close to me who are vulnerable, or all of these. I can feel split between putting my time and effort into what's needed at home, and what's needed at work. I might feel confused or overwhelmed, or feel guilty about having to put one set of needs above the other; or feel guilty about not meeting either set of needs.

Developing ideas

Other struggles were concerned with themes of connection and isolation, identity, adaptation, threat, exhaustion and burnout, and authority. Exits were included on the list, as a way of offering ideas for addressing the struggles, but it was importantly not the focus of the list. We tried to embody the CAT ideas of close description and doing with rather than making this an advice-giving tool, of which there were already many. Exit themes were principally around connection with others, self-compassion, normalising and recognising our shared humanity in our experiences of the struggles.

Feedback was sought and additions made from the initial consultees. The list was then circulated via professional networks, Twitter and Facebook, with an invitation to others to use it as they wished in their own workplaces. The list was then used widely by others, particularly psychologists and therapists, in supporting their own teams. They used it in varied ways, but the commonest was to scaffold reflective practice conversations in their own teams. The list appears to help helpers to start those conversations, and help the 'helped' to speak about their experiences. Many users had no specialist CAT knowledge, and one of its strengths is in its accessibility to a non-CAT audience. The most prominent feedback theme was that people found the list validated their own experiences; many then found themselves able to think more creatively about how to respond. The list was descriptively focused, rather than problem focused: the struggles are not necessarily 'dysfunctional' and the catalytic effect it had was more to do with self-recognition and validation than problem solving. It is an example of the application of CAT ideas in a timely way to a broad audience, to support reflective practice at work and better staff wellbeing.

Summary

The richness of the CAT model is its increasing adaptiveness to ongoing challenges in the workplace. The Helper's Dance List is likely to be a useful reflective tool for those in helping roles and a valuable aid for unlocking rich information. The study described in this chapter was a small sample size focusing upon one service, however, the findings from it provide a framework from which to aid 'reflection on reflection'. The wealth of exits provided suggested it would be a useful experience for staff teams to reflect together using the Helper's Dance List to share their feelings and ways of coping and to help build beneficial relationships in a staff team on an ongoing basis The preliminary results indicated that the 'Helper's Dance List' can be a valuable tool for professionals looking to explore and work with morale and relationships amongst staff teams. In keeping with the evolving nature of the CAT approach this has inspired the Covid Struggles List.

As staff feel their greatest challenge comes from systems and external influences out of their control, CAT can be a useful tool to map out these dynamics as well as helping people reflect on the dances they take part in as a result. More generally, CAT-inspired tools such as the 'Helpers Dance List' and the 'Covid Struggles List' provide a dynamic and accessible way to help develop conversations between staff and as such scaffold the development of relational awareness.

Chapter 10: CAT-informed Supervision of CAT-informed reflective practice in a forensic setting – 'Map and Talk'

Alison Bickerdike, Nicola Kemp and Clare Bingham

Introduction

This chapter discusses supervision of reflective practice in forensic settings. We consider some of the literature around this area, and the key ingredients and processes supervision of reflective practice seeks to address. This is followed by an exploration of how the CAT model is congruous with many of the required functions and processes of supervision of reflective practice. The supervision structures developed in our own service (East London NHS Foundation Trust Forensic Directorate) for CAT based 'Map and talk' monthly reflective practice groups (RPGs) are outlined, followed by some CAT-informed reflections exploring the challenges facilitators bring and how our model of supervision supports and responds to this. Finally, we consider some wider issues raised in the chapter, and point to future directions.

1. Introduction and literature review

The challenging and complex nature of working in forensic settings is widely recognised in both practice and the literature (eg Mitzman, 2010; Adshead, 2012; Shannon, 2017). Service users have often experienced significant trauma, neglect and disrupted attachments throughout their lives, leading to limited repertoires of reciprocal role procedures and dissociated self-states. For example, seeking power/dominance or perfect care to avoid unbearably painful feelings and enacting abusive or neglectful roles to self and others when this is not met. As staff working in these settings, we can often join 'the dance' (Potter, 2014, 2020) with our service users in unhelpful or damaging ways. This can result in a myriad of consequences, from burnout and work dissatisfaction to traumatization and boundary violations. As well as the relational dynamics between staff and service users, working in long-term institutional settings can impact hugely on teams, organizations and wider systems. The experience of powerlessness, isolation and stigma can resonate across all levels of an organization, such as the spotlight being shifted to power imbalances within teams (Heneghan *et al*, 2014).

As a result, supervision is essential in these settings, to protect the supervisee from enacting harmful patterns and to promote collaborative working across the system (Shannon, 2016). The requirement for direct clinical supervision is acknowledged at local and national levels, and within the professional code of conduct of a number of disciplines. However, at the time of writing there are no stipulations about the supervision of reflective practice. This is surprising since reflective practice has increasingly become a key intervention in helping staff teams manage the complexity and emotional impact of their work, with the ultimate aim of providing effective care to our service users. Equally there is relatively little written in the literature about supervision to deliver reflective practice, either in forensic or other types of settings. This is also striking considering the multi-faceted and complex processes involved in facilitating reflective practice, particularly in group settings (which is often the format in forensic and other psychiatric inpatient settings).

The relational nature of reflective practice and supervision: models of supervision

Although there are limited guidelines about supervision for reflective practice facilitators, we can draw on the rich literature about supervision in general and CAT more specifically to help understand some of the key ingredients. Delivering reflective practice is relational, focusing on the dynamics between service users, staff, teams and wider systems and within the RPG itself. Several key influential models of supervision focus on the importance of the relational. Holloway's (1995) Systems Approach model is multi-faceted with the supervisory relationship being at the core. The model includes the characteristics of the client, therapist and supervisor as well as the context in which the therapy is taking place as important factors in supervision. Furthermore, Holloway presents the range of tasks and functions (resulting in 25 possible task-function combinations) that can take place during the supervision process (see Table 1, below).

Table 1: Tasks and functions of supervision (Holloway's systems approach model)

Functions	Tasks
1. Monitoring/evaluating	1. Counselling skills
2. Instructing/advising	2. Case conceptualisation
3. Modelling	3. Professional role
4. Consulting/exploring	4. Emotional awareness
5. Supporting/sharing	5. Self-reflection

Hawkins and Shohet's (2012) Seven-Eyed Process model also focuses on the importance of relationships, both the therapist's relationship with the client and with the supervisor. They describe the different lens ('eye') or modes a supervisor can use when focusing on either the therapist–client matrix or the therapist–supervisor matrix. They suggest that a supervisor should become skilled in using each mode and know when to switch between the different eyes (which they refer to as 'helicopter ability'). Similar to Holloway's model, Hawkins and Shohet (2012) emphasise and incorporate the importance of context in which the therapy and supervision takes place.

Table 2 Seven Eyed Process Model (Hawkins & Shohet, 2012)

Client–therapist matrix	Eye 1 – Focus on the client
	Eye 2 – Focus on the interventions/strategies used by therapist
	Eye 3 – Focus on the client–therapist relationship
Therapist–supervisor matrix	Eye 4 – Focus on the therapist
	Eye 5 – Focus on the therapist–supervisor relationship
	Eye 6 – Focus on the supervisor's processes
Context	Eye 7 – Focus on wider contexts

The components of both models are highly applicable to reflective practice supervision, considering the different processes a supervisor may need to shift between depending on the needs/developmental level of the group and the importance of thinking about context, such as the role and impact of organizational issues.

CAT and supervision of reflective practice

The CAT model's relational focus and associated concepts and techniques fit well as both an approach to reflective practice/consultation (Walsh, 1996; Marshall *et al*, 2013; Carradice, 2017; Potter, 2010, 2014, 2020; Kemp *et al*, 2017) and supervision (Pickvance, 2017; Carradice, 2017). For example, helping group participants and facilitators understand relational dynamics in terms of reciprocal role procedures or drawing on understanding of multiple positions and state shifts to help understand why teams can feel polarised. Another important function of reflective practice supervision is to provide a restorative and caring role for the facilitators, building compassionate self-to-self reciprocal roles (Carradice, 2017).

Supervision of reflective practice facilitators can be delivered either individually or in a group. However, a group setting for reflective practice supervision is advantageous, mirroring the RPG itself. Since its conception, the CAT model has included therapy supervision in groups for a number of reasons, including learning from others, the richness of multiple voices from different backgrounds that can help name and explore diversity and inequality issues, and challenging the authority of a single supervisor

(Ryle & Kerr, 2002; Blunden & Beard, 2017; Pickvance, 2017). The expertise and understanding that has been developed in this area can apply to the supervision of RPGs. For example, the understanding of parallel processes in CAT supervision groups can enrich understanding of what is happening in therapy (Pickvance, 2017; Nehmad, 2017). This refers to when the unrecognised relational dynamic (reciprocal role procedures) between a therapist and client is enacted in the relationship between the supervisor and therapist or other members of the group or vice versa. In group reflective practice supervision, parallel processes may represent what is happening at different levels of the system (Carradice, 2017). Furthermore, group supervision can embrace and harness the multiple positions and perspectives that the facilitators are trying to encourage and contain in RPGs, helping to understand the whole picture rather than its individual parts.

2. The 'Map and talk' approach: supervision structure

Our approach has been to train and support multidisciplinary staff to become reflective practice facilitators. We emphasise selection, training, supervision and oversight of the development of competencies, rather than assuming these competencies belong to only one discipline. The importance of multidisciplinary working in a forensic setting meant we were keen to develop a structure emphasising collaboration and shared ownership.

'Map and talk' RPGs are facilitated by multidisciplinary staff from across the Forensic Directorate. New facilitators respond to an open invitation to multidisciplinary staff (Band 7 and above) to become 'Map and talk' facilitators, with the support of their line manager. 'Map and talk' facilitators attend an initial two-day facilitator training originally developed by Steve Potter and the authors. This training outlines the theory behind the approach, of the 'Map and talk' model, and presents opportunity for reflection and practice. Multidisciplinary pairs of trained facilitators are allocated to each ward/team across the Directorate. As well as discipline we consider a range of factors when pairing co-facilitators including breadth of experience, gender and ethnicity, aiming for diversity over uniformity within the pairs. All facilitators work within the Forensic Directorate, but are not allocated to wards on which they have clinical duties. Each ward/team has a 'Map and talk' RPG session at their monthly multidisciplinary team away day, facilitated by the same facilitator pair, providing a longer-term continuity to the RPGs, and the opportunity for the pairs to develop an ongoing reflective relationship with the groups and each other.

All facilitators volunteer to become facilitators. There is an explicit discussion throughout the project of the various 'hats' worn by facilitators, in order to specifically help facilitators acknowledge and manage their different roles within the system. Training is provided for participants of RPGs around 'what is reflective practice, and what it is not', thereby establishing the boundaries of the groups, helping facilitators and participants have a clear understanding of the remit and expectations of RPGs, and to establish ground rules/expectations of these. The level of seniority we require in terms of banding means that our reflective practice facilitators have considerable forensic mental health service, group facilitation, staff management, reflective practice or therapeutic experience, and we support ongoing development of this for example using the competency framework in Chapter 5. This is one way of assisting oversight of training needs, benchmark standards and good governance procedures in this respect.

The training is embedded, supported and updated through a robust supervision structure (Figure 2). Each pair of facilitators attend one of three monthly supervision groups; one group comprising five pairs (held at the LSU) and two groups comprising six pairs each (held at the MSU). Supervision groups are closed – the pairs attending remain consistent. Each group is supervised by a multidisciplinary pair of supervisors, mirroring the ward-based groups. The three supervisor pairs have monthly external supervision, creating a three-level iterative reflective process in the supervision structure (Figure 2). We have additionally developed governance guidelines, training for teams (participants) about the 'Map and talk' model, and ongoing training events for facilitators. There is a collaborative relationship with the Directorate trauma informed response team who offer additional support for teams in the context of serious incidents, to ensure the two approaches are complementary of each other. We have completed several qualitative and quantitative evaluations of the 'Map and talk' project (McGregor, 2017; Tuck, 2017), and specifically the experiences of participants and facilitators.

Supervision group sessions follow a similar format to the 'Map and talk' RPGs themselves – each facilitator/pair in turn describes a moment from their delivery of 'Map and talk' over the past month. Group discussion and reflection, using the 'Map and talk' model, enables the group to notice and name the enacted reciprocal role procedures, various positions, widening the lens and deepening reflection. Mapping in the supervision groups and reflecting on this process also deepens technical understanding and experience of the model, and enables the group to learn from each other. Often, the groups provide a space to notice the common themes elicited throughout the system, the relationships between these and wider aspects of the organization and beyond, and the opportunity to think together about wider social, political and cultural resonances.

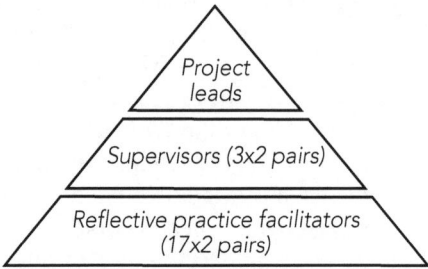

Figure 2: Supervision structure 'Map and talk'

The 'Map and talk' supervision structure uses the CAT framework to address many of the functions and processes outlined in the introduction to this chapter:

- Supervision sessions are theory driven, relational, and within a safe regular structure (closed group sessions, at the same time and day every month)
- Supervision sessions provide an opportunity for supervisors and project leads to ensure processes of clinical governance and evaluation, and for overseeing and maintaining competencies (Monitoring/Evaluating, Holloway, 1995)
- Supervision sessions provide an opportunity for ongoing training in the theory and model of 'Map and talk', offer the opportunity for facilitators to ask about and develop technical expertise in the model and receive feedback about the application of the model and theory (Instructing/Advising, Holloway, 1995)
- Supervision sessions provide the opportunity for (Modelling, Holloway, 1995)
- Using the 'Map and talk' template collaboratively enables the ongoing assimilation of multiple positions, the safe discussion of difference without blame (the dance not the dancer) as well as a means of noticing and naming the more difficult and evasive patterns that are commonly re-enacted in forensic settings to protect staff and service users from trauma and violence. This promotes the supervisee's capacity for self-reflection about a given moment (Consulting/Exploring, Holloway, 1995)
- Supervision sessions support an iterative process of reflection taking place with an increasingly wider lens on the Forensic Directorate
- Supervision sessions maintain emotional support for facilitators, supervisors and groups (Supporting/Sharing, Holloway, 1995).

The functions of supervision are not independent but strongly relate to each other.

3. Themes from supervision

The following figures use the 'Map and talk' template to describe our reflections on the relational themes elicited in supervision sessions, and how these might relate to the functions and processes of supervision outlined previously.

The quest for perfect control, and perfect care

A frequently named reciprocal role procedure in supervision groups was, in response to a high emotion/threat/anxiety/anger moment the pull to provide a 'Fix'. Our facilitators felt a great deal of responsibility for the teams, their experiences and feelings. The felt sense of responsibility to fix was intrinsically linked to 'making things safe', for others and therefore by extension for ourselves, often in the presence of underlying trauma, and associated overwhelming emotion, fear of violence, or chaos. In the forensic setting there are default means/structures for doing this particularly through controlling and restricting: a pull to reach *perfect control*. In pursuit of this, 'doing to' can be default, but inhibitive of collaborative engagement, processing and reflection, and 'doing with'. This sets in motion a tension for facilitators between controlling and feeling: trying to maintain space for reflection, and feeling, at the same time as a pull to action/structure/intellectual solutions.

At other times facilitators also described a pull to protect the groups, to become a rescuer, to provide *perfect care*. This was demanding and exhausting.

When *perfect care* and *perfect control* inevitably were unattainable or unsustainable, facilitators would often experience a self-protective temptation to give up, avoid, or cut off. However, this also triggered unbearable feelings of guilt in relation to a perceived abandoning. This perpetuated the pull to mitigate this, leading to a vicious circle of fixing, rescuing, failing and abandoning, an exhausting process, but very difficult to let go. 'Soldiering on' is another well-worn procedure in the NHS and in forensic settings. One example, among many, of this is many of our facilitators, ourselves included, considered the monthly 'Map and talk' groups when planning leave, afraid and unable to let them go/miss them.

The above processes emphasise the importance of supervision as a means to help facilitators recognise, understand and manage the high emotional and cognitive impact of delivering reflective practice.

Chapter 10: CAT-informed Supervision of CAT-informed reflective practice in a forensic setting – 'Map and Talk'

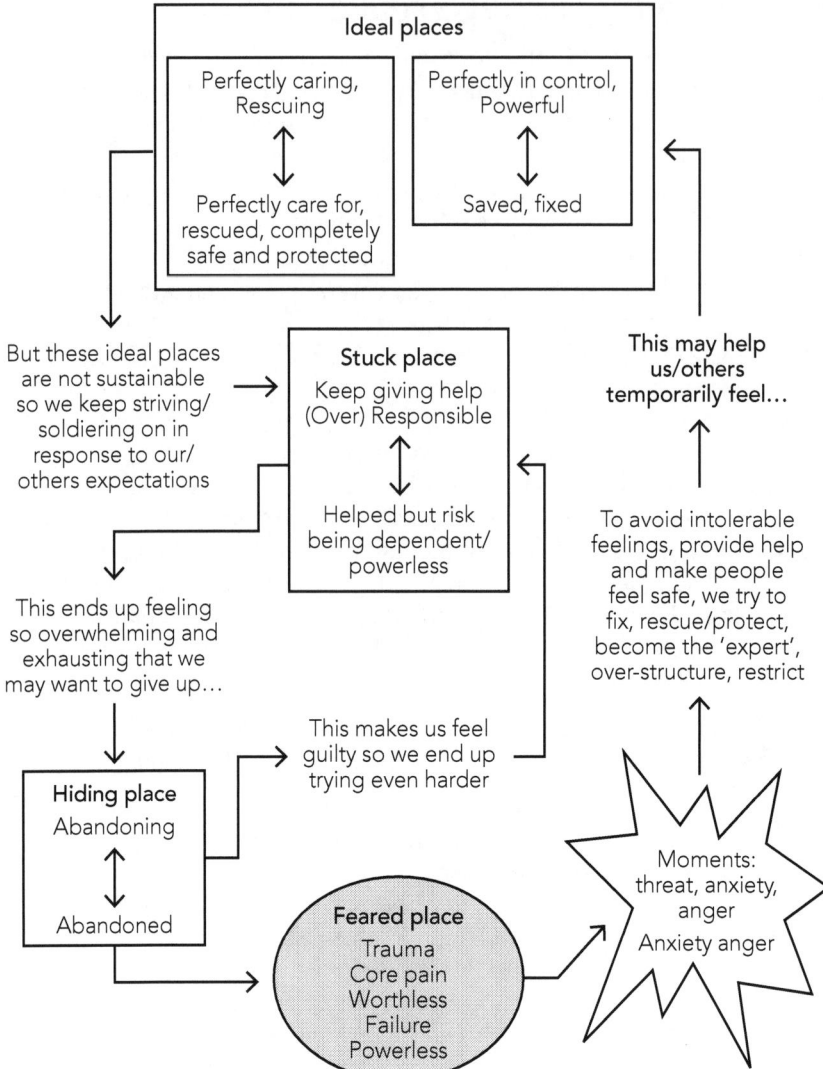

Dilemmas: Mapper anxiety and perfect competence (Figure 4)

Failure to achieve *perfect care* or *control* could be internalised by facilitators: what did a failure to fix trigger/represent/mean for facilitators themselves? This was often expressed in supervision through focus on the technical aspects of the model, such as expressing worries that their maps were not good enough. Importantly facilitators *sense* of this competency, that is to say their confidence, also had an impact on this. We collectively coined the term for this 'mapper anxiety'.

Ideal places

Perfectly competent ↕ **Fixed Admiring**

← Achieving this can lead to feeling ←

Perfectly caring, Rescuing ↕ **Perfectly cared for Rescued Completely safe and protected**

Perfectly in control, Powerful ↕ **Saved, Fixed**

When we cannot get to or stay in this ideal place we may experience anxiety… → **Mapper Anxiety**

And risk/fear

Battling place
Critical
Challenging
↕
Failure
Rubbish
Incompetent
Unconfident

But this can hinder expression of difficult feelings and reflection →

Hiding place
Silencing
Disconnecting
Less empathic
↕
Silenced
Cut-off
Misunderstood
Invalidated

Stuck place
'Doing to' by:
Over-engineering
Imposing too much structure
Too much intellectualising
↕
'Done to'

To avoid the associated anxiety and fear, we may strive to go to the ideal places by…

Feared place
Trauma
Core pain
Worthless
Failure
Powerless

In supervision groups, facilitators often discussed the relationship between anxiety and the risk of 'over engineering' in response, seeking *perfect competency* to mitigate against the fear of failure. This again created a tension for facilitators – the impact of structure could sometimes feel at odds with allowing the group ownership of the content (the risk of 'doing to' rather than 'doing with'). That is to say, focus on the technical aspects of the model, can itself be at the expense of allowing sufficient space for the expressions of difficult feelings.

The dilemmas outlined in these maps speak to the tensions involved in maintaining the diverse functions of supervision groups outlined earlier (monitoring/evaluating; instructing/advising; modelling; consulting/ exploring and supporting/sharing, Holloway, 1995). As described in Hawkins and Shohet's (2012) model, being able to select what supervision area to focus on and shifting perspective appropriately between them depending on the needs of the supervisees ('helicopter ability') is a complex skill in itself. Mapping is an important means of identifying, reconciling and understanding these: to provide adequate technical and competence training and oversight, as well as a reflective and experiential space. A suffocating intellectualising structure was to be avoided (leading as it could to the position of silencing to silenced), albeit a structure was itself also necessary for the safe containment and naming of overwhelming feelings. It was noticed in the supervision groups that sometimes 'the gaps in the map can be as important as the words'.

Colluding vs colliding, divisions, anger and blame (figure 5)

Another conflict (dilemma) commonly named in the process of facilitation was that elicited by awareness of avoidance of discussion of particular issues by the group in sessions, and facilitators' desire to enable the group to express this. This could feel daunting, to name difficult emotions could feel attacking, challenging, exposing. However equally to *not* address these observations, could again lead to concerns about 'not doing a good job', neglecting, abandoning, failing. In this way facilitators often felt poised between collision and collusion.

The reciprocal role procedures elicited in RPGs often travelled through faultlines of division: of seniority, discipline, experience, ethnicity, gender, in groups and in supervision. Feeling under threat, powerless, inadequate or undervalued, as service users, members of the groups, facilitators and as supervisors can lead to responses such as shutting down, avoidance, or alternatively blaming or attacking. This could lead to silencing or ruptures between facilitating pairs, between facilitators and supervisors, or facilitators and participants, as it can between staff and service users, or groups of staff.

Naming and mapping of divisions in groups and in supervision groups ultimately enabled them to be expressed and explored, but was not always easy, comfortable or possible. The selection of multidisciplinary facilitating pairs as complementary along some of these divisions is helpful in this – allowing the pair to accommodate multiple positions between them.

Complementing each other rather than being in competition with each other, pairs often successfully noticed named and modelled the process of this for their groups, and reflected on this in the supervision sessions. The respect for and explicit attention to diversity of discipline, ethnicity, gender, age and therefore experience in our facilitator mix translates into our consideration of the breadth and diversity of competencies required for reflective practice facilitation.

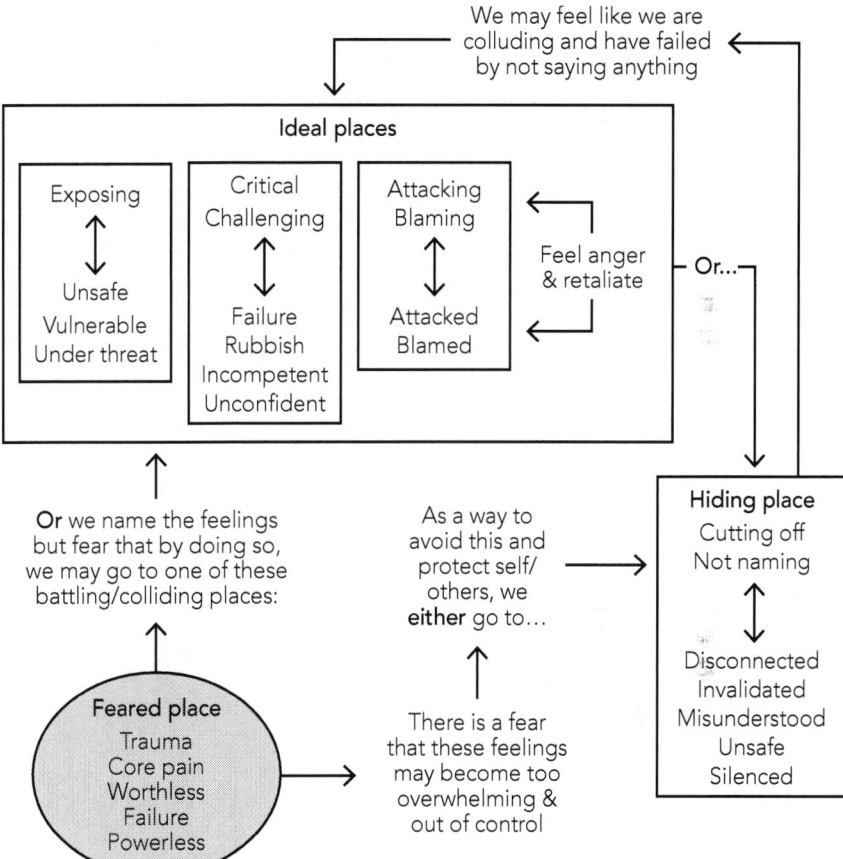

Exits – reflective group processes: noticing naming and negotiating (Figure 6)

The use of mapping in the supervision groups helps facilitators to *notice, name and negotiate* these processes as they experience them in the RPGs. It helps make sense of the dilemmas, the interactions between 'positions', facilitating safe recognition of what might be thought of as 'harmful' or 'bad' feelings in a way that contextualises and empathises, therefore encourages noncritical naming. The idea of 'the dance not the dancer' further supports this, and the rule of thirds enables reflections to be drawn on the parallel processes impacting on this across the system. The process of noticing, naming and negotiating hopefully enables participants in the RPGs and facilitators in the supervision groups to experience an attuned, challenging but containing role, which is reciprocated by their feeling heard, safe and understood.

It should be noted that the 'Hoped for place' in Figure 6 is more realistic than the 'Ideal places', but it is impossible for any of us to be there *all of the time*. There will often be times when we are invited to, and join, different 'dances' and shift to another position. The key is to notice and name when this is happening, so that we can move back to our 'Hoped for place' or 'Good enough' places sooner.

Supervision sessions, through mapping, aim to provide an intellectual, emotional and relational understanding of these processes, addressing the specific functions and tasks of supervision and reflective practice, as well as making links to parallel processes in the wider systems. The use of the 'Map and talk' template in RPGs and supervision helps facilitators further maintain and develop competencies and technical expertise.

The multidisciplinary make up of RPGs, facilitators and supervisors and therefore representation of all voices across these groups is fundamental to the representation of multiple voices and perspective at all levels, and therefore the additional effective noticing and naming of divisions where possible too.

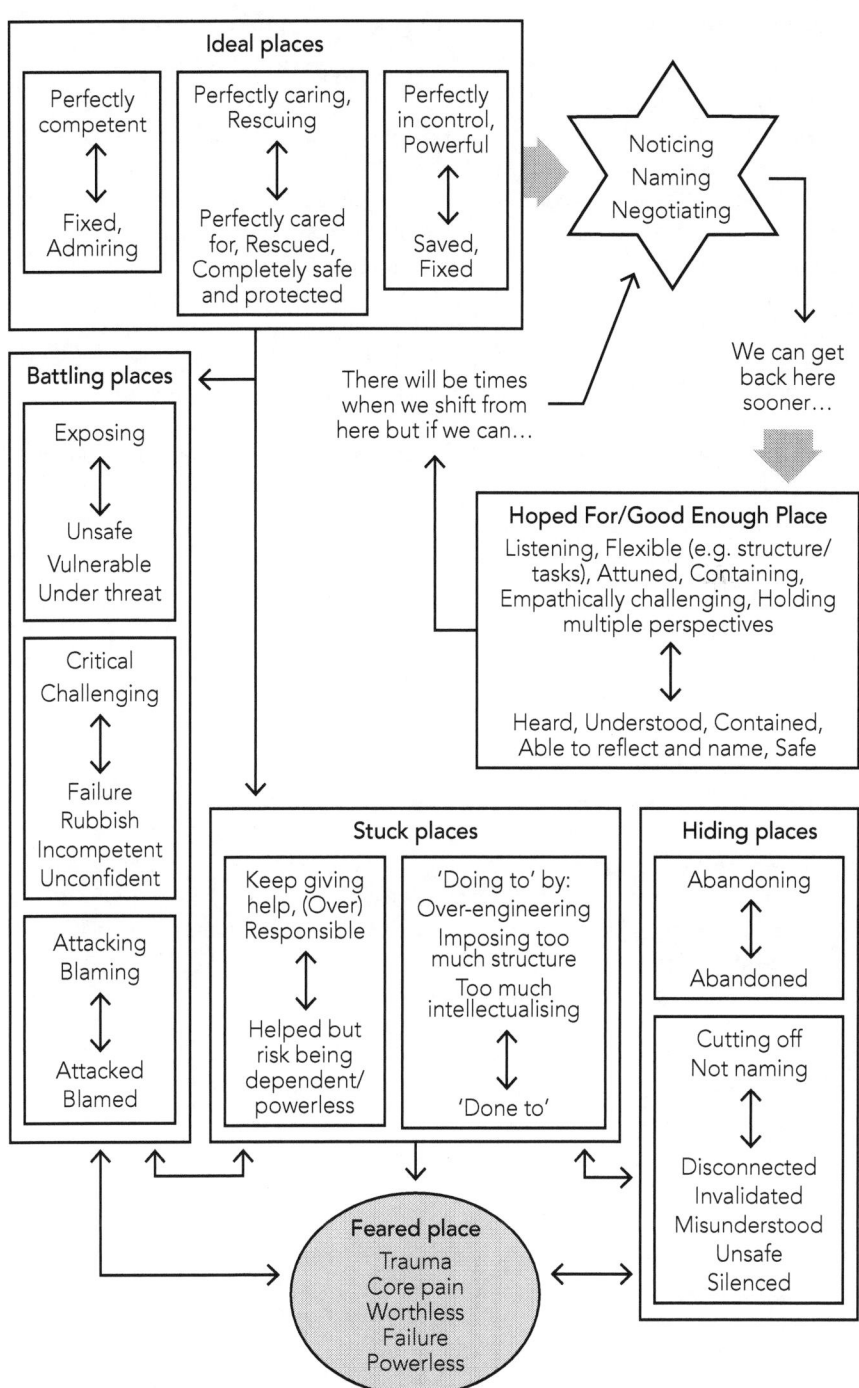

Wider re-enactments across the supervision structure

The supervision themes mapped out above originated in the 'Map and talk' RPGs, resonated through the supervision groups themselves, and were therefore experienced just as acutely by supervisors. As supervisors we were caught in the same enactments, feeling responsible for containment, feeling the pull to fix, wondering if we were 'up to the job' and competent and confident enough to maintain the safety of the sessions. Were we achieving the balance between structure, theory, competency training and reflection/processing? As supervisors we would also find ourselves striving to help facilitators feel safe, feeling responsible for the effective and contained delivery of 'Map and talk', and to also contain the unprocessed, traumatic traces/incidents and memories that are being noticed and named, or not, throughout the system. We felt the dilemmas: between 'exposing' when we think a facilitator/pair is not naming difficult feelings, and colluding when we did not feel 'brave' enough to name this; concerned about unsafely exposing others when too close to a trauma; striving to maintain a collaborative approach, perhaps at times at the expense of 'doing to', when that is what is required. The iterative supervision structure in which supervisors map supervision sessions in external supervision, captures these same patterns and offers supervisors the space and model to reflect on their experiences of the supervision groups.

A particular challenge for supervisors is that of non-attendance at supervision sessions, and how to manage this. We underline the expectation of supervision attendance as a necessary and important part of safe practice as a reflective practice facilitator. We recognise that there may be multiple reasons for non-attendance: sometimes practical (organizational obstacles to attendance such as a lack of dedicated time in job plans) and sometimes relational (for example, it is likely that at times non-attendance at supervision may be a means of 'hiding' or 'avoiding'). We address this through individual contact with facilitators where non-attendance has been an issue. However, to further address this we have also completed a Quality Improvement Initiative to explore in greater depth the drivers behind non-attendance at supervision. This process involves hypothesis generating, information gathering, ideas testing and evaluation. Through anonymous survey as well as discussion with facilitators in groups, we explored the 'drivers' of 'Map and talk' supervision attendance including: facilitators experience of supervision (including perceived safety and support); facilitators understanding of supervision (in terms of expectations in relation to the various functions of supervision outlined in this chapter); and organizational aspects of the 'Map and talk' project in terms of those which support attendance at supervision (for example time to facilitate reflective practice, attend supervision). This is currently a work in progress, which we anticipate will lead to further positive development in some of the structures in place to support the 'Map and talk' project.

4. Power, inequality, Covid-19 and the bigger picture

As described above, responses to feelings of threat and anxiety are often enacted through the inequities contained within the larger structures in which we work and live. It is all too easy for the structures we have to address and acknowledge these issues to further replicate the dynamics of power and hierarchy which are a feature of forensic systems. The experience of dynamics in groups between group members, or subgroups of members, which replicate damaging and toxic aspects of social inequality around discipline, power, ethnicity, gender and sexuality are important to notice and name where possible, but often trigger uncomfortable feelings in facilitators too. We are all involved in experiences of inequality, perhaps in privileged positions feeling responsible, guilty and paralysed, finding ourselves participating in a system in ways which are extremely dissonant to the way in which we would like to believe we participate. Or, alternatively, experiencing anger, frustration and fear at the impact of inequality and powerlessness we experience as we try to survive, change or call out a system where we do not experience equal treatment, respect or privilege. The chronic and pervasive nature of the inequalities to be found in the UK, the mental health system, the forensic mental health system, are something to which we do all contribute, as staff as well as citizens we are also part of these systems and this can be painful to reconcile. This pain or discomfort can often lead to silence and a fear of expressing feelings, which can lead to the perpetuation of the very situations we wish to counter.

These dynamics are particularly enacted in group sessions around for example how inequalities can impact on who in a group/team is silenced, who feels responsible for speaking, for fixing, who feels neglected, who talks in 'Map and talk' RPGs. They are enacted in response to the strong hierarchical nature which continues to exist in most forensic inpatient settings.

The impact of Covid-19 and the resurgent attention and awareness of the impact of inequalities this has raised has given awareness and articulation to these dynamics. These inequalities, too long and too often ignored/overlooked/unspoken, particularly as reported by our Black and Minority Ethnic (BAME) staff and service users, were further exacerbated and thrown into stark relief by this process. For example, in a very small but active way, the impact of Covid-19 on the need (revealing stark differences in the ability and opportunity), to work from home in terms of positions in the institution, autonomy over working practices and resources to do so, starkly divided many of our teams in terms of discipline, ethnicity, gender and seniority, and this was reflected in the 'Map and talk' sessions themselves as they sought to adapt to more virtual ways of working. The impact of gender on perceived ability to manage violence and aggression has also been a theme of groups particularly during periods of acute stress and violence in the setting. There are many and far more examples of this, which deserve greater exploration, and with greater opportunity for the conversation to be owned by all.

With respect to these issues, facilitators commonly face the dilemma of how to enable participation without over-exposing or making people feel unsafe, without making assumptions about others' experiences, or trying to speak for others as opposed to attending to the obstacles to equal participation. 'Map and talk' can provide a structure to name stark differences in experience, but embarking on this remains a challenge, requiring an established culture of safety and containment which can itself be difficult. All being 'in it together' as far as possible in terms of the structures we have described we believe is a helpful start, but as is being able to acknowledge that sometimes we are not 'all in it together.' 'Map and talk' is proving a valuable way to have a dialogue together in the midst of great inequality and difference, and to respond to wider relational dynamics our services mirror from the wider social, political and cultural environments. If not too optimistic, hopefully this can be the starting point to also effect change.

Conclusions

This chapter has reviewed the multiple processes and functions of supervision of reflective practice, and how the CAT model as applied to reflective practice is a suitable and effective means to deliver this. We have described our own model of reflective practice and supervision, and how we try to incorporate theory, structure, monitoring and evaluation, with training and support and opportunity for reflection, across an iterative structure, and how the 'Map and talk' model itself is an integral part of this. We described how multidisciplinary relationships are integral to this, as well as our emphasis on multidisciplinary pairs as facilitators of reflective practice. Supervision of reflective practice must address the need for structure, training and competency but also the importance of shared thinking time, safety and emotional processing. This is in acknowledgement of the visceral and traumatic experiences we endure in forensic settings and that attempts to over sanitise can be harmful, but equally to be aware of the impact of trauma and the need to manage the discussion of this. The driving nature of trauma, violence, overwhelming emotional experiences of anger and fear in all of the processes outlined in this chapter are a feature of the service we work in and the ongoing experience and impact of this on our service users and staff. As well as a need for reflective emotional processing there is also need at times to be 'doing to' and to be directive and for didactic approaches.

We are writing this chapter after six years of 'Map and talk' in East London. We have tried to describe the rationale behind our approach but are aware that in a developing field this is only one way of approaching supervision of reflective practice. It is apparent that we approached this in our service from the 'ground up'. Our driving emphasis has been on 'doing with' not 'doing to', and a desire to create a common language for all disciplines and capitalise on the incredible expertise of our staff. However, in reality a balance is needed, and sometimes 'doing to' is needed. Ongoing evaluation and a self-critical perspective are important to keep this in mind. We also have to be humble about our own blindspots and to recognise our own privileged positions in the system. Although the model gives the opportunity to have these discussions, there are also many obstacles to this.

This chapter has focused on the supervision groups, but this needs to be accompanied by other governance procedures which maintain the safety and integrity of our reflective practice delivery. As the field develops in terms of understanding the competencies and requirements of reflective practice facilitators, we continue to develop our own structures in collaboration with others involved in the same area. We certainly hope that the work others in this volume are doing, will provide assistance in terms of outlining helpful criteria to support the assessment, development and maintenance of core reflective practice competencies of our skilled facilitators, provide a benchmark to assist with ongoing evaluation of these competencies, to enable us to continue to monitor and oversee safe delivery of reflective practice in our service. We hope to develop a robust competency framework to better assess evaluate and support our reflective practice facilitators to maintain and develop the necessary skills to deliver reflective practice safely, as well as to continue to assess the delivery of reflective practice sessions themselves, and ensure good practice. Maintaining fidelity to the CAT model is important through both the oversight of the project, as well as the ongoing development in CAT and other competencies of our range of facilitators and supervisors. We continue to recognise the importance of ongoing independent evaluation of the experiences of our participants and facilitators in order to keep on top of evaluation of the experience of reflective practice in our service, as well as to contribute to the literature.

The groups at all levels of the system provide a zooming out/helicopter view of the directorate and wider systems which is helpful in understanding our own positions, whatever they may be in this, and recognising that what feels like ours alone is often shared with others. This has never been more important than during the current year. 'Map and talk' has provided a means of naming the difficult emotions and dilemmas elicited by the impact of Covid-19 on the interface between personal and professional. During this pandemic our RPG and supervision sessions were attended better than ever, and the content at times was emotional, honest and challenging, as we would expect. As a national health service and a country we have found ourselves in the midst of a number of conflicting processes, the hero worshipping of the NHS, in the face of a lack of PPE, and under-investment and undervaluing of other care staff; the highlighting of inequalities which are increasing with many in the country facing extremely difficult times physically, psychologically and economically. We have all experienced a roller coaster year of emotions, personally and professionally. 'Map and talk', an inclusive space to have conversations from different perspectives has never felt so important, but has also perhaps never been so difficult.

Acknowledgements: We are extremely grateful to our fellow 'Map and talk' supervisors: Dadai Gwendoline Dandato, Teresa Wolowiec, Lorna Downing and Alison O'Reilly for conversations and maps developed in supervision sessions which led to the conclusions in this chapter. Additionally, to Steve Potter for his ongoing guidance and support in this process, and all our dedicated Reflective Practice facilitators past and present, and staff who participate in the RPGs. We are appreciative of the support given to us by East London Foundation Trust and particularly the Forensic Directorate in our ongoing delivery of 'Map and talk'.

PART 3: Reflective practice and the wider organization

Chapter 11: When forensic services go astray – what can CAT offer at a system level?

David Harvey

Introduction

Forensic services work with service users who pose potential risk of harm to others, and who often have multiple, chronic and interrelated needs. At times, these services struggle to function optimally, which can contribute to prolonged stays in overly restrictive conditions, mismanagement of risk, inappropriate intervention planning or active harm or neglect by services. The premise of this chapter is that these 'surface problems' may need to be re-conceptualised as inadvertent consequences of the emotional demands of the work and the ways in which the systems, and the workforce, respond and organise themselves to protect against this. This can manifest like trauma responses at a systems level. To support forensic services to manage these powerful pressures, and the inadvertent harm they can cause to staff, service users and the wider public, we need a framework to be able to understand and make sense of wider system functioning. The Multiple Self State Model is Cognitive Analytic Therapy (CAT)'s framework of how trauma impacts on an individual. Here the framework is applied to forensic systems and used to highlight areas of focus and action to minimise the disruption that can be caused when forensic system go astray.

What does it look like when forensic systems go astray?

Forensic services include high, medium and low secure inpatient care as well as community and outpatient services. Service users in secure care will be detained under the Mental Health Act and in most cases will have committed an offence or pose a risk of harm to others (NHS Confederation, 2012). Within these services there is compassionate care, rehabilitative multi-agency working, comprehensive case management, thoughtful risk assessment, thorough discharge planning and effective public protection practices, all in highly complex situations that require the perennial tension between 'care' and 'control' to be intricately balanced (Hamilton, 2010; Rubitel & Reiss, 2010). However forensic systems can go astray and lose their way sometimes with extreme harm coming to the public (for example, see South East Coast Strategic Health Authority (2006) and Ministry of Justice (2020). Organizational abuse or neglect can also occur as seen in high secure hospitals in the UK in the 1990s and more recently when Jimmy Saville had free rein and access to keys meaning he was able to abuse the most vulnerable (Quinsey, 1999; Mersey Care NHS Trust, 2014; BBC, 1999; Department of Health, 2014). Forensic systems can go astray in other ways that are more subtle or insidious and so are easier to overlook. Inefficiencies in pathways leave men and women at inappropriate levels of security for too long – subject to repeated assessments, lack of progress to the community, duplication of interventions, and victims of therapeutic or case management drift (Kasmi *et al*, 2020; Centre for Mental Health, 2013). This has been attributed to individual units adopting their own implicit or explicit criteria; inconsistencies in the application of admission criteria; not admitting service users with little chance of moving on; and delays due to differences in opinions between individual practitioners across services (Völlm *et al*, 2018; Hare-Duke *et al*, 2018; Coid *et al*, 2001). 'Long stay' service users[2] make up 23.5% of the high secure population and 18.1% of medium secure, with 20% staying longer than 20 years and data indicating length of stay may be on the rise (Hare-Duke, Furtado, Gou & Völlm, 2018). Given that secure care accounts for over 1% of the entire NHS budget and 10% of all the mental health budget with an overall spend of £1.2 billion (Rutherford & Duggan, 2008; Walker *et al*, 2012) there are ethical and financial reasons to explore the challenges forensic services face in delivering timely pathways of care.

In what contexts are forensic systems likely to go astray?

Clinical experience and research evidence suggest that forensic systems are most likely to go astray when working with service users whose criminogenic or clinical needs are multiple and complex. Men and women in this cohort may be characterised by any constellation of features including; attracting a diagnosis of 'personality disorder' (especially 'anti-social' or 'borderline'); being labelled as having 'treatment resistant schizophrenia'; having a learning disability and/or ASD diagnosis; having assaulted staff or committed violent or sexual offences in institutional settings; displaying self-harm/suicidal behaviours; having previous or current substance misuse problems; low motivation/readiness for treatment; and use of seclusion (Völlm *et al*, 2018; Tetley *et al*, 2012; Hare-Duke *et al*, 2018). This group of service users may also experience physical health problems, have lost custody of their children, have limited accommodation options, poor education and employment

---

2   Defined as having been in medium secure for more than five years; high secure for more than ten years; or high and medium for more than 15

opportunities and low levels of financial resource/security. Therefore, multiple services, agencies and commissioning arrangements are often involved meaning that probation, police, mental health services, physical health services, substance misuse services, housing providers, local authorities, employment/education support, parenting/children's services and advocacy and benefit agencies all lead to additional 'system complexity'. This cohort of service users, more often than not, have been neglected, brutalised and dehumanised by those who should have protected, nurtured and cared for them (Liddle, Boswell, Wright, & Francis, 2016). As a result, the notion of help, support or limits from another person is plagued with implicit assumptions that they will be neglected, brutalised and dehumanised all over again. It is not surprising therefore that they engage in ways that are ambivalent, dismissive, untrusting and conflictive, all of which pose profoundly challenging threats to any sense of competence or usefulness in the workforce. For this client group, meaningful 'intrapsychic' change may be slow, precarious or even unlikely accompanied by multiple setbacks leaving professionals and services confused, exacerbated, demotivated or burnt out. Yet this vulnerable group of service users will have little choice but to depend on the workforce and the system behaving in a co-ordinated, considered, unified, consistent way that optimises its efficiency in meeting their needs, managing risk proportionately and helping them lead a meaningful life (Mind, 2018).

When working in these contexts, with professionals feeling overwhelmed and optimism ebbing away, clinicians may find themselves pushing for some form of 'intrapsychic' change in service users – we may see medications frequently changed or a pressure to offer psychological interventions repeatedly or eternally with the hope of changing behaviour. Whilst well intentioned, such repetitive or 'coerced' psychological interventions (especially for those who are unlikely to gain meaningful or sustainable benefit) may in fact be iatrogenic or, due to non-completion or poor outcomes, be cost-ineffective and undermine staff and client morale (Jones, 2007; Tetley *et al*, 2012). We need additional ways of approaching such complex problems and their underlying drivers. It is suggested here that instead of solely focusing on 'problematic service user behaviour', we could widen our focus to include 'problematic system behaviour' and how this can unintentionally contribute to mismanagement of risk, prolonged stays in overly restrictive conditions or active harm or neglect by services.

Re-conceptualising 'surface problems' in forensic systems

There are times when examples of forensic systems going astray as outlined above can be helpfully reconceptualised as mirroring trauma responses, but at a system-level. However, before exploring this in further detail there is a critical caveat – money. An under-resourced forensic system will not be able to function optimally. The political should not be reduced to the psychological by re-conceptualising the impact of poor financial investment as psychological phenomenon at a systems level. Just as in our direct work with service users, we have a responsibility to recognise that the roots of 'dysfunction' can be systematic economic deprivation (Jansson, 2017). Assuming that a system is appropriately funded, the invitation here is to consider re-framing 'surface problems' seen in forensic systems.

Forensic work is emotional and anxiety-provoking and yet is rarely acknowledged as such on a day-to-day basis. Professionals are expected to engage with powerful feelings, manage physical and psychological threat to themselves whilst making authentic connections, hear horrific accounts, think about harrowing personal histories, manage destructive urges and behaviours of service users (and staff), and yet still make complex decisions and effect change. Social and political pressures serve to sustain an unrealistic fantasy that risk of harm can be 'treated' and so eradicated. This is upheld by a pernicious, and often undiscussed, expectation that we will be shamed and humiliated should we make a mistake or be 'wrong'. Unclear or conflicting aims of the agencies we work in can mean grappling with goals of rehabilitation, care, punishment, control or public protection simultaneously provoking further complexity and anxieties. There are adversarial legal processes, statutory frameworks, ministerial scrutiny, or forensic cross examination in exposing forums, such as Courts, tribunals or parole hearings. Amongst all this there is no manualised, universally agreed approach when working with service users whose needs and risks are complex and multiple, and whose engagement is ambivalent, aggressive or forced upon them. Quite simply professionals do not always know how best to help, which can stir up an underlying, yet rarely acknowledged, sense of helplessness, confusion and incompetence. It is therefore hardly surprising that systematic review findings indicate work-related stress in forensic mental health professionals is a cause for concern (Brown *et al*, 2017).

In order to function teams, services and organizations will come to manage these pressures and anxieties as best they can. They may do so unconsciously *via their responses to problems, the cultures they cultivate or the decisions, procedures, policies and structures they adopt and endorse through formal channels*. Yet in doing this they may contribute to the maintenance of unthoughtful, fragmented and rigid service provision and culture leading to the emergence of 'surface problems' (Menzies, 1960; Bion, 1968; Ballatt & Campling, 2011). System behaviours that unintentionally come about to protect staff and systems from anxiety thus ensuring their own psychological survival (but impairing overall functioning) have been referred to as social defences (Menzies, 1960). This kind of functioning can parallel the impact of trauma but at a system and workforce level: rigid and repetitive responses, avoidance of emotion, oppression of alternative perspectives, mistrust, and relationships underpinned by blame, control, domination or neglect, all contributing to chronic or transient 'dysfunctionality' and the emergence of 'surface problems'. (Bloom, 2010a, 2010b; Lowdell and Adshead, 2009; Barrett, 2011; Zagier Roberts, 1994). When in the thick of it these powerful forces can feel overwhelming and confusing. There is a need to understand and make sense of them – a process CAT calls *reformulation*. This helps improve functioning by reducing the need for (system) behaviour that occurs to contain confusion or anxiety (Ryle & Kerr, 2002; Thompson *et al*, 2008; Holmes, 2014).

CAT as a framework for making sense of 'surface problems'

Psychoanalytic concepts have been the most influential ones to make sense of system (mis)behaviour to date, such as defences, inner conflict, innate instincts, impulses, fantasy, projection, projective identification or paranoid-schizoid functioning (eg Menzies, 1960; Obholzer & Roberts, 1994; Lodwell & Adshead, 2009). However, these concepts are imprecise and inaccessible to the majority thus reinforcing unhelpful power dynamics (Ryle, 1998). Those who understand and use these ideas can be perceived as powerful, critical or persecutory, whilst the use of interpretation can undermine the untapped capacity of others for self-reflection heightening self-doubt and self-blame (Ryle, 1994). Moreover, these concepts provide no explicit framework for those without specialist training and knowledge, despite the importance of structure and frameworks when working with clinical complexity and powerful staff and organizational responses (Liveslely, 2003; Moore, 2020; Ewers *et al*, 2002; Main, 1957; Johnston & Paley, 2013).

CAT as a framework outside of the therapy room has focused on client difficulties interacting with the relational tendencies of professionals and systems leading to wider difficulties, which Kerr (1999) called *contextual reformulation*. Excellent CAT frameworks have been developed to inform indirect clinical intervention in forensic settings (see Marshall *et al*, 2014; Annesley & Jones, 2016) and beyond reducing confusion, improving shared understandings, reducing stress, having clearer aims in case management and helping staff make sense of complex clinical presentations and the powerful responses they can provoke (Kerr, 1999; Kerr *et al*, 2007; Kellett *et al*, 2014; Shannon 2016; Shannon, 2017; Thompson *et al*, 2008). CAT has also been used as a framework to make sense of professional or organizational dynamics in general terms (with less of a focus on functioning in relation to a specific client or direct clinical work). Walsh (1996) emphasises CAT's capacity as a conceptual framework to make sense of system problems by fully describing the dynamics and patterns. CAT has been used in:

- staff wellbeing and staff performance (Appleby, 2003; Moss & Tanner, 2013; Carson & Bristow, 2015)
- service strategy, HR and leadership processes and service operations (Shannon et al, 2016 & 2017; Shannon, 2020).

As Ryle (1994; 1998) advocated in therapy, it is suggested here that there needs to be a down to earth, demonstrable, practical, direct and collaborative framework for forensic services to accurately and wholly describe their own system problems in a non-blaming, supportive and containing way thus exploring what may be required to avoid making things worse (Dunn and Parry, 1997).

The multiple-self states model: the CAT model of trauma

The multiple self states model (MSSM) (Ryle, 1997) is the CAT framework of how trauma can impact on an individual (Pollock, 2001). It suggests early life trauma, along with biological and genetic predispositions, impacts on the psychological functioning of a person at three different but inter-related levels[3]: limited or interrupted reflective capacity; fragmentation; and rigid, reduced ways of relating to self and others (Ryle & Kerr, 2002). The MSSM has mostly been applied to therapy with people who may attract a diagnosis of various types of 'personality disorder' (Ryle, 2002; Nehmad, 1997; Shannon et al, 2006; Manson et al, 2017; Pollock, 2006)[4]. However, there is merit in using this framework to make sense of 'traumatized' system behaviour, which can contribute to 'surface problems' in forensic services, along the three same levels: limited or interrupted reflective capacity (of the system); fragmentation (of the system); and restricted and rigid responses (of the system) – as depicted in the figure below.

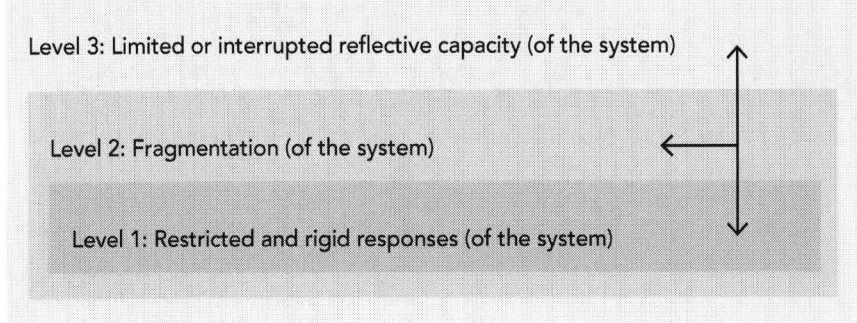

---

3   Some of the MSSM literature refers to levels of 'damage'. Given the importance CAT gives to how language builds thought and so intra-and interpersonal experiences and dialogue (Vygotsky, 1986; Bakhtin, 1929/1985), the term 'impact' has been used as opposed to 'damage' thus moving away from disease or deficiency models and in doing so reflecting CAT's curious stance of noticing phenomena from a more neutral, non-judgmental position.

4   In this chapter the emphasis is not on the traumatic origins or developmental processes that lead to these difficulties at an individual level (or how to manage them in a therapy setting), all of which is discussed in the key texts on MSSM by Ryle (1997), Pollock (2001) and Ryle & Kerr (2002), in addition to the particularly helpful outline given by Hayward and McCurrie (2008).

For the remainder of this chapter each of three levels are used to conceptualise forensic systems going astray and what kind of action may be helpful in response to re-focus on service user care, pathways, staff well-being and support or risk management.

Level 3: Limited or interrupted reflective capacity of the system

At a system level problems with reflective capacity are the struggle to notice difficulties or consider the needs, desires, hopes, aims, perspectives, feelings and thoughts (or 'state of mind' or 'internal world') of different teams, services or agencies (as outlined at an individual level in Holmes, 2014; Bateman & Fonagy, 2008). This means it can be difficult to notice and accurately describe what may be happening for, and between, all parties.

> *Gordon was hoping to be discharged from low secure care soon. His inpatient team agreed he was ready. The forensic community team believed he could be supported by a generic community mental health team. A referral was made but swiftly rejected citing that his risks were too high and he was a 'forensic patient' and the policy was he should be taken into the forensic community caseload. The low secure inpatient and forensic community team were irritated with this lack of flexibility and it exacerbated historic divisions between the services. After increasingly fractious communication, it had to be escalated to senior management. Similar dynamics merged there due to long standing frustrations at interfaces between services and organizations. Preoccupation with this issue meant that the Local Authority and housing providers had not been invited to MDT meetings to explore joint-discharge planning. Gordon's discharge was delayed.*

The services around Gordon are showing signs of limited reflective capacity. Each team is understandably caught up in the emotion as opposed to stopping to think about their own emotional experience or that of the other team. Exercising reflective capacity here would involve staff noticing and freely talking about their reactions or perceptions and hypothesising about the reactions or perceptions of others, and then considering how all this may influence the responses, plans, decisions, culture or policies that impact on Gordon's pathway. This ability is dynamic and under stress or high arousal can easily become interrupted and skewed temporarily or, under chronic stress, enduringly. Where this happens there is less likelihood that a team or system will notice itself or others responding unhelpfully and considering the reasons for this. An important aim is therefore to help teams and services create, sustain or recalibrate reflective thinking or what has been called the 'team mind' (Barrett, 2011). In the example above, a first step could be noticing and naming the fragmentation emerging around Gordon's care and starting to hypothesise in balanced, curious, complete ways about the experience and perceptions of each part of the system and how this may be driving such responses.

Regular, reflective practice groups help develop and sustain the reflective capacity in clinical teams. However, this will rarely be enough because frontline teams have limited scope to remedy the deeper and wider problems inherent in forensic services. Wider problems often emerge at the interface between clinical and operational staff; between frontline teams and management; or between different teams, services or agencies. It is, therefore, necessary to enhance the reflective capacity, of the whole system by embedding it culturally and structurally. Role modelling reflective approaches in ad hoc ways may contribute to cultural shifts – simply making links between emotions and responses in straight forward ways when making plans may help. For example, in a meeting between senior managers about Gordon's pathway, it may be helpful simply to state, *'There's still a lot of anxiety and suspicion around this maybe that's why the relationship between services is so poor. Maybe we need to ask them their experience.'* Yet this kind consideration of 'states of mind' or role modelling (by those who are able or interested to work in this way) is unlikely to be sufficient and wider *structural support* is likely be required. However, in operational, corporate or commissioning streams of work, reflective conversations may not be prioritised or even understood and the rationale can feel unclear or unwelcomed. The following may be helpful:

- Ensuring that reflective groups are embedded and protected in team structures and routines by operational managers
- Explicit agreed values and behaviours in service strategy focusing on reflective approaches and a clear rationale for this
- Terms of references for all meetings and groups that welcome honest perspective sharing, predict possible tensions or differences of opinion and values a joint responsibility to pay these attention and resolve them together
- Reflective approaches are named as key in operational policy and procedure – such as, in risk meetings, referral meetings or governance meetings
- Standard agenda items in meetings that focus on the experience, feedback and perspective of staff, service users and wider stakeholders (including other agencies, teams etc.) to help understand their 'state of mind'
- Commissioning acknowledgment of reflective practice and ways to monitor this via reporting mechanisms and embed this across all provision including the commissioning process

The rationale for reflective capacity that moves beyond tokenistic acknowledgement must be clear. In addition to staff wellbeing and support, reflective practice, at times, needs to be linked to clear and explicit ways to shift approaches or take action otherwise it can be seen to be indulgent and useless (Barrett, 2011). Being clear on this rationale can avoid derision, frustration, dismissal and an ultimate lack of buy-in from those with the authority to legitimise reflective approaches in service provision and system functioning. Reflective capacity is the 'starting point' of noticing and understanding dysfunctional fragmentation or rigidity within a team, service or system. These issues must be 'noticed' and understood in balanced, whole ways as a first step before planning how best to respond in integrated and flexible ways (as discussed below in relation to level 2 and 1, respectively).

Level 2: Impact, fragmentation

Noticing, understanding and addressing system fragmentation in forensic services is (or should be) core business. Necessary natural boundaries and structural divisions in and between services can be exacerbated by operational, organizational and emotional pressures. Fragmentation can occur between wards; departments; professional groups; hospital and community provision; or levels of security. When working with clients whose needs are multiple we will also see a range of organizations and agencies involved creating further structural divisions and greater diversity of service approaches and cultures creating fertile ground for fragmentation. Unaddressed fragmentation inhibits: a system wide approach, multidisciplinary or multi-agency working, co-ordinated service responses, fluid pathways and planned transitions for service users. It also impairs responding to complex clinical and risk presentations that require a range of expertise.

> *Across the (fictional) region of Aldwater forensic services were commissioned and delivered based on specialist pathways through secure care depending on diagnosis. This was to provide expert specialist support and intervention. Small, pathway specific teams were formed each managing the respective referral processes. Over time disagreement and resentment became more frequent amongst the different teams about which pathways a service user should be accepted into. This was especially the case for the service users whose needs and presentations were dynamic, challenged services or were not compatible with discrete categories. Debate and disagreements often led to delays in transfers and tensions between pathway leads leading to poor communication.*

In Aldwater forensic services there are signs of system fragmentation – absolute, dichotomous, black-or-white approaches and a tendency to become overly focused on one's own internal functioning and activity losing sight of the 'bigger picture' and service user experience. A key task in the face of such system fragmentation is sufficient integration. What this means in practical terms can vary widely depending on context. In line with the CAT model, it can often be important to develop an 'integrated' version of events through complete, whole descriptions of issues that emerge at the boundary between parts of a system instead of biased or partial accounts. For example, in the previous example, how did Gordon's team make sense of the response of the community team? Was it partial in construing them as just awkward and unprofessional, or was it a more complete description also taking into account their possible anxieties about managing forensic risk and the high caseloads they have to manage? Similarly, did the forensic teams have the opportunity to think about the drivers behind their own responses? If they did, perhaps it came to light that they felt envious and exasperated because other parts of the system had the option to avoid working with forensic risks – leading to feelings of frustration. Whatever their nature, such fuller descriptions can open new, integrated ways of thinking about issues that arise between services, increasing the chances of more balanced responses.

At times system fragmentation within forensic service delivery is organizationally-sanctioned or operationally-encouraged. Where fragmentation is inherent within how services are designed or delivered it can be fruitful to consider how this fragmentation may, in part, be understood as an inadvertent way to manage complex emotional reactions within the workforce but be detrimental for service users. In Aldwater, what started out as considered, reasonable policy, over time, may have become to decline referrals for those who challenge a sense of control, competence and expertise within the workforce. This operational, categorical service design may have allowed staff to avoid some of the emotional challenges inherent in forensic work with those who have complex, transdiagnostic needs, but in doing so frustrated service user pathways. It is not suggested here that services are mindlessly designed purely to meet the needs of the workforce but the invitation is to ensure there is enough reflective capacity to notice and question where this may be the case. Embedding reflective approaches into operational decisions and service planning may assist some of these conversations and ideas to be considered in careful, thoughtful ways. Where sanctioned fragmentation is required then structures around the parts of the system can serve to ensure sufficient integration, joint-working or collaboration.

Sufficient system integration will usually require some structural support to minimise and monitor the ongoing pull to fragment and retreat into silos or unnecessary specialisms, especially if the work to be done together becomes controversial or contested (as will often be the case at interfaces in forensic services). For example, in Aldwater sufficient integration may be achieved via one overall governance and monitoring structure, blended operational management arrangements across all the pathways, one joint point of referral or joint assessments and pathway planning for service users whose needs were not compatible with the service delivery model. Further system interventions to encourage integration may include:

- Joint regular forums where different parts of a system can come together and review success of any joint working, but also be honest about tensions and problems at interfaces
- Active reviews of working at interfaces (or partnership working/multi-agency working/joint-working)
- Where working at an interface is regular, consideration can be given to joint governance arrangements, joint project work or joint strategies clearly legitimised by those with authority to do so
- Formal monitoring of attendance in clinical or business meetings ensuring that all relevant parties are present consistently and addressing persistent absences through reaching out to understand this
- Sharing practice and organizational knowledge or expertise to increase understanding of different areas of work between services, agencies or professional groups
- Clear review processes, audits or evaluations focusing the experience, learning and efficacy of joint-working arrangements or working at interfaces
- Careful consideration being given to introducing further fragmentation within forensics systems with open healthy debate about perceived needs and disadvantages of this

If there is sufficient reflective capacity in a system to notice unhelpful fragmentation, strive to understand it (taking into account various perspectives and experiences) and then jointly aim to address it through adequate integration, then this may increase the chances of flexible and innovative responses to service user needs and risks (level 1). An overall aim therefore could be for forensic services to be made up of a workforce and structures that recognise the importance of integration and joint working and expect this to be frequently jeopardised because of the necessary structural divisions, which can be easily exacerbated by the emotional pressure in the work.

Level 1: Restricted and rigid responses

According to the MSSM model a lack of physical or psychological safety in formative periods can lead to limited and rigid ways of relating, known as reciprocal role procedures (Pollock, 2001). Sometimes forensic services and systems function in limited or rigid ways. Obviously, any system (especially one managing risk of harm) needs structure and agreed procedures to run smoothly and safely. In forensic services balancing this with flexibility is paramount. However, when the balance tips too far towards rigidity it can be important to have some way of conceptualising this to indicate ways forward. In CAT terms overly rigid practice could be seen as a reciprocal role procedure (or relational pattern) to manage, and ward off, the potential anxiety of being cast into unbearable (imagined, anticipated or actual) 'roles'. For example, in Gordon's case perhaps the general community team experienced forensic services as 'abandoning, relinquishing responsibility' and so felt 'anxious, overwhelmed' at the prospect of working with a service user from secure care. The seemingly reasonable policy of service users from secure care being supported by a forensic community team may in fact manage these anxieties, but prevent fluid, person-centred pathways out of secure care based on individualised need. Reducing anxiety may have allowed more flexible responses. This could be achieved by offering some teaching to the general community team on working with forensic risks, or sharing how secure care services had come to understand Gordon's risk potential, risk escalation pattern and how to respond. Ongoing support and consultation may also have been a more flexible way to facilitate his pathway out of secure care. Similarly, in Aldwater there was potential for rigid and limited responses to referrals and pathway planning. Specialism and expertise can inadvertently tip from being helpful for specific presentations and needs to being rigid and protective for services by providing a supposedly sound rationale to decline referrals that cast professionals into the roles of 'overwhelmed, exacerbated, unsure or hopeless'. In essence, it can be helpful to maintain a healthy scepticism and openness to thinking that, sometimes, policy or procedures can enact and bolster rigid ways of relating with other services and service users, by affording the workforce, and system, subjectively safer and more containing 'roles' associated with feeling powerful, absolute competence, control, expertise, self-protection or power thus quelling unsettling feelings or experiences. An inadvertent consequence can be reduced capacity to respond flexibly taking into account the different perspectives and aims of all stakeholders, especially in novel situations and this can hamper progress along a pathway for a service user or disrupt proportionate risk management and positive risk taking. Flexible ways of managing the process in Aldwater may have been to encourage a shared sense of responsibility and flexibility across all teams through cross-working, reciprocal consultation, shadowing opportunities, mutual CPD sessions, joint supervision arrangements or jointly-developed contingency plans if after admission it emerged that a service user's needs were not well met on specific pathway despite the best efforts.

Flexible ways of delivering services, providing care and engaging with service users and other parts of the system may help overcome rigid or restricted responses, which are at times legitimised by apparently reasonable organizational process. However, any venture that sets out to introduce new ways of thinking or providing services should also acknowledge that innovation and creativity can be profoundly threatening and unsettling for the status quo because it poses the possibility of removing 'system coping mechanisms'. This means that in forensic services flexibility, innovation and creativity will be frustrated, jeopardised, impinged upon or disrupted by wider system responses. This may not necessarily be out of malice from elsewhere in a system and ideally should be responded to with understanding, acceptance, assertiveness and perseverance. We need to help the system feel supported, contained and assured – allowing creative, flexible, innovative options of operating to feel safe and tolerable. This can be done by ensuring anxieties are carefully contained by thoughtful, flexible and responsive structures and processes (see Harvey & Tuohy, 2020). Overall an important aim at level one is to develop a workforce and structures that value innovative, flexible, individualised and creative practices whilst understanding these can be understandably anxiety provoking and so will often be impinged upon by system responses. Encouraging this within service provision may be assisted by:

- Striving for innovative quality improvement through safe, carefully planned and proportionate experimenting and learning
- Leaders and those with authority encouraging and sanctioning safe ways of being innovative, creative and flexible
- Establishing networks of staff and service users that disseminate learning from innovative, creative and flexible practices, including to commissioners – this may be co-produced case studies
- Considering additional, responsive clinical governance arrangements or enhanced support around creative or innovate initiatives especially at times of struggle
- Formal service evaluation focusing on the impact of innovative projects or ideas
- An acknowledgement in Terms of References for relevant governance or operational meetings that system behaviour, including via sanctioned policies and procedures, may come about to manage emotional reactions in the workforce and state a commitment to talk about this where it may emerge
- Paying careful attention to structure and support needs around the workforce if new, flexible ways of working are to be adopted

Conclusion

The aim of this chapter has been to invite practitioners, managers and wider stakeholders to helpfully question, enquire and explore the ways in which forensic systems think about themselves and their behaviour. Forensic services grapple with complex clinical, risk and legal scenarios in healthcare. The multitude of pressures that these systems must work with can at times lead to them going astray and one way to conceptualise these problems is as parallels to trauma responses, but at a system level. The CAT model of trauma may provide a map to navigate these issues, which when experienced first-hand can feel overwhelming, confusing and insurmountable. If those within and around forensic services can ensure there is structure to notice when problems emerge and to try and understand the varied perspectives involved, there is greater chance of 'seeing' and understanding fragmentation or excessive rigidity in service responses. This can help take action to create enough system integration or sufficient system flexibility to stay on track in meeting service user need to help the men and women we are here to support make progress back into their community in a safe and timely manner.

Chapter 12: Leadership and Cognitive Analytic Therapy

Part one – relational dynamics and culture

Jenny Marshall

Introduction

The NHS is under significant pressure with a climate of austerity and staffing shortages. With a growing need to meet performance indicators and to develop service improvements, the culture of the NHS has been gaining increased attention, particularly in relation to service failings. The founding value of the NHS was and still remains compassion and the importance of compassionate leadership has been highlighted as integral to embedding these values throughout the organization. However, the 2019 NHS survey suggests that these values are far from embedded within the culture and much work remains as to how to embed and sustain these values in light of the pressures that the organization is under. The components of compassion and the nature of the task can be easily articulated but the practicalities of translating this into clinical practice and the day-to-day business of the organization is less clear. It is proposed here that Cognitive Analytic Therapy (CAT) is a reflective model which would be well suited to the task. In this Chapter I will discuss leadership relational dynamics and how these can influence culture. In Chapter 13, I will focus on my own personal and professional reflections on a journey through leadership using CAT concepts.

Part 1: What can CAT bring to leadership?

The role of senior leadership teams has been identified as crucial in setting the culture of the organization. The Mid Staffordshire review in 2013 highlighted, following the discovery of appalling suffering of many patients, an insidious negative culture involving a tolerance of poor standards and a disengagement from managerial and leadership responsibilities. The report identified the need for common culture and values of the NHS to be applied at all levels of the organization, but of particular importance is the example set by leaders in relation to ethics, standards and conduct in a similar vein to those expected from frontline staff. Similarly, the review into the abuse which took place at Winterbourne View in 2012 highlighted the bigger leadership and cultural challenge of promoting compassionate care across the system alongside enabling staff to feel able to speak out when they see poor care taking place.

Research on leadership in today's NHS (Anandaciva *et al*, 2018) highlights high vacancy rates and turnover of senior positions which have a significant impact on culture, staff engagement and performance. It is the stories from the senior leadership within the NHS which give meaning to some of the reasons behind high vacancy rates and turnover. All those interviewed spoke about difficult financial and operational pressures to the extent that some felt the roles were no longer possible. These pressures, a combination of prolonged austerity, increasing demand for services and growing shortages of clinical staff were described as having created a *'near toxic cocktail of pressures for senior NHS leaders'* (p27). It was felt that the challenging financial and operational climate had led to an increase in regulatory requests and controls and as a consequence, impacted on local autonomy and decision making. Interviewees articulated this to be *'sucking authority up to higher levels…we spend time training and recruiting talented people then we do not let them lead'* (p29). It was noted that the most emotive part of the interviews was about the current performance environment where the language used was described as that of violence, *'regulatory firing squads, politicians swinging axes and the language of vulnerability, of leaders feeling exposed and isolated'* (p32). The leadership model was described as *'you must do everything and will be judged on your ability to achieve it and you have no friends'* (p32). Of further concern were the references to the internal world of the leader *'I am viewed by everyone around me to be resilient. I'm the CEO with a smile on her face. The happy, steady, calm CEO. But that's not what's always going on inside'* (p43).

These patterns were echoed by interviews in the Chief Executive's Tale (Timmins, 2016), describing regulation which *'favours process rather than outcome'*, systemic bullying from all directions (politics of health, media, regulation and financial constraints), themes which are *'signals of a system that is buckling under a heady cocktail of factors that we ignore at our peril'* (p79). These are not the only interviews or documents which raise such concerns, Gerada (2014) wrote:

> 'I believe that there is something profoundly wrong with the NHS today. The health service's prevailing culture is one of fear even though it's staff are meant to espouse kindness and compassion. The service is becoming a place where staff feel attacked, unloved and abandoned by their political and managerial leaders'
> (p348).

Given the descriptions of the leadership culture described above, it is no wonder that the story of staff is one of significant challenges: the NHS survey (2019) showed that 40.3% of staff reported feeling unwell as a result of work related stress over the last 12 months. There were significant relational difficulties reported with 54% of relationships feeling strained at times and 12.3% reporting bullying from managers and 19% from colleagues. In addition, there were significant issues related to how staff perceived their involvement in organizational change processes.

Senior leaders know that a positive, engaged workforce will deliver high quality care but it has been suggested that the environment for this to exist in needs to challenge national bodies, regulators, the media and local communities to shift their attitudes and for what they consider systemic bullying to stop in order for vibrant innovative practice to thrive (Timmins, 2016).

Cognitive Analytic Therapy and leadership

Relational models have been increasingly used to support teams and have benefits associated with being a common language, minimising problematic team dynamics, stress and burnout (Kerr *et al*, 2003; Kerr *et al*, 2007). The use of a Cognitive Analytic model has demonstrated improvements with perceived skill level, improvements in communication and morale within the team, perceived improvement in team function and apparent improvement in the experience of patients (Freshwater & Kerr, 2006; Kerr *et al*, 2007; Thompson *et al*, 2008). However, the focus has tended to be on supporting frontline staff and less is known about the benefits with managers and senior leadership teams.

Carston and Bristow (2015) describe possible benefits of using CAT in collaboration with management in the NHS; to help individuals, colleagues, leaders and teams. They highlighted that the same concepts used in the CAT model to describe the world and ourselves in relation to it as interacting systems, can be used for understanding organizations. Shannon *et al* (2017) describes examples of using CAT within a management structure with specific reference to the relational difficulties that go with directing a team of staff. This example highlights the way a manager applied some of the concepts to recognise their relational patterns and usual style of coping/reacting in a crisis (blaming) and then to revise their style of coping/reacting (calm, confident, contained). Coleby and Freshwater (2019) identify the importance of dialogue and mapping with senior managers to support clinicians, to retain compassion and to *'keep the whole map in mind as senior colleagues grapple with personal challenges of managing and allocating a limited resource in the face of widespread and complex needs in our society'* (p15).

Through his work with organizations and teams using CAT concepts, Potter (2020) has developed the concept of the one third's rule. The one thirds rule suggests that any given interaction or relational dynamic is influenced by one third the individual's own relational patterns that they are bringing to the interaction (the world within me), one third the interaction with others (the world between us) and one third the dynamics within the wider team/organization/culture (the world around us). Traditionally working with frontline staff, the focus can't remain on just the service user (individual formulation without reference to the relational dynamics involved in the caring relationship), or on understanding dynamics between staff teams and patients, (the world between us) without considering the wider context of the service, or whole organization, (the world around us).

Our leaders whether in the NHS or other settings are first and foremost human beings. They have their own histories and experiences which have formed the basis for who they are, how they relate to others and how they have survived. The same as anyone else, our leaders will have their own relational patterns which they bring into the workplace and which play out in the same way that they do for staff and patients alike.

Our patterns of relating are developed early in childhood through relations and dialogue with significant others. They are internalised and played out in relation to ourselves and others throughout life. For an individual raised with critical parents with high standards for achievement, the individual may internalise an expectation that others will criticise. Procedures such as avoidance or overworking may develop to avoid criticism but inadvertently pull others into a critical role.

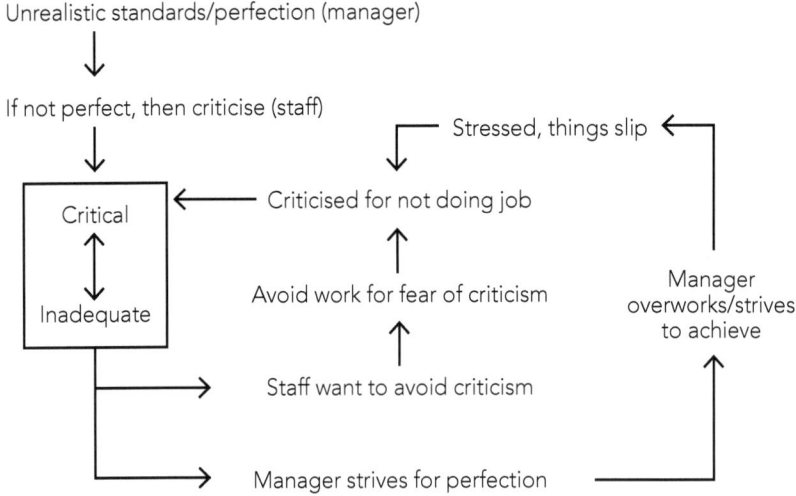

Played out in the workplace these patterns have the potential to be harmful to the self and in leaders they have the potential to influence, develop and nurture a compassionate culture in the same way they have the potential to be a destructive or harmful influence. In the same way that a leadership culture of compassionately caring and supporting with clear boundaries and expectations can nurture a positive culture, a leadership culture or leaders with a more critical or attacking relational style will influence the culture in a more negative way.

If we are to truly understand how cultures can be nurtured or harmed, this requires us to look beyond our leaders to understanding the relational dynamics at all layers of the organizations we work in, from frontline dynamics played out between service users and staff teams, to leaders and leadership dynamics, to the wider organization and political context.

Creating conditions for safety: the overarching relational model as scaffolding

There are many ways to develop a culture of reflective practice. Within CAT the concept of 'push where it moves' is important in determining where to start such initiatives. In some services, starting 'bottom-up' with frontline staff and in doing this, demonstrating good outcomes and 'buy in' may build a case for developing the reflective practice with managers and senior leaders. In other services, there may be perceived value in starting to build a reflective culture 'top-down' with the senior leadership teams given their influence on culture. This is explored in Walsh and Freshwater (in press) in their chapter on using CAT to make sense of organizational hurt. Additionally, Chapter 7 in this book explores alternative ways of developing and embedding reflective practice in more detail with specific reference to different forensic services.

Within any team whether frontline staff, managers or leaders, there is a need to build a sense of safety in order to reflect. This takes time and can be particularly challenging if being started within a crisis. In a crisis people will naturally feel under threat and as a result may shut down and be unable to use the space. Being unable to use the space may be observed in different ways; practical issues such as people not attending, not adhering to time boundaries or not feeling able to speak. These may be easier to manage by reinforcing the time boundaries. Other more complex issues to manage may be related to difficulties reflecting on self. In any group experiencing the emotional impact of their work, there may be expected a period of 'telling their story' in order to feel heard and validated. In a well-functioning group, this is likely to settle down once members feel safe and are then able to reflect on the one thirds rule, focusing in on the parts they can change, what I bring to the relational dynamic and my exits. The aim therefore is to create a safe culture of reflective practice as business as usual so that in a crisis it is easier to use the space and difficult conversations can take place.

Zone of proximal development: culture change takes time

The Vygotskian (1978) concept of the zone of proximal development (ZPD) is a core part of CAT. Therapy aims to work within the ZPD in order to enable service users to actively participate in a change process alongside a therapist, making sense of their difficulties in light of their life story whilst avoiding either overwhelming their skill, emotional capacities or self-understanding or fostering a dependency without any real change (Brown, Walsh & Laganis, 2020).

This model can also be applied to reflective practice. Reflecting on relational dynamics, be it with individuals, clinical, management or leadership teams, is to work with vulnerability. Core themes such as safety or feeling unsafe, power, control or feeling powerless and feelings of competence/good enough or inadequacy/shame are present. A reflective practice group which only validates without encouraging the group or individuals to consider their part within the relational dynamics is unlikely to create any meaningful change within the individual, team or organization. In a similar vein, there can be a pull to change too much too quickly, to rescue teams in difficulty; to be the expert who can fix things, but if we go beyond a person or team's skills, emotional capacities or self-understanding, this is likely to be unhelpful and could trigger a blocking response, shame or unmanageable emotions. Individuals or teams can feel undermined, attacked or overwhelmed and may withdraw or retaliate. Remaining attuned to the group is one of the core competencies for reflective practice facilitators and more detail relating to competencies can be found in chapter 5 on competencies.

Creating connection and dialogue

A focus on creating meaningful connection and dialogue with leaders is a priority. All too often with leaders, the focus may be on business; sticking to an agenda, and being task focused. There may have been few opportunities for coming together as human beings and reflecting on the experience of being a leader. Sharing such experiences in a safe and supportive way whilst being mindful of the groups ZPD, is a key part of reflective practice for leaders.

> 'The loneliness of leadership is a big issue, especially when you are being asked to deliver the impossible with little forgiveness.'
> (Anandaciva et al, 2018, p 63)

We are always on the map

Leadership by it's very nature requires great risk; developing excellent services involves using creativity and innovation, and risks failure. The current climate can be perceived as one of judgement and scrutiny; the care quality commission (CQC) evaluating services with ratings ranging from outstanding to inadequate to name just one example. The value of supervision and help for the helpers has already been discussed in Chapters 9 and 10. The need for both these functions is even more important for leaders.

Potter (2020) has developed through mapping with teams, ways of holding these different positions through 'hide and seek with hopes and fears'. He describes holding in mind 'what I really, really want' with the counterposition 'what I really, really don't want'. Even just these two positions for leaders can be helpful to reflect on the hopes and fears for leaders; hopes for excellent services for service users (possibly with an outstanding CQC rating to recognise this), fears for a service failing their service users (with humiliation and shame of services seen as inadequate). With these positions named, leaders can start to reflect on what is difficult, how do we cope or how do we try to achieve what we want or avoid what we don't want. Through such dialogue, it may become possible for leaders to recognise how, often it is the way that we go about trying to achieve our goals that can be problematic. For example, just as an individual goal of trying to have some control is reasonable, going about it by rebelling may be counterproductive.

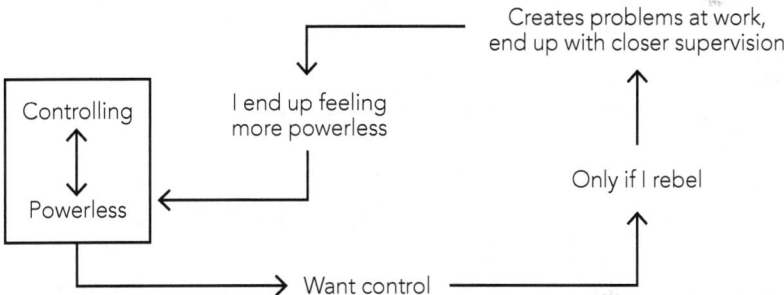

In a similar way, a leader who strives to achieve high standards but goes about it by overworking, trying to do everything, never switching off and burning out with stress may be counterproductive.

Some patterns may be easier for leaders to identify with; for example, those dynamics which are primarily driven by a 'self to self' relationship such as the example above of internalised high expectations leading to an internal dialogue about working harder and doing everything, never switching off.

Those relational dynamics which may be more challenging to identify with may be those which negatively affect others or the service. For example, leaders becoming more controlling or bullying in response to an environment of performance management and scrutiny or at the other end of the spectrum, leaders overly focusing on supporting and caring for staff but at the expense of challenging poor practice.

However, when services are receiving feedback about the quality of care or from staff experiences, there needs to be a culture where leaders can reflect on being pulled into problematic relational dynamics with a recognition that 'we will end up on the map'. There is a long way to go to create a culture where leaders are truly supported to learn from mistakes, to get back up again after a 'failure' and to truly reflect on how this happened. As Brown (2015) talks about in her book on leadership, taking risks requires vulnerability and she quotes the famous speech from Roosevelt (1910), saying in the end,

> 'it is not the critic who counts; not the man who points out how the strong man stumbles or where the doer of deeds could have done them better. The credit belongs to the man who is actually in the arena, whose face is marred by dust and sweat and blood; who strives valiantly.'

It is only with this kind of culture, that smaller mistakes or near misses can be learnt from with the hope that in doing so, this helps to prevent more serious failings.

All parts of the picture

Working within organizations, we encourage others to consider the wider organizational context and this can lead to separation between frontline staff and managers/leaders. Uniquely, CAT can offer us the opportunity to consider all parts of the picture. This is similar to Potter's (2020) concept of hovering, in which he talks about *'hovering like a hawk or helicopter... seeing here and there and taking in different points of view'* (p27). He describes how 'it brings multiple possibilities to life of seeing more than one perspective at the same time'.

Within leadership roles there are complexities being grappled with; service and team dynamics and individual management dynamics. Leaders or managers will typically hear one part of a story but yet are expected to make complex decisions. Instead, leaders can use mapping to consider many parts of a story or many positions on the map. His use of the one-thirds rule challenges us not to put all of the blame on the system, others or ourselves but encourages us to explore interactions and dynamics at play. When working at a leadership level, a core part of the role is the culture which is being created but it is only in being able to consider all parts of the picture, that we can start to truly understand the culture and work to improve or change it. This also includes holding a sense of organizational history. The narrative of organizations and individuals needs to be held with an ability to zoom in to the problems, look at them and reflect as well as the ability to zoom out making sense of them in light of history and the organizational or individual narrative. The ability to stand back is crucial; not to be reactive and only see one part of the picture.

Organizational reformulation: Our shared past organizational experiences and how they play out now

There are a number of tools used within CAT which can also be adapted to support teams and organizations with understanding organizational life, organizational stories and leadership team dynamics. I will describe below three specific tools which I have applied to organizational reformulation and found helpful.

1. Sequential Diagrammatic Reformulation (SDR)

The SDR is a visual summary of the core relational patterns and aims to map out both helpful relational patterns and those which perpetuate difficulties. Used with teams or organizations, mapping can help to hold the conversation and to focus on exploring the narratives and relational dynamics at play.

The figure below uses the stories of leaders (Anandaciva *et al*, 2018) and develops them into a provisional adapted sequential diagrammatic reformulation (SDR) or 'map'. This aims to identify core relational patterns within the leaders interviewed and provisionally illustrates possible procedures which could be maintaining these relational patterns. This is an example of the type of 'map' which can be developed with managerial and leadership teams. Exits are illustrated as one way of showing how change can be achieved.

Chapter 12: Leadership and Cognitive Analytic Therapy

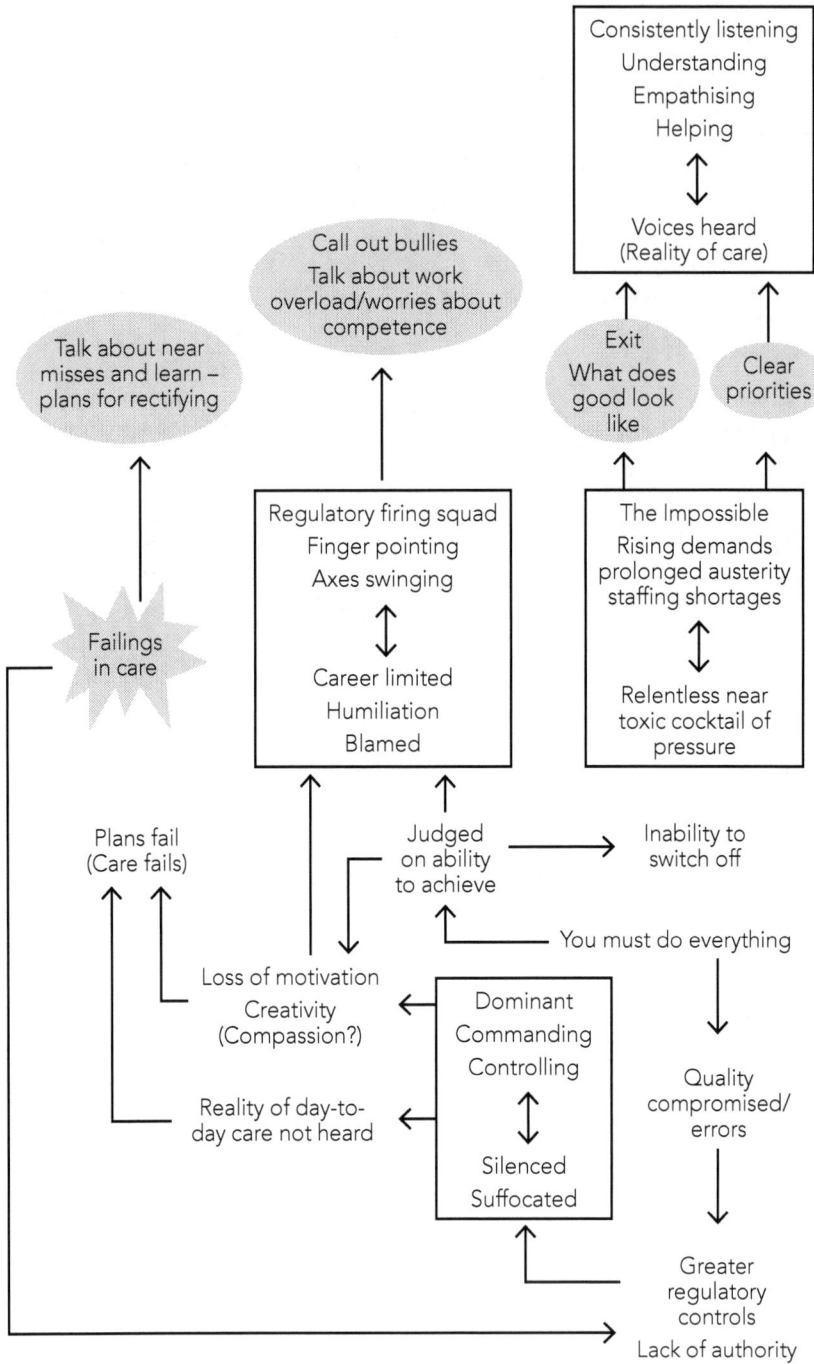

2. Written reformulations: the use of letters

Within CAT there is a tradition of writing reformulation letters which centres on the target problem patterns which are the focus of the therapy, but sits these in context of the history and how they are enacted in the here and now within therapy and within life. There is less written about the use of writing to facilitate reflective capacity in teams.

A therapeutic letter to a leadership team alongside a map could hold the conversation and help process the emotions associated, anchoring the important issues or challenges within a narrative history.

Example of organizational change

Managers or leaders may find themselves frustrated or angry at staff who are perceived as being 'difficult' or 'resistant' to change. Of course, this is valid; staff come to work to do a job and it is understandable that a manager or leader would be frustrated when staff do not hold up their end of the bargain. However, this is just one part of the picture. From some staff perspectives, organizational change brings loss: of relationships, of safety, of services they have passionately invested in and a loss of identity as roles change. This can elicit powerful feelings of grief, of feeling devalued and unimportant and of feeling unsafe and uncertain. A relationally informed service would take time to acknowledge and validate these feelings; leaders may find themselves having more empathy with staff, staff may feel heard and appreciated and have a voice. Acknowledging the hurt and loss as well as hope and a vision for the future can create a new more compassionate narrative.

An organizational reformulation can be a powerful tool to support staff through organizational change. In my experience, mapping can often help with the story telling and managers and leaders can take the first step to share how their work feels for them. This may be the first time they have had this experience and if this is the case, we as facilitators are hugely privileged to hear this. It falls to us to communicate how we have really listened to them. Letters in this case can give a really powerful message that we have truly heard and tried to understand and this can have a similar emotional resonance to the reformulation letter in therapy.

3. The boundary seesaw model as applied to leadership/management

Hamilton (2009) developed the boundary seesaw model in response to the dilemma of providing security and care in forensic services. She described common themes within forensic settings in how staff set and manage boundaries. At one end of the seesaw, a more controlling style of relating, which involved keeping an emotional distance and an over focus on rules, regulations and tasks with very inflexible boundaries. This could pull responses such as a superficial compliance, active rebellion or battles for power and control. At the other end of the spectrum was a style characterised as a pacifier or super carer, indulging patients and fostering an overdependence. The negotiator was identified as more of a middle ground, with clarity about negotiable and non-negotiable boundaries within a collaborative professional relationship which is not too close and not too distant. Although individuals may be more drawn to one style over the other depending on their relational patterns developed in childhood and influenced throughout life, there is also movement up and down the spectrum depending on other relational dynamics.

This model has a lot of relevance to leadership and management. There is a challenge in management and leadership in balancing both compassion and wellbeing with performance. Although general relational patterns go beyond these three styles of relating, given these were prominent themes within staff in forensic services, it is not beyond the realms of possibility that these are also themes found within leaders in forensic services and that this is a spectrum through which leaders move up and down. For example, the life experiences of the manager/leader could determine whether they were pulled more to controlling or protecting. Additionally, considering Potters (2020) three-part rule, we might consider how the organizational culture and the team or individual would interact with the leaders relational style to 'pull' a particular style of management/leadership. Using this model, one leader might display a more controlling style of leadership as this may be a feature of their relational style. Another leader might be pulled to an over focus on controlling performance measures in response to a lack of boundaries and clear expectations in the culture. One leader might have a prominent overinvolved relational style whereas another might shift into it temporarily as needed to support an individual struggling in their staff team. Similar to therapy, questions leaders might ask themselves either in trying to understand their own relational style or in trying to understand an organization or team in difficulty, are is this a familiar place I find myself in? Is it comfortable? Or is this out of character for me, not a usual place I find myself? Such questions help both self-reflection and supporting others in reflecting on what is them (my relational patterns), what is others (their relational pattern) and what is related to the wider context (organizational or cultural relational patterns).

The model highlights that our relational style needs to sit within these structures. The 'negotiator' manages relational distance by developing closeness within boundaries, and clear expectations and fixed and flexible limits. An aspiration to a 'healthy organization' has been suggested as requiring four components: a clear primary task needed to survive, clear structure of roles and responsibilities, shared principles of how we do what we do, informed by why we do what we do and a space to reflect on the emotional impact of the work, (Personality Disorder Knowledge and Understanding Framework, 2007). Relational leadership and the use of the CAT model has to sit in this context and the 'negotiator' style of management would very clearly require these components to be present.

Leading in a crisis

It is impossible to write this chapter without acknowledging the significant impact of the COVID-19 pandemic which occurred during this time.

In trying to create safety, the pandemic has taken away a lot of control from individuals. This was on a societal level with national lockdowns and restrictions on movement and social contact, and specific to healthcare with the establishment of command-and-control structures, all designed to keep people safe and minimise risk. These themes will have elicited a range of reactions depending on each individual, their relationship with power and control and their characteristic ways of coping. Take, for example, an individual who was raised by a controlling parent. One individual in this situation may have felt stifled and squashed but resentfully complied and remained safe but frustrated. Another may have felt powerless and angry and have rebelled leaving them feeling powerful but in conflict or having further power taken away. The narrative told by staff may be one of anger and not feeling valued or feeling powerless with no autonomy. A manager or leader may feel frustrated with the person who complies but complains behind closed doors, feeling powerless to support their staff member as they will not voice it. They may feel undermined and angry with the staff member who is rebelling and not adhering to management advice. The narrative told by the manager may be one of frustration at not being respected or of feeling undermined.

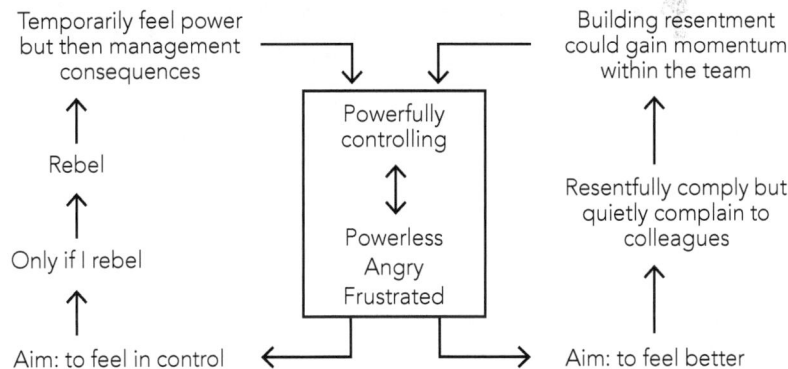

These patterns being played out in the workplace are likely to detract from the core business of providing care. More than ever the role of leaders needs to hold in mind relational dynamics within us, between us and around us to get the full picture.

The pandemic brought an additional dynamic to the fore. By its very nature, it undermined everyone's sense of safety on a primitive and fundamental level. The invisible threat which could be located anywhere but where risk increased through physical contact and physical proximity challenged many healthy procedures we have about safety seeking. To seek safety from someone who could be a threat or that we could be a threat to left many people with a huge sense of loss and grief.

In times of threat, our characteristic ways of coping and surviving, developed in early childhood and played out through our lives are triggered. In a pandemic where to be close is to be dangerous, this could almost be perceived as triggering a trauma response within the workplace. The pull to seek closeness with colleagues whilst simultaneously needing to stay apart to keep safe mirrors a trauma response and can create an automatic survival response; fight, flight or freeze. As described above, within the workplace it is likely that all responses will be seen – the staff member who rebels in response to control (fight), the staff member who takes flight (calling in sick) and the staff who are overwhelmed (freeze). As leaders and managers being relationally aware and having an understanding of how individual's develop their coping and survival mechanisms will help foster compassion for individuals and teams they are managing and leading.

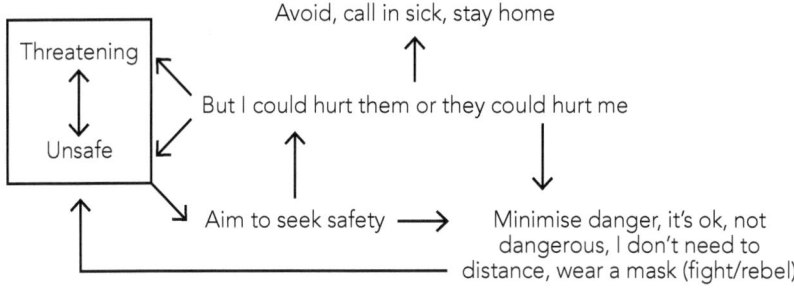

A manager or leader in a crisis is in the position of needing to make difficult decisions or implement difficult decisions. In a highly pressured situation with new and constantly changing advice and practice and where these decisions need to be made at a faster pace than ever, there is likely to be little space for reflection and reflection is difficult to do alone or without connection. The importance of leadership relationships comes to the fore in crisis situations. Similar to clinical work in a forensic setting, during a pandemic with command-and-control structures, we are dealing with themes of control and power and there is the potential within this for fragmentation and splitting within teams. The boundary seesaw model (as mentioned in the previous section) (Hamilton, 2010) may been able to offer valuable insights to leaders and managers; the need for safety and consistency is crucial, for managers and leaders to be able to offer compassionate leadership but this needs to coexist with the organizations clear primary goal, shared principles, and clear roles and responsibilities.

Similar to the starting point of my journey with reflective practice, in my experience, reflection in a crisis if it is not part of usual business, is difficult if not impossible. However, it is also extremely difficult to create a sense of safety if there are not clear goals, shared principles and roles and responsibilities. Defences may be high, people are likely to feel threatened and unsafe and it is hard to make space to reflect or to feel safe enough to do so if space is provided. Given the significant role of leadership in crisis situations, it is absolutely crucial that learning from this pandemic includes recognition of the need for relationally safe and reflective leadership teams with a long-term commitment to relationally informed reflective practice coexisting with principles for a healthy organization.

Conclusion

There are significant challenges for the NHS and for healthcare services. Leadership is crucial in setting the culture but the stories of our leaders tell of the toll their work can take on them personally and emotionally. Our leaders are people first and foremost and as people we flourish in a supportive, containing, compassionate environment. Providing such an environment for others without having it yourself is hugely challenging if not impossible. These are lessons we need to listen to. CAT tools can offer leaders a model for relational awareness and tools for supporting leadership teams to take steps in telling their stories, creating shared understanding and thinking together about how to create compassionate cultures.

Chapter 13: Leadership and Cognitive Analytic Therapy

Part two – a personal and professional journey

Jenny Marshall

Introduction

Cognitive Analytic Therapy (CAT) and leadership is not a training course which you attend, receive a certificate and therefore have the skills to use CAT concepts to lead. My journey is not by any means a finished journey; similar to therapy, it is lifelong learning and reflection. Within this section, I aim to discuss core aspects of CAT which I have found to be integral to a leadership role when thinking about myself as a leader, others as leaders and the system and culture of leadership around me.

The history…

CAT recognises that we are socially formed and that our relational patterns are influenced by significant figures in our lives, predominantly in childhood but throughout life as well. Our leadership styles therefore are not only influenced by our relational patterns developed as children but by other influential people in our lives and at work. Whilst my professional career has been influenced by many people, the scaffolding for my journey with CAT and leadership began long before I trained as a CAT practitioner with two individuals carving a path of leadership and influence in very different ways. I feel I want to share something of them in order to touch on the idea that leadership development is as relational as our individual personality styles are. CAT as a model is often thought of as intergenerational and I believe our leadership styles have a similar heritage. I have been fortunate enough over many years to have the benefits of working with both external (Steve Potter, CAT Psychotherapist, Supervisor and Trainer) and internal consultants, (Kate Freshwater, Consultant Psychologist and CAT Lead for a learning disabilities and mental health trust).The combination of these roles has been instrumental in scaffolding both the structures of CAT development within leadership teams I have worked with, and the emotional scaffolding and containment offered to me over many years to develop into a leadership role using CAT. They have their own stories to tell but I will share a brief snapshot of their thoughts and influences here to give some background to the influence they had when we worked collaboratively together to pioneer some of the leadership work.

Steve: *In those early days when the CAT approach was taking shape there was a multidisciplinary outlook among the people drawn to Tony Ryle's leadership. It was an approach with open borders that brought different ideas and methods together in a new integration. At the same time, it was bringing people from different backgrounds together in an open dialogue. To borrow Ian Kerr's phrase it was, whether working directly with patients or indirectly with teams, a contextual approach. There is something about the relational integration of ideas in CAT that gives it face validity and gives those steeped in it the confidence to speak of the dynamics of mental health treatments in an open and common sense way.*

Kate: *A group analyst colleague once said to me "You know what your problem is Kate? You can't let go of things". He probably had a point, with regard to both my car and relationship regularly breaking down – but it's not been all bad. The accessibility and usefulness of CAT that I have witnessed over the years has fuelled my tenacity to keep on keeping on at people with regard to the benefits of CAT both as a therapy and contextual model. No doubt my CAT promotion comments are sometimes as unwelcome as my colleague's unsolicited advice, but it has been easy to be passionate and persistent about CAT when I have seen so many people helped by it, and so many good souls drawn to it. I'm pleased I didn't let go of it. Usually, it has been unpredicted windows of opportunity (as well as wearing them down!) that reaped more benefits to the development of CAT in our organization, rather than formal process such as writing proposals for service development.*

Probably the most important example of this was in my early days of CAT work, when I was invited to present an intro to CAT to the Trust board as part of their visit to a service. Last on the agenda for the day, I was informed that things had over-run and there would not be enough time for the presentation. My usual placation/avoidance traps would have led me to go home, but with recent life events having loosened my map, I walked into the board room and asked if I could just have 20 minutes of their time, given the preparation and importance of the topic. This led to a further meeting with the Chief Executive and service targets set for CAT, and was probably the most pivotal moment in my many years of CAT work.

As an internal consultant, the building of the CAT work on a Trust-wide basis by Kate, provided both a practical structure and also perhaps more importantly, supervision, coaching, mentoring and support which was instrumental to the later developments of reflective practice both within the service I worked in and also my own leadership journey.

Some years later, I started my journey with practitioner training through the Association of Cognitive Analytic Therapy (ACAT). My CAT training was initially funded with the understanding that the training would be used not only to provide therapy but to offer training and support for the frontline nursing staff. The emotional demands of working in forensic services were being increasingly acknowledged with particular emphasis on the nature of the trauma staff are exposed to. I had been working in forensic services for a number of years and previous experience of running reflective practice groups had been that they were usually requested in a crisis. However, I had observed that, in a crisis, staff anxieties were usually high and there was often a fear of criticism or scrutiny which made it difficult for the reflective space to feel safe and for staff to be able to use the space to share or acknowledge difficult feelings. As a consequence, learning in or after a crisis was often limited. This experience profoundly influenced the development of an overarching relational model which aimed at embedding training and reflective practice as 'everyday business', (Marshall *et al*, 2014).

It was at this point that I was introduced to Steve who had been building a network of practitioners interested in the relational approach as applied to teams, particularly in forensic settings. In the early days of the work Steve did with myself and Kate, I felt great trepidation about mapping with teams; observing the process I did not know how he was taking messy maps and turning them into something meaningful. Until I had the 'light bulb moment': he did not know where he was going with it either but was trusting in the process of co-creating narratives with the aid of words shared on paper or white board.

Building scaffolding and a basis for safety

Building an overarching relational model and a culture of reflective practice required significant scaffolding from the outset. It involved gaining support from the senior leadership team for the initiative. Although I didn't 'take the bull by the horns' by interrupting the directors, I was aware that the scope of the plan and support for a proposal to train the service in a relational model and ongoing reflective practice was ambitious to say the least. I remember thinking at the time 'what have I got to lose' and so I wonder how much of a theme about such projects and developments is driven by the willingness to take a gamble, put yourself out there and risk failing? Once the senior leadership team had approved the initiative, collaborative relationships with managers who could support the translation of the vision into reality were needed. This involved releasing teams of staff to attend training and supporting staff attending regular reflective practice sessions.

What had been an original five-year plan was extended beyond this as the service expanded and as with staff changes and turnover, emphasis was placed on both initial training for staff and embedding and sustaining reflective practice for those wards who had received the training. As with the expansion of many projects, at some point there becomes a need to recognise we cannot do it all singlehandedly and it is required for there to be sufficient people dedicated and motivated, and I believe with the tenacity illustrated by Kate earlier to take over the reins. With these qualities and a recognition of the importance of the relationships with managers who manage the practical issues related to attendance, reflective groups will hopefully go on even without us, taking on a life of their own and becoming the norm.

Over the years of sustained reflective practice, I observed that managers rarely attended reflective practice but would instead often support the ward to enable nurses to attend. I was struck by their selflessness within this, protecting a space for staff at the expense of space for themselves. I began to float ideas about offering training using the CAT model for managers, informally initially but this was enough to see it was worth pursuing. This led to the leadership and management team supporting a proposal to offer reflective practice for managers following a similar programme of training to the ward teams including the following themes:

A. General awareness of relational dynamics
B. Self-awareness – my own relational dynamics/patterns
C. Leadership relational dynamics/patterns – those I lead within the service
D. Leadership relational dynamics/patterns – those I relate to outside the service (wider trust/other trusts (NCM).
E. Leadership team dynamics
F. Follow up reflective practice groups on a monthly basis

During the training days, the managers reflected on the CAT model and described how despite not attending reflective practice groups, they felt 'we speak the language'. Building a reflective culture from the bottom-up had allowed for a wider appreciation of reflective practice. The managers spoke about how they felt the model 'gives a voice to staff who are there all the time' as well as 'the space to stand back'. It appeared from the managers that using the CAT model for reflective practice had become 'the way we do things around here'. This culture change, if it could be described in this way, allowed for the reflective practice to been seen as a welcome and safe initiative for managers and senior leaders within the scaffolding of reflective practice throughout the service rather than threatening as can be the case if reflective practice is implemented as part of a response to crisis.

Creating connection and dialogue

In all the teams I have worked with, frontline staff, managers and leaders, one of the most consistent pieces of feedback has been the value of coming together as a team, having safe connection and dialogue can enable managers and leaders to realise that they are not alone in the way they feel. In particular, following one of the training sessions, where the managers shared the pressures of their role (to be manager, leader, mentor, pastoral supporter, nurse), one person spoke up to say, 'I thought it was just me, I didn't realise everyone else felt this way too'. This was a bitter-sweet experience for me, simultaneously hearing the value of our training as the specific loneliness of being the only psychologist manager resonated with me. Ward managers naturally have peers. For psychologists, allied health professionals or other heads of services or directors they may be the only one in their position. Whatever the title, it is important to remember the humanity of each individual leader and to consider how connected they are and the space for reflective dialogue that each leader has. This may be more apparent for leaders who do not have well-functioning leadership teams but even with the best functioning teams, the benefit of having support networks cannot be understated.

It is easy to feel alone as a leader, but if we define ourselves as leaders, managers, psychologists, nurses, we are putting barriers up and highlighting difference. We are all human and being reminded of our common humanity can help us not to feel so alone. Reflective practice can be more than reflecting on the dynamics of our interactions and our relational pattern, it is an opportunity for dialogue and connection, for coming together rather than being divided.

> *'If I relate to others from the perspective of myself as someone different – A Buddhist, Tibetan and so on- I will then create walls to keep me apart from others. And if I relate to others thinking I am the Dalai Lama, I will create the basis for my own separation and loneliness. After all there is only one Dalai Lama in the entire world. In contrast, if I see myself primarily in terms of my fellow human, I will then have more than seven billion people who I can feel deep connection with. And this is wonderful isn't it? what do you need to fear or worry about when you have seven billion other people who are with you?'*
> (Dalai Lama & Desmond Tutu, 2016, p100)

The quote above I feel represents the ethos we are trying to create with an overarching reflective practice model. Within groups it can be easy to only see your individual or group perspective. Within a compassionate culture, we are trying to see ourselves as humans. It is well accepted that we need to show empathy for our service users and increasingly that we need to recognise and support frontline staff with the emotional demands of the role. It is less talked about in relation to the need to walk in the director's shoes or manager's shoes. If and when we can shift from blame directed at our service users, colleagues, managers or directors and step outside of our experience to consider 'what is going on for me, for that individual or team or in the organization' we will be creating a compassionate culture.

One of the unexpected outcomes of all my work both with frontline staff and leaders and managers has been my own shift in empathy. We hope that training and reflective practice will help staff with empathy for their patients and for each other, but I have been struck time and again at how hearing the staff stories of their work lives, leaves me with a deeper emotional understanding, empathy and connection for them. As facilitators I believe we are 'in this' with them, not separate facilitators untouched by their experiences.

The tricky part... being on the map

As leaders, if we are connecting and building relationships and in dialogue with others, we are part of the relational dynamics and culture. One of the most personally challenging parts of this work has not been the delivery of the training and reflective practice workshops. Listening to groups whether frontline or leadership, getting alongside and making sense through mapping together has always been something which comes easier to me. My experience of this for many years has been being both an internal (working within the service) and external (being slightly removed from the team by not being ward based) consultant. Taking up this dual position, whilst not quite fitting in either category, has enabled me to have the benefits of both; strategically able to influence and generate 'buy in' to the overarching relational model from my internal role and relationships, whilst being separate enough to be able to 'hover' and observe team dynamics without being too much 'in them'. However, one of the key differences in bringing the reflective model to leadership, has been that in being senior enough to be able to 'sell' the model to those in such positions, I have also been more 'in' the dynamics and 'on the map'. In the caring profession and in leadership, we bring our high hopes, expectations, we bring our compassion and passion and we bring our striving to do better for the people we serve. But as leaders we lead and we follow. We make decisions and we carry out decisions made by others. We are in the public eye, both with our teams, our services, and externally from commissioners, the media and the public. We are exposed for the decisions we make and those we do not make. We can be named, blamed and shamed and we hope not to be on the receiving end of 'axes swinging, fingers pointing with career ending humiliation' (Anandaciva et al, 2018) as so succinctly described by the leaders in the NHS. We do this work because it matters and because we believe in it but if we do it whole heartedly, it is exposing, it accesses our core pain and it hurts.

The most challenging part of my leadership journey has been leading through the pandemic. At their core, forensic services are involved in managing risk in order to protect others. In doing this, the environments can be perceived as controlling and restrictive. The core aspect of control is over freedom, the service users, detained under the Mental Health Act are unable to leave. Services control whether they can have leave, where to, and how long for. Qualities of protection and control are working alongside each other simultaneously and are experienced differently by different individuals. The pandemic brought with it a very similar dynamic. Control over liberty through lockdown was the best example, dictating whether you could leave your home, for how long, where to and who you could see had a lot of parallels with forensic services particularly as it was in the interest of trying to control the virus and save lives, in essence to protect. In the wider population, this was viewed by some as protecting, by others as controlling. Leading through the pandemic in forensic services brought these dynamics to the fore, all of a sudden I was viewed as either controlling or protecting staff in relation to wearing PPE, social distancing, limiting office space, changing job roles whilst being simultaneously helpless, having these restrictions and changes imposed from the government and filtered down.

As already discussed in the previous chapter, in a crisis situation, where individuals feel under threat and feel unsafe, it is likely to be difficult to reflect. In such a situation, it can be increasingly hard to see more than just your own perspective, to see the dynamics at play in the wider organization and with others as well as your own dynamics which you are bringing. There is an increased likelihood that we will end up on the map, and not be able to see it. On top of this, with the need to keep physical distance, the sense of loneliness as a leader was heightened.

This left me wondering how I would be able to write or speak about leadership with integrity when I have so much to learn and when I can get it wrong.

One of the first realisations in relation to this was that we are not leadership experts. The nature of CAT is collaborative and in the same way we would see our service users as their own experts by experience within therapy. Applying the same principle, to leadership, we are not claiming to be leadership experts. Using CAT within leadership teams involves a side-by-side journey with the organization, a journey of vulnerability. This for me both emphasises the importance of the scaffolding to provide a safe basis for reflection as mentioned, but also the importance of an awareness and experience of working within the zone of proximal development. I have known and understood the concept of ZPD on a theoretical level and to a certain extent within therapy for some time. However, the concept was brought to life in relation to my own experiences of working both within my ZPD in relation to reflective practice and awareness of self and also a contrasting experience of being pushed outside of my ZPD. The first example was when I was working with a trainer who demonstrated 'mapping the moment' using an example which had just occurred. One momentary interaction which I had not given any significance to was suddenly on the white board in front of the group illustrating my core relational patterns. Within the context of our co-trainer relationship and some self-awareness, this was within my ZPD. It brought new insight but in a safe environment. In contrast, my second experience, a one-off team reflective practice session which was provided without any scaffolding or follow up highlighted some of the more problematic procedures. Without the scaffolding of safe ongoing reflective practice, this felt too risky and did not lead to sustained team or individual change. Outside of my ZPD, my felt experience was that this was demoralising and unsafe. For me, this was a helpful reminder of the need to stay closely attuned to individuals and teams when running reflective practice. Particularly when teams are not functioning, there can be a pressure to make change but meaningful change takes time and needs to be at the right pace or individuals/teams can shut down.

My second realisation in relation to being on the map as a leader, related to some underlying assumptions about myself. I noticed a very powerful sense of being a fraud. How could I espouse relational leadership if I myself was unknowingly on the map, pulled into problematic relational dynamics? It was at this point that I realised that although for years I had been teaching with a slide which stated 'we are always on the map', I was not prepared for this to be so true, and for the first time, I fully realised why my co-trainer included this slide.

I wondered about why it was so much easier to consider being on the map as a therapist as opposed to as a leader. There are many possible reasons for this but to highlight a few, I considered the safe space or scaffolding provided in CAT supervision where there is an expectation that this is discussed and reflected on within therapy and in contrast, the absence of this type of reflection within management supervisions or leadership cultures. I also thought about the importance of shared experiences, and how both my supervisors had openly used many personal examples of being on the map which had fostered an acknowledgement that we are all human, a side-by-side curiosity about interactions and dynamics and a sense of safety in exploring these issues. If you are on the map in a supportive and reflective culture, with compassionate colleagues, as had been my experience in CAT supervision, this can be a safe learning experience, an opportunity to get things wrong and repair them; reparation being key to growth.

However, being on the map without support and compassion within the organization may end up feeling like you are under attack. Again, this served to emphasise the importance to me when considering any relational dynamics, that all aspects of the picture are taken into account and that as senior leaders we are able to hold the one thirds rule in mind; what is going on within us, between us and around us.

The ending...CAT exits

I started these two chapters (part 1) considering the current climate in the NHS according to leaders (Figure 1) and the need for compassionate leadership embraced in a meaningful and sustainable way. Like many concepts, it is easy to talk about compassionate leadership and it is easy to talk about suggested exits on the leadership map such as having clear priorities, calling out bullies, talking about workload and worries about competence. It is much harder to do as it is tied up in our own relational patterns and procedures. Returning to the three- part rule, compassionate leadership needs to reflect on what the individual brings, the team or others and the wider organizational context.

The **wider organizational context** may involve trying to achieve the impossible and this may create in leaders a near toxic cocktail of pressure. There may be greater regulatory controls which can feel dominating and controlling. This **requires recognition of this as a relational dynamic and the impact from a wider systemic organizational level involving internal and external leaders becoming aware and considering organizational exits from this.**

Staff (including leaders) may feel silenced, suffocated, experiencing a loss of motivation and creativity and may rebel or disengage. This requires an **embedded relational approach with commitment to sustaining reflective practice** so that staff can not only feel safe enough to explore this and feel heard but so they can start to understand the wider organizational context, and their response and part within this. Staff may not have total control over changing this but recognising their part may bring about small change. The enormity of this task should not be underestimated. It is far easier for staff to blame upwards than it is to consider however small, the part they may play in problematic relational dynamics. Creating reflective capacity can take a significant amount of time and commitment from the organization both to embed and sustain and even with the infrastructures in place, some staff will find this easier than others, or will find the group setting safer than others.

On an individual relational level, understanding our own relational patterns will make a difference. Common relational patterns identified in the helpers dance list (such as never feeling good enough and coping by trying even harder, or caring/looking after others but ending up neglecting self) are prominent in the helping profession and likely to be present in leaders. Individual awareness can help either through **reflective practice or through personal therapy**. For example, feeling a relentless near toxic cocktail of pressure not only requires an organizational and team approach but it also requires an individual response to being able to put our own boundaries in, recognition of the need to take care of ourselves as carers and leaders and the ability to ask for help. The ability to do this, for some may come easy but for others is likely to require the self-awareness to recognise the striving procedure, tendency for self-neglect or procedure of coping alone before exits can be put in place. It is important to remember that our relational patterns are developed early in childhood and one of the principles underpinning the message 'we are always on the map' is that we are not always aware when we are repeating problematic patterns. Patterns such as striving may serve us well in some circumstances but particularly under a crisis such as the pandemic, may end up being extremely harmful and may be linked with work related stress, high sickness rates. Individual recovery from this is likely to depend on the wider organizational context and team/colleagues; if the scaffolding is present for a compassionate reflective culture, this may be recognised and revised. However, in the context described by senior leaders in the NHS, if we are judged on our ability to succeed or we face a regulatory firing squad or finger pointing, this may feel humiliating, blaming and bullying.

As I draw this chapter to a close, it falls to me to share my own exits from a personal leadership struggle. Steve Potter (2020) uses an analogy of a flat tyre to describe how themes of helplessness which can be common in organizations, can become intertwined with feeling useless. A flat tyre and feelings of helplessness in being able to fix this can easily be resolved with help but if I judge myself as being useless for not being able to fix it creates 'a kind of wounded sense of self where I am the flat tyre which is a much more difficult repair job since I am the cause of the puncture'. When stranded at the side of the road with no way to get home, we would usually call for help. In a leadership position, this emphasises the importance of networks not just of professional relationships but those scaffolding relationships which will come when you call for help and whilst they may not be able to fix the tyre, they may wait with you, honestly, patiently and compassionately until the puncture is repaired. When we feel punctured, it is likely that this will go to the heart of our core pain, after all, we are people first before leaders. In these situations, we will need people; personal professional and therapists who can remind us that this is not all of us, and that there are other parts of ourselves, our healthy self is still there. We need to be reminded of these parts of ourselves in order to heal.

My leadership journey, is by no means finished and it has been the most challenging, rewarding and difficult journey of my career. As with therapy, developing a leadership culture takes time. Like therapy it is dependent on the social context. This journey has been ongoing for over 20 years and it feels as though I and my colleagues have only scratched the surface in thinking contextually and relationally about it. There are many other voices of leaders out there and if we want to truly understand leadership culture we need to hear them. If we can start a dialogue, to explore relational leadership we will be starting to build the framework and scaffolding for a different NHS.

Chapter 14: Concluding thoughts

A dialogue between the editors

Jenny Marshall, Jamie Kirkland and Steve Potter

Introduction

In this chapter we hope to reflect on the book as a whole, and using the one thirds rule, reflect on what was going on within us, between us and around us during the writing of the book. It is an invitation to the reader to start a dialogue with us about reflective practice.

Where did this (the book) start?

Probably a lot longer ago, but our thoughts went back to the coming together of a group of people in the U.K. all working in forensic services. Whilst the group were geographically diverse, stretching from Edinburgh and Glasgow in Scotland down to Devon and East London in England, we were united by a common desire to work relationally. Each group had been working separately, developing relational thinking and reflective practice using Cognitive Analytic Therapy concepts in diverse ways.

This led to the first forensic CAT conference which was themed as a 'Shared Thinking Space'. We never expected it to take off the way it did but we found ourselves hosting a conference which was sold out with a waiting list. There was so much enthusiasm and a real appetite for thinking space and reflective practice.

In some ways we wanted the book to reflect and capture the energy and voices from this conference. There, we had debated through the planning stage about the programme and the importance of trying to make sure that, whilst theory and evidence are important, it should not dominate at the expense of space to think during the day. Within the book we have tried to strike a balance of theory and evidence but have taken time to reflect on the process of writing the book too.

We wondered if the diversity in voices at the conference would be heard as disparate voices, a collection of valuable but separate initiatives and experiences. Actually, we have found, and we hope the reader does too, that even though the voices are telling their own stories, in many ways, they are reflecting common themes, their creativity has shone through and has not been stifled but all have been anchored and scaffolded by the CAT model.

What were you seeking to achieve with the book?

Following the conference we hoped that this project would achieve a few modest goals by keeping alive ideas from a collection of people at the conference in the face of constant challenges. We wanted to capture enthusiasm in the field of forensics for a CAT-informed approach to reflective practice. We wanted to strike a balance between the tension of creativity and permission to adapt the approach but also to guide those approaching reflective practice with a feeling that they are following some principles for good practice and have some scaffolding. As such we find the CAT model can be an anchor but it also allows people to develop and create.

We captured this by hearing different voices in the chapter contributors, but there were similarities in what we heard. We feel it was 'a comfortable experience of similarities'. As the process moved on, we became less wary of this, not so much a backslapping exercise where writers simply agree with each other. Rather, with CAT as an anchor, a creative but similar approach. In order to do so we had to learn, as editors, to accept what was being produced but also shape this work. We wondered if it paralleled 'mappers anxiety' – where to enter a reflective practice session with a preconceived idea as to what would be said risked missing out on voices and unexpected directions in the conversation. We had to learn to trust the voices.

'How do you sustain reflective practice?'

It was hard to sustain that enthusiasm following the conference. It somehow created a momentary haven from the reality of day-to-day work. On returning to business as usual within healthcare and forensic work, it was hard to protect the time to take forward some of the hopes we had following the conference. This was often mentioned as a central dilemma in sustaining reflective practice.

This is a real challenge, there will always be a crisis, some much worse than others. The pandemic has been a real feature of this book but others have been there in the background, Black Lives Matter, Brexit and there will always be others. This is why reflective practice is so important, we need to hold a space to think as we navigate our way through the complexities, our own experiences, those in our near vicinity and the wider context in which we live and work.

In sustaining reflective practice, much like the first conference, we have to consider failure, it not working, events getting in the way. We may have grand plans which do not come to fruition. But do we even need grand plans? We talk about a few examples of 'grand plans' in the book with some of the proposals and overarching models but what are we really trying to do? We have learnt through experience and through watching other like-minded people, that this really is about the long view, culture change takes years and can be thought of as collections of moments of meaningful dialogue, connection and reflection.

> *Jenny: This came to the fore throughout the writing of the book. Jamie, you took up multiple positions during the writing of the book and shared your example of not just your usual role but being on the frontline on the wards, giving me an example of a therapeutic ward conversation. Really, this is the heart of what we are trying to do. CAT chats are a really accessible example of this. This led to thinking about reflective space for our service users, do we have this and if not, why not, we should. This is what we hope the book will do, generate ideas and develop a life of its own.*

> *Jamie: In our dialogue, Jenny, you spoke of how you had run a session for service users on reflective practice through recovery college. I wondered if I had had an unoriginal thought – but this was not the effect. It was a connection, in dialogue, about how clinicians (Jamie and Jenny) working in different places are using the anchor of a CAT approach to create a community for reflective practice.*

What has been the process of writing the book?

> *Jenny: Similar to mapping we think at the beginning there was writers anxiety. A lot was unknown, perhaps the book wouldn't even happen. It was a leap of faith in saying yes, taking a risk to put ourselves out there and risk failing. My lightbulb moment mapping with Steve early on was realising that he didn't know where he was going with it, there was no preconceived end point he was trying to get to, he trusted the process of mapping. I think we have trusted the process of writing both for us and for the other writers in the book.*

What has been your relationship with each other?

It has developed over time. We found little and often has worked best, perhaps like reflective practice. There has been a reservoir of trust, to explore gut feelings and hold our own anxieties and fears as well as celebrating the achievement from every author in the book. At points it has been hard to think and difficult to look at the book.

> *Jenny: It has been these points at which I have been able to hover above and notice, it is hard to think, I seem to be avoiding the book, perhaps I had better give Jamie a call. There have been mistakes along the way but I think we both knew the frustration this caused and I think we managed to 'name the dance' not 'blame the dancer'. We both appreciated the kindness in this. Again, this is what we hope for,*

> we all make mistakes but perhaps if there was more kindness and forgiveness?
>
> **Jamie:** *We cannot underestimate how important it was to check-in. It was important to have a calmer voice (Jenny), and felt like a CAT chat using 'raw' words to get the gut feeling out and then work with this. The benefits of having the 'other' – when there are times one cannot think the reaching out has allowed for space to think and reset, then begin again. Also having differing skills to get things done was helpful. The usual tension of working together has partly been helped with checking in, not assuming where the other is at. But these were 'little and often'.*

We therefore applied these ideas to the writing of the book. We had to recognise pressures for the writers and how we hold or let go and when to gently push. Not everyone can give when they have a deadline, circumstances change, energies sap. Just as in reflective practice, not each member of the group can always be 'present' when they have competing work and personal lives. So the book is not an end point, rather an invitation to build a dialogue around reflective practice.

What are your hopes for the book?

This is not a finished product. It has been difficult to draw to a close as with a reflective culture, it is an ideal, not a destination you reach. Hopefully, this can be a platform to bring more dialogue and for people to feel they can move out of the therapy room and work more with the environment. We hope it has been accessible and that whilst trying to provide some structure and theory and reflection on competency, that it will not stifle creativity. We hope this resonates with people but is not too mysterious, we want people to give it a go and to give some tools and frameworks for this.

We can be optimistic, after all this is the final chapter and we don't want it to be a damp squib! We need to simultaneously acknowledge that some of these initiatives might not get off the ground or they might hit hurdles and fail. When we think of failure it is hard to think about being face down on the floor and people prefer stories about getting back up again. We want this to be an optimistic final chapter but need to acknowledge that isn't always how it goes and that can be ok too. We have told many success stories in this book but perhaps there is more that could be said about those failures too. They also might not be failures, if we shift our perspective to collections of therapeutic moments, they may be enough to sow a seed which is returned to later when the time is right. This may be another book or collection, not for now.

What is missing from the book?

It is rooted in the forensic community but there are many other voices and key figures in reflective practice outside forensic services and so we need to hear their voices. We lost some people along the way so we did not get to hear their voices. Our frontline staff are missing but their voices are perhaps the most important.

> **Jenny:** *Steve recalls Dave from the very first training we did together. Over 30 people squashed in a hot room together but the warmth with which we all engaged. I (Jenny) have been trying to get him to speak with me for a while now. I'll keep trying! His is an important voice, perhaps an unsung hero for the role he has played in my work behind the scenes and there will be others like this.*
>
> **Jamie:** *I am curious how we try to be collaborative in our approach but we do not always get representation across professions. Yet it was the nursing assistant that sat in a CAT chat, engaged with the developing map about an offender and that person's loneliness and said, 'so what he really needs is PRN chat!'.*

Finally, you, the reader of course is missing. We talk about show don't tell and we hope we have done enough of this in the book. It can be hard to get across the emotional resonance that this work can have. Someone recently described the sharing of letters in teams as so powerful you could hear a pin drop. That is the real sense of needing to experience this rather than have it done to you. We want this book to be an invitation for a dialogue.

What are you proud of and where now?

We have got voices within the book sharing their experiences. We feared that we would not have them, but it really has been co-produced and we are proud of this. There has been trust in the collaborative process through distance and time. We hope the book has felt like one author but many voices and if we have achieved this then we will be really proud of it. We have survived the unknown and uncertainty; it has been difficult to be too proud in case it didn't happen, in some respects holding both positions has simultaneously spurred us on and kept us grounded in the hard slog.

We have been perhaps guilty of trying CAT as a reflective and contextual model. It is still taught as eight individual cases during practitioner training and we are hoping that this book can be a platform for the development of reflective practice considering issues such as competencies, supervision and frameworks.

We are proud of this work, mapping and working with the relational environment, encouraging people to reflect relationally and trying to make a model for reflective practice accessible. We hope (and would be proud if we achieve this) that the reader will hear this as a down to earth, accessible approach and feel they can develop their own style a position in dialogue with themselves, their teams and their organizations. We don't want it to be mysterious. Culture change comes in different ways and contexts, we can make a difference in a series of therapeutic moments and encounters as well as through the vision of five, ten year or longer-term plans.

Tony Ryle was interviewed shortly before his death and asked how he saw the CAT community developing. He created a therapeutic model that at the heart of it was relational and he shunned being seen as 'the expert'. He did not want the model to stop developing when he died. He wanted multiple voices to be heard. His words were: 'Don't mourn, organise'.

We want this book to be just the beginning. We want it to organise the CAT community around thinking about reflective practice using this model. We want to share our innovations in these developments.

Readers will react, we will promote it, we want to discuss it and get into dialogue with others. The book is a platform to do this.

References

ACAT (2000) *The Psychotherapy File. An Aid to Understanding Ourselves Better*. ACAT, Dorset.

Adlam, J. (2016) *"Not keeping it in the family"* – *A mentalisation-based approach to facilitating Reflective Practice Groups for multi-disciplinary staff teams in forensic settings* (Ghent). Conference paper.

Adshead, G. (1998) Psychiatric staff as attachment figures. Understanding management problems in psychiatric services in the light of attachment theory. *British Journal of Psychiatry*, 172, pp64–69.

Adshead, G. (2012) 'Mirror Mirror': Parallel processes in forensic institutions. In J. Adlam, A. Aiyegbusi, P. Kleinot, A. Motz & C. Scanlon (Eds) *The Therapeutic Milieu Under Fire: Security and insecurity in forensic mental health*. London & Philadelphia: Jessica Kingsley.

Aitken, C.J. & Schloss, J.A. (1994) *Occupational Stress and Burnout Amongst Staff Working with People with an Intellectual Disability*. Chichester: John Wiley.

Anandaciva, S., Ward, D., Randhawa, M. & Edge, R. (2018) *Leadership in Today's NHS: Delivering the impossible*. London: The King's Fund, NHS Providers. Available at: https://www.kingsfund.org.uk/sites/default/files/2018-07/Leadership_in_todays_NHS.pdf [Accessed: 15 June 2020]

Annesley, P. & Jones, L. (2016) The 4P's model: A Cognitive Analytic Therapy (CAT) derived tool to assist individuals and staff groups in their everyday clinical practice with people with complex presentations. *Reformulation*, Summer, pp40–43.

Appleby, K. (2003) Cognitive Analytic Therapy – its influence on my practice in the occupational health speciality within a clinical psychology and counselling service. *Reformulation*, Spring, pp18–24.

Bakhtin, M. (1929/1985) *Problems of Dostoyevsky's Poetics* (C. Emerson, Trans.). Minneapolis: University of Minnesota Press.

Ballatt, J. & Campling, P. (2011) *Intelligent kindness: Reforming the culture of healthcare*. London: RCPsych publications.

Barker, D., Tansey, L., Newman, E. & Quayle, E. (In preparation) Training forensic mental health nurses in Cognitive Analytic Therapy (CAT) principles: a qualitative exploration of the impact on complex case conceptualisation and implications for practice. *Qualitative Health Research*.

Barnes, N. (2016) Learning with young people about being. *Reformulation*, 46, pp11–18.

Barrett, J. (2011) Sustainable organizations in health and social care: Developing a 'team mind'. In: A. Rubitel and D. Reiss (Eds) *Containment in the Community: Supportive frameworks for thinking about antisocial behaviour and mental health*. The Portman Papers. London: Karnac Books, pp45–68.

Bascal, H.A. (1972) Balint groups: training or treatment? *Psychiatry in Medicine*, 3, pp373–378.

Bateman, A. & Fonagy, P. (2008) Comorbid antisocial and borderline personality disorders: mentalization-based treatment. *Journal of Clinical Psychology*, In Session, February 2008.

Benson, J. (2018) *Working More Creatively with Groups* (4th edition). Oxford: Routledge.

Binks, C., Jones, F. W. & Knight, K. (2013) Facilitating reflective practice groups in clinical psychology training: a phenomenological study. *Reflective Practice: International & Multidisciplinary Perspectives*, 14 (3), pp305–318.

Bion, W.R. (1962) *Learning from Experience*. London: William Heinemann Medical Books.

Bion, W.R. (1968) *Experience in Groups*. London: Tavistock Publications.

Bledin, K. (2019) Support for staff support groups: a role for group analysts. *Group Analysis*, 52 (3), pp339–349.

Blom-Cooper, L. (1995) *The Falling Shadow: One Patient's Mental Health Care*, 1978–3. Bloomsbury Academic.

Bloom, S. L. (2010a) Trauma-organized systems and parallel process. In: N. Tehrani (Ed) *Managing Trauma in the Workplace – Supporting Workers and the Organisation*. London: Routledge, pp139–153.

Bloom, S. L. (2010b) Sanctuary: an operating system for living organizations. In: N. Tehrani (Ed) *Managing Trauma in the Workplace – Supporting Workers and the Organisation*. London: Routledge, pp235–251.

Blunden. J. & Beard, H. (2017) 'CAT group supervision: the social model in action'. In: D. Pickvance (Ed) *Cognitive Analytic Supervision: A relational approach*. Abingdon: Routledge, pp125–136.

British Association for Counselling & Psychotherapy (2018) What Happens in Therapy? Leicestershire: British Association for Counselling & Psychotherapy. Retrieved from: http://www.itsgoodtotalk.org.uk/what-is-therapy

British Broadcasting Corporation (1999) 'UK Hospital's troubled past.' [Online] [Accessed 12 Feb 2020] Available at: http://news.bbc.co.uk/1/hi/uk/253288.stm

Brown, B. (2015) *Rising Strong*. UK: Penguin Random House.

Brown, D., Igoumenou, A., Mortlock, A., Gupta, N. & Das, M. (2017) Work-related stress in forensic mental health professionals: a systematic review. *Journal of Forensic Practice*, 19 (3) pp227–238.

Brown, R., Walsh, L. and Laganis, C. (2020) Catalyse Executive. The Zone of Proximal Development (ZPD) (Vygotsky 1978) in relation to Cognitive Analytic Therapy (CAT). (Twitter) 24 February 2020.

Calvert, R. and Kellett, S. (2014) Cognitive analytic therapy: A review of the outcome evidence base for treatment. *Psychology and Psychotherapy: Theory, Research and Practice*, 87, pp253–277.

Camus, A. (1942) *The Outsider*. London. Penguin.

Carradice, A. (2004) Applying cognitive analytic therapy to guide indirect working, *Reformulation*, 23(Autumn), pp18–23.

Carradice, A. (2004) Applying CAT to guide indirect working. Reformulation, theory and practice in CAT. *Reformulation*, 23, pp16–23.

Carradice, A. (2013) 'Five-session CAT' consultancy: Using CAT to guide care planning with people diagnosed with personality disorder within community mental health teams. *Clinical Psychology & Psychotherapy*, 20, pp359–367.

Carradice, A. (2017) 'Supervising CAT consultancy in mental health teams'. In: D. Pickvance (Ed) *Cognitive Analytic Supervision: A relational approach*. Abingdon: Routledge, pp209–221.

Carson, R. & Bristow, J. (2015) Collaborating with management in the NHS in difficult times. *Reformulation*, Summer, pp30–36.

Centre for Mental Health (2013) Briefing note: secure services. [Online] [Accessed 03 Jan 2020]. Available at: https://www.centreformentalhealth.org.uk/sites/default/files/201809/securecare.pdf

Chen, Q., Liang, M., Li, Y., Guo, J., Fei, D., Wang, L., He, L., Sheng, C., Cai, Y., Li, X., Wang, J. & Zhang, Z. (2020) Mental health care for medical staff in China during the COVID-19 outbreak. The Lancet Psychiatry, Volume 7, Issue 4, e15 – e16. https://doi.org/10.1016/S2215-0366(20)30078-X

Clarke, S., Thomas, P. & James, K. (2013) Cognitive analytic therapy for personality disorder: a randomised controlled trial. *British Journal of Psychiatry*, 202, pp129–134.

Coid, J., Kahtan, N., Gault, S., Cook, A. & Jarman, B. (2001) Medium secure forensic psychiatry services: Comparison of seven English health regions. *British Journal of Psychiatry*, 178(1) pp55–61.

Coldwell, J. B. & Naismith, L. (1989) 'Violent incidents on special care wards in a special hospital'. *Medicine, Science and the Law*, 29, pp116–123.

Coleby, J. and Freshwater, K. (2019) The Idealised Care Smokescreen: How the Tools we share can be used to attack. *Reformulation*, Summer, pp13–16.

Community Team. *Reformulation*, Summer, pp38–44.

Craissati, J., Minoudis, P., Shaw, J., Chuan, S., Simons, S. & Joseph, N. (2015) Working with offenders with personality disorder, A practitioners guide. NHS England: National Offender Management Service. Available at: https://www.england.nhs.uk/commissioning/wp-content/uploads/sites/12/2015/10/work-offndrs-persnlty-disorder-oct15.pdf [Accessed: 11 June 2019]

Dawber, C. (2013a) Reflective practice groups for nurses: A consultation liaison psychiatry nursing initiative: Part 1 – the model. *International journal of mental health nursing* 22 (2), pp135–144.

Dawber, C. (2013b) Reflective practice groups for nurses: A consultation liaison psychiatry nursing initiative: Part 2 – the evaluation. *International Journal of Mental Health Nursing*, 22, pp241–248.

Department of Health (2012) *Transforming Care: A National Response to Winterbourne View Hospital*. Whitehall.

Department of Health (2012) Transforming Care: A National Response to Winterbourne View Hospital. Whitehall. Available at: https://assets.publishing.service.gov.uk/government/uploads/system/uploads/attachment_data/file/213215/final-report.pdf [Accessed: 10 September 2020]

Department of Health (2014) Jimmy Savile Investigation: Broadmoor Hospital Report to the West London Mental Health NHS Trust and the Department of Health. Accessed: April 2020 via:https://assets.publishing.service.gov.uk/government/uploads/system/uploads/attachment_data/file/323458/Broadmoor_report.pdf

Department of Health (2002) Policy Implementation Guidance for Adult Acute inpatient Care Provision, p 33. Available at: http://www.p3-info.es/PDF/MHpolicy.pdf [Accessed: 30 October 2019]

Department of Health (2006) From Values to Action – The Chief Nursing Officer's Review of Mental Health Nursing. Available at: http://webarchive.nationalarchives.gov.uk/20130104234335/http://www.dh.gov.uk/prod_consum_dh/groups/dh_digitalassets/@dh/@en/documents/digitalasset/dh_4133840.pdf [Accessed: 15 March 2020]

Department of Health (2007) New ways of working for applied psychologists in health and social care: Working psychologically in teams. London: Department of Health. Available at: https://www.wiltshirepsychology.co.uk/Working%20Psychologically%20in%20Teams.pdf [Accessed: 15 March 2020]

Department of Health (2012) Transforming Care: A National Response to Winterbourne View Hospital. Whitehall. Available at: https://assets.publishing.service.gov.uk/government/uploads/system/uploads/attachment_data/file/213215/final-report.pdf [Accessed: 14.01.2021]

Dickey, L.A., Truten, J., Gross, L.M. & Deitrick, L.M. (2011) Promotion of staff resiliency and interdisciplinary team cohesion through two small-group narrative exchange models designed to facilitate patient- and family-centered care. *Journal of Communication in Health Care*, 4, pp126–138.

Dokter, H.J., Duivenvoorden, J.J. & Verhage, F. (1986) Changes in the attitude of general practitioners as a result of participation in a Balint group. *Family Practice*, 3, pp155–160.

Doyle, P., Tansey, L. & Kirkland, J. (2019) A Repertory Grid study of CAT group formulation in a forensic setting. *International Journal of Cognitive Analytic Therapy and Relational Mental Health*, 3, pp69–93.

Dunn, M. & Parry, G. (1997) A formulated care plan approach to caring for people with borderline personality disorder in a community mental health service setting. *Clinical Psychology Forum*, 104, pp19–22.

Dunn, M. & Parry, G. (1997) A reformulated care plan approach to caring for people with borderline personality disorder in a community mental health service setting. *Clinical Psychology Forum*, 104, pp19–22.

Dunn, M. & Parry, G. (1997) A reformulated care plan approach to caring for people with borderline personality disorder in a community mental health service setting. *Clinical Psychology Forum*, 104, pp19–22.

Erikson, E. (1963) *Eight ages of man. In: Childhood and society* (2nd edition). New York: Norton.

Evans, M. (2016) *Making Room for Madness in Mental Health: The Psychoanalytic Understanding of Psychotic of Psychotic Communication*. 1st ed. London: Routledge.

Ewers, P., Bradshaw, T., McGovern, J. & Ewers, B. (2002) Does training in psychosocial interventions reduce burnout rates in forensic nurses? *Journal of Advanced Nursing*, 37, pp470–476.

Fallon, P., Bluglass R., Edwards B. & Daniels, G. (1999) Report of the Committee into the Personality Disorder Unit, Ashworth Special Hospital. Department of Health. Available at: https://www.gov.uk/government/uploads/system/uploads/attachment_data/file/265696/4194.pdf [Accessed: 27 March 2020]

Fook, J. & Gardner, F. (2007) *Practising Critical Reflection. A Resource Handbook*. Maidenhead: McGraw Hill Education and Open University Press.

Fook, J. & Gardner, F. (2013) *Critical Reflection in Context. Applications in Health and Social Care*. London & New York: Routledge.

Freshwater, K. & Kerr, I. (2006) CAT Skills Training in Mental Health Settings. *Reformulation*, Summer, pp17–18.

Gabbard, G.O. (2010) *Long-term Psychodynamic Psychotherapy: A basic text*. Washington, DC: American Psychiatric Publication.

General Medical Council (2013) Good Medical Practice. General Medical Council. Available at: http://www.gmc-uk.org/static/documents/content/GMP.pdf [Accessed: 27 March 2020]

Gerada, C. (2014) Something is profoundly wrong with the NHS today. *British Medical Journal*, pp348.

Goleman, D. (1995) *Emotional Intelligence: Why It Can Matter More Than IQ*. New York: Bantam Books.

Goleman, D. (2006) *Social Intelligence: The New Science of Human Relationships*. New York: Bantam Books.

Hamilton, L. (2010) 'The boundary seesaw model: good fences make for good neighbours.' In: A. Tennant and K. Howells (Eds) *Using Time, Not Doing Time: Practitioner Perspectives on Personality Disorder and Risk*. Chichester: John Wiley, pp181–194.

Hare Duke, L., Furtado, V., Guo, B. & Völlm, B. A. (2018) Long-stay in forensic-psychiatric care in the UK. *Social psychiatry and psychiatric epidemiology*, 53 (3) pp313–321.

Harley, D. (2017) *Independent evaluation of reflective practice groups provided by the Psychotherapy Department* (NHS Lothian) for general psychiatric services. Edinburgh: Health Improvement Scotland.

Hartman, D. & Kitson, N. (1995) An examination of a staff group at a supra-regional deaf unit. *The Psychiatrist*, 19 (2), pp82–83.

Harvey, D. & Tuohy, B. (2020) 'Partnership working.' In: J. Ramsden, S. Prince and J. Blazedell (Eds) *Working effectively with 'Personality Disorder': Contemporary and critical approaches to clinical and organisational practice*. Shoreham-by-Sea: Pavilion.

Hawkins, P. & Shohet, R. (2012) *Supervision in the Helping Professions* (4th edition). Maidenhead: Open University Press.

Hayward, M. & McCurrie, C. (2008) Metaprocedures in Normal Development and in Therapy. *Reformulation*, Summer, pp42–45.000

Heffron, M. C., Reynolds, D. & Talbot, B. (2016) Reflecting together: reflective functioning as a focus for deepening group supervision. *Infant Mental Health Journal*, 37 (6) pp628–639.

Heneghan, C., Wright, J. & Watson, G. (2014) Clinical psychologists' experiences of reflective staff groups in inpatient psychiatric settings: a mixed methods study. *Clinical Psychology and Psychotherapy*, 21, pp324–340.

Hepple, J. (2015) CAT Reflective Practice Groups, *Reformulation*, Winter, pp22–25.

Hepple, J. (2019) CAT reflective practice groups, *Reformulation* 51, pp22–25.

Hepple, J. & Sutton, L. (2004) *Cognitive Analytic Therapy and Later Life: New perspectives on old age*. Oxford: Routledge.

Hermans, H. (2001) The dialogical self: toward a theory of personal and cultural positioning. *Culture and Psychology*, 7, pp243–281.

Holloway, E. L. (1995) *Clinical Supervision: A systems approach*. Thousand Oaks, CA: Sage Publications.

Holmes, J. (2014) 'Attachment theory in therapeutic practice.' In: A. N. Danquah and K. Berry (Eds) *Attachment Theory in Adult Mental Health*. Oxford: Routledge.

Hope, R. (2004) Ten Essential Shared Capabilities. A framework for the whole mental health workforce. London: Department Of Health. Available at: http://www.cmecic.org/resources/Education_Training_and_Development/The%20ten%20essential%20shared%20capabilities%20-%20a%20framework%20for%20the%20whole%20of%20the%20mental%20health%20workforce.pdf [Accessed: 20 March 2020]

Horney, K. (1945/1992) *Our Inner Conflicts*. New York: Norton.

Janis, F.L. (1972) 'Groupthink.' In: E. Griffin (Ed) (1991) *A First Look at Communication Theory* (1st edition). New York. McGrawHill, pp235–246.

Jansson, Å. (2017) 'From self-help to CBT: regulating emotion in a (neo)liberal world.' [Online] [accessed 02 Sep 2020] Available at: https://emotionsblog.history.qmul.ac.uk/2017/12/from-self-help-to-cbt-regulating-emotion-in-a-neoliberal-world/

Jefferis, S. (2020) http://tinyurl.com/CovidStrugglesMay2020.

Jenaway, A. & Mortlock, D. (2008) service innovation: offering cognitive analytic therapy in a child and adolescent mental health service, *Reformulation*, 30, pp31–32.

Johnson, A.H., Nease, D.E., Jr, Milberg, L.C. & Addison, R.B. (2004) Essential characteristics of effective Balint group leadership. *Family Medicine*, 36, pp253–259.

Johnson, S., Lloyd-Evans, B., Howard, L., Osborn, D. & Slade, M. (2010) 'Where next with residential alternatives to admission?' *The British Journal of Psychiatry*, 197, pp52–54.

Johnston, J. & Paley, G. (2013) Mirror mirror on the ward: who is the unfairest of them all? Reflections on reflective practice groups in acute psychiatric settings, *Psychoanalytic Psychotherapy*, 27 (2) pp170–186.

Johnstone, L., Whomsley, S., Cole, S. & Oliver, N. (2011) Good practice guidelines on the use of psychological formulation. Leicester: British Psychological Society. Available at: http://www.sisdca.it/public/pdf/DCP-Guidelines-for-Formulation-2011.pdf [Accessed:19.02.2021]

Jones, A. and Childs, D. (2007) Reformulating the NHS reforms, *Reformulation*, Summer, pp7–10.

Jones, J. (2014) A Report for the Centre for Social Work Practice on Reflective Practice Group Models in Social Work. London, Centre for Social Work Practice. Available at: https://www.brighton-hove.gov.uk/sites/default/files/migrated/article/inline/reflective-practice-report-11.05.15.pdf [Accessed: 10 August 2020]

Jones, L. (2007) Iatrogenic interventions with personality disordered offenders, *Psychology, Crime & Law*, 13 (1) pp69–79.

Kasmi, Y., Duggan, C. & Völlm, B. (2020) A comparison of long-term medium secure patients within NHS and private and charitable sector units in England, *Criminal Behaviour and Mental Health*, 30, pp38–49.

Kellett, S., Wilbram, M., Davis, C. & Hardy, G. (2014) Team consultancy using cognitive analytic therapy: a controlled study in assertive outreach, *Journal of Psychiatric and Mental Health Nursing*, 21, pp687–697.

Kemp, N., Bickerdike, A. & Bingham, C. (2017) 'Map and Talk' – A cognitive analytic therapy informed approach to reflective practice in a forensic setting. *International Journal of Cognitive Analytic Therapy and Relational Mental Health*, 1 (1) pp147–163.

Kerr, I. B. (1999) Cognitive analytic therapy for borderline personality disorder in the context of a community mental health team: individual and organisational psycho dynamic implications. British Journal of Psychotherapy, 15 (4) pp425–37.

Kerr, I. B., Birkett, P. B. & Chanen, A. (2005) Clinical and service implications of a cognitive analytic therapy model of psychosis. *Australian and New Zealand Journal of psychiatry*, 37, pp515–523.

Kerr, I., Dent-Brown, K. & Parry, G. (2007). Psychotherapy and mental health teams, *International Review of Psychiatry*, 19, pp63–80.

Kirkland, J. (2016) *Policy and Guidance on Reflective Practice Group Sessions. Governance Group, Directorate of Forensic Mental Health and Learning Disabilities*. Glasgow: NHS Greater Glasgow & Clyde.

Kirkland, J. & Baron, E. (2014) Using a cognitive analytic approach to formulate a complex sexual and violent offender to inform multi-agency working: developing a shared understanding. *Journal of Sexual Aggression*, 21 (3) pp394–405. (doi: 10.1080/13552600.2014.939596)

Kjeldman, D., Hjolmström, I. & Rosenqvist, U. (2004) Balint training makes gps thrive better in their job. *Patient Education and Counselling*, 55, pp230–235.

Kurtz, A. (2020) *How to Run Reflective Practice Groups: A guide for healthcare professionals.* Abingdon: Routledge.

Lees, A. (2017) *Evaluation of Reflective Practice Groups Project: Brighton & Hove Children's Services.* London: Centre for Social Work Practice. Available at: https://cris.winchester.ac.uk/ws/portalfiles/portal/356526/824824_Lees_ReflectivePracticeGroupEvaluation_original.pdf [Accessed: 10 August 2020]

Leiman, M. (1992) The concept of sign in the work of Vygotsky, Winnicott and Bakhtin: Further integration of object relations theory and activity theory. *British Journal of Medical Psychology*, 65, pp209–221.

Leiman, M. (2002) Towards semiotic dialogism: The role of sign mediation in the dialogical self. *Theory and Psychology*, 12 (2) pp221–234.

Liddle, M., Boswell, G., Wright, S., Francis, V. & Perry, R. (2016) 'Beyond Youth Custody – trauma and young offenders: A review of the research and practice literature.' [Online] [Accessed 08 June 2018] Available at: http://www.beyondyouthcustody.net/wp-content/uploads/Trauma-and-young-offenders-a-review-of-the-research-and-practice-literature.pdf

Livesley, J. (2003) *Practical Management of Personality Disorder.* New York: Guilford Press.

Livesley, W. J. (2012) Integrated treatment: A conceptual framework for an evidence-based approach to the treatment of personality disorder. *Journal of Personality Disorders*, 26 (1) pp17–42.

Lloyd, J. (2011) Consulting with staff teams. *Clinical Psychology and People with Learning Disabilities*, 9 (1) pp22–31.

Lloyd, J. & Clayton, P. (2013) Cognitive Analytic Therapy for People with Intellectual Disabilities and their Carers. London: Jessica Kingsley Publishers.

Lowdell, A. & Adshead, G. (2009) 'The best defence: Institutional defences against anxiety in forensic services.' In: A. Aiyegbusi and J. Clarke-Moore (Eds) *Therapeutic Relationships with Offenders: An Introduction to the Psychodynamics of Forensic Mental Health Nursing.* London: Jessica Kingsley Publishers, pp53–68.

Macallister, P. & Jacobs, C. (2012) *College Centre for Quality Improvement – Standards for Psychotherapy in Medium Secure Units.* Royal College of Psychiatrists. Available at: https://www.rcpsych.ac.uk/pdf/Standards_for_Psychotherapy_in_MSUs_June2012.pdf [Accessed: 10 September 2020]

Main, T. F. (1957) The Ailment. *British Journal of Medical Psychology*, 30, pp129–145.

Manson, K., Lad, S. & Cavieres, M. (2017) Developing a CAT understanding of anti-social personality disorder (ASPD), *Reformulation*, Summer, pp42–48.

Marshall, J., Freshwater, K. & Potter, S. (2013) Adaptions of a CAT skills course. *Reformulation*, Winter, pp6–8.

Marshall, J., Freshwater, K. & Potter, S. (2014) Using cognitive analytic therapy within a forensic setting: an overarching relational model. *Forensic Update 2014 Annual Compendium*, pp132–137.

Marshall, J., Freshwater, K. and Potter, S. (2014) Using cognitive analytic therapy within a forensic setting: an overarching relational model, *BPS Forensic Update*, 115, pp46–51.

Mason, T. (2002) Forensic psychiatric nursing: a literature review and thematic analysis of role tensions, *Journal of Psychiatry and Mental Health Nursing*, 9 (5) pp511–520.

McAvoy, P. (2012) Significant events in ward-based reflective practice groups. Doctorate of Clinical Psychology, University of Leeds.

McGregor, C. (2017) (Unpublished dissertation) 'A Service Evaluation of 'Map and Talk' Reflective Practice.' *MSc Clinical Forensic Psychology Dissertation*, Institute of Psychiatry, Psychology and Neuroscience, Kings College London.

McLaughlin, Á., Casey, B. & McMahon, A. (2019) Planning and implementing group supervision: a case study from homeless social care practice, *Journal of Social Work Practice*, 33 (3) pp281–295.

McVey, J. & Jones, T. (2012) Assessing the value of facilitated reflective practice groups. *Cancer Nursing Practice*, 11 (8) pp32–37.

Mental Welfare Commission (2009) 'Too Close To See – Summary of Our Investigation into the Deficiencies of the Care and Treatment of Mr F. Mental Welfare Commission. Mental Welfare Commission.' Available at: http://www.mwcscot.org.uk/media/52063/Too%20Close%20to%20See%20Mr%20F%20Summary.pdf [Accessed on 10 September 2020]

Menzies, I. (1960) The functioning of social systems as a defence against anxiety: Report on a study of the nursing service of a general hospital, *Human Relations*, 13 (2) pp95–121.

Mersey Care NHS Trust (2014) Internal investigation into allegations made by four people relating to Jimmy Savile at Moss Side Hospital (previously part of Ashworth Hospital, Mersey Care NHS Trust). Available at: http://data.parliament.uk/DepositedPapers/Files/DEP2014-0919/03_Ashworth_Hospital_-_Lib_Doc_-_Report.pdf [Accessed 02 Feb 2020]

Midstaffordshire NHS Foundation Trust Public Inquiry (2013) *Report of the Mid Staffordshire NHS Foundation Trust Public Inquiry*. London: The Stationery Office. Available at: https://assets.publishing.service.gov.uk/government/uploads/system/uploads/attachment_data/file/279124/0947.pdf [Accessed: 10 March 2020]

MIND (2018) 'Shining lights in dark corners of people's lives': A Consensus Statement for people with complex mental health difficulties who are diagnosed with a personality disorder. Retrieved from https:// www.mind.org.uk/media/21163353/consensus-statement-final.pdf

Ministry of Justice (2020) 'Probation Serious Further Offence Review in the Case of Joseph McCann.' Available at: https://assets.publishing.service.gov.uk/government/uploads/system/uploads/attachment_data/file/870617/sfo-review-joseph-mccann.pdf [Accessed 03 March 2020]

Mitzman, S. F. (2010) Cognitive analytic therapy and the role of brief assessment and contextual reformulation: the jigsaw puzzle of offending, *Reformulation*, 34 (Summer), pp26–30.

Moore, E. (2012) Personality disorder: its impact on staff and the role of supervision, *Advances in Psychiatric Treatment*, 18 (1) pp44–55.

Moore, E. (2020) Trauma-informed practice: repairing harm via restorative resolution, *Trauma Informed Care in Forensic Settings Conference*, 30 January 2020, Newark.

Moss, M. & Tanner, C. (2013) CAT as a model for development of leadership skills, *Reformulation*, Winter, pp11–14.

Moylan, D. (1994) The dangers of contagion: projective identification processes in institutions. In: A. Obholzer and V. Roberts (Eds) *The Unconscious at Work: Individual and Organizational Stress in the Human Services*. London: Routledge.

Mulhall, J. (2015) A CAT-informed approach to a time-limited (closed) group within an adolescent inpatient setting, *Reformulation*, Winter, pp20–28.

Murrell, K. A. (1998) The experience of facilitation in reflective groups: A phenomenological study, *Nurse Education Today*, 18 (4) pp303–309.

National Education Scotland (2020) 'Matrix – A guide to delivering evidence-based psychological therapies in Scotland.' Available at: https://www.nes.scot.nhs.uk/our-work/matrix-a-guide-to-delivering-evidence-based-psychological-therapies-in-scotland/ [Accessed 28 January 2021]

Nehmad, A. (2017) 'The healthy supervisor: A CAT understanding of the process of psychotherapy supervision'. In: D. Pickvance (Ed) *Cognitive Analytic Supervision: A relational approach*. Abingdon: Routledge.

Nehmad, A. (1997) CAT and narcissism: the missing chapter, *Reformulation*, Winter, pp3–9.

NHS Confederation (2012) Defining mental health services: Promoting effective commissioning and supporting QIPP. Available at: https://www.nhsconfed.org/~/media/Confederation/Files/Publications/Documents/Defining_mental_health_services.pdf [Accessed on 18 Oct 2020]

References

NHS Education for Scotland (2011) 10 Essential Shared Capabilities for Mental Health Practice; Learning Materials. NHS Education for Scotland. Available at: http://www.nes.scot.nhs.uk/media/351385/10_essential_shared_capabilities_2011.pdf [Accessed 10 June 2020]

NHS Scotland Forensic Group (2016) Position Paper on Psychological Approaches to Personality Disorder in Forensic Mental Health Settings. School of Forensic Mental Health: Forensic Network. Available at: https://www.forensicnetwork.scot.nhs.uk/wp-content/uploads/Principles-of-Structured-Clinical-Care.pdf?x82981 [Accessed 5 May 2020]

O'Neill, L., Johnson, J. & Mandela, R. (2019) Reflective practice groups: Are they useful for liaison psychiatry nurses working within the Emergency Department? *Archives of Psychiatric Nursing*, 33, pp85–92.

Obholzer, A. & Zagier Roberts, V. (1994) *The Unconscious at Work: Individual and Organizational Stress in the Human Services*. London: Routledge.

Onyett, S., Pillinger, T. & Mujen, M. (1997) Job satisfaction and Burnout among members of Community Mental Health Teams, *Journal of Mental Health*, 6 (1).

Patrick, J., Kirkland, K., Maclean, C., Polnay, A., Russell, K. & Cawthorne, P. (2018) *Matrix Reflective Practice Framework*. NHS Scotland Forensic Network, School of Forensic Mental Health. Available at: https://www.forensicnetwork.scot.nhs.uk/wp-content/uploads/Matrix-Reflective-Practice-Framework.pdf?x82981 [Accessed: 10 June 2020]

Pickvance, D. (2017) (Ed) *Cognitive analytic supervision: A relational approach*. Abingdon: Routledge.

Platzer, H., Blake, D. & Ashford, D. (2000a) An evaluation of process and outcomes from learning through reflective practice groups on a post-registration nursing course, *Journal of Advanced Nursing*, 31, pp689–695.

Platzer, H., Blake, D. & Ashford, D. (2000b) Barriers to learning from reflection: a study of the use of groupwork with post-registration nurses, *Journal of Advanced Nursing*, 31, pp1001–1008.

Pollock, P. (2001) 'CAT and the multiple self-states model of trauma. In P. Pollock (Ed) *Cognitive Analytic Therapy for Adult Survivors of Childhood Abuse: Approaches to Treatment and Case Management*. Chichester: Wiley.

Pollock, P. H., Stowell-Smith, M. & Gopfert, M. (2006) *Cognitive Analytic Therapy for Offender: A new approach to forensic psychotherapy*. London: Routledge.

Pollock, P.H. (2006) 'CAT for a rapist with a psychopathic personality disorder.' In: P.H. Pollock, M. Stowell-Smith and M. Gopfert (Eds) *Cognitive Analytic Therapy for Offender: A New Approach to Forensic Psychotherapy)*. Oxford: Routledge, pp186–220.

Potter, S. (1999) A personal view of a ACAT, Reformulation, *ACAT News* Winter, pp2–5.

Potter, S. (2010) Words with arrows: The benefits of mapping whilst talking', *Reformulation*, 34, pp37–45.

Potter, S. (2013) 'The helper's dance list.' In: J. Lloyd and P. Clayton (2013) *Cognitive Analytic Therapy for People with Intellectual Disabilities and their Carers*. London: Jessica Kingsley Publishers, pp89–121.

Potter, S. (2020) *Therapy With a Map: A cognitive analytic approach to helping relationships*. Shoreham by Sea: Pavilion Publishing, p77.

Powell, T. & Howard, R. (2006) Reflective practice comes of age in Birmingham, *Clinical Psychology Forum*, 67, pp34–37.

Price, A. (2004). Encouraging reflection and critical thinking in practice, *Nursing Standard*, 18 (47) pp46–52.

Quinsey, V. (1999) Report of the committee of inquiry into the personality disorder unit, ashworth special hospital, Vol. 1, *Journal of Forensic Psychiatry*, 10 (3) pp635–648

Ramm, M. (2010) *Cognitive Analytic Therapy at the Orchard Clinic Medium Secure Unit for Mentally Disordered Offenders*. DCP Scotland, No. 3.

Reid, Y., Johnson, S., Morant, N., Kuipers, E., Szmukler, G., Thornicroft, G., Bebbington, P. & Prosser, D. (1999) Explanations of stress and satisfaction in mental health professionals: a qualitative study, *Social Psychiatry and Psychiatric Epidemiology*, 34, pp301–308.

Roth, A.D. & Pilling, S. (2009) *A Competence Framework for the Supervision of Psychological Therapies*. London: University College, London. Available at: www.ucl.ac.uk/pals/research/clinical-educational-and-health-psychology/research-groups/core/competence-frameworks-8

Royal College of Psychiatrists, Quality Network for Forensic Improvements (2015) *See, Think, Act – Your Guide to Relational Security* (2nd edition). London: Royal College of Psychiatrists. Available at: https://www.rcpsych.ac.uk/pdf/STA_hndbk_2ndEd_Web_2.pdf [Accessed: 5 May 2020]

Rubitel, D. & Reiss, A. (2010) *Containment in the Community: Supportive Frameworks for Thinking about Antisocial Behaviour and Mental Health*, London: Routledge.

Ruch, G. (2007a) Reflective practice in contemporary child-care social work: the role of containment, *British Journal of Social Work*, 37, pp659–680.

Ruch, G. (2007b) 'Thoughtful' practice: child care social work and the role of case discussion, *Child and Family Social Work*, 12, pp370–379.

Ruch, G. (2009) Identifying 'the critical' in a relationship-based model of reflection, *European Journal of Social Work*, 12 (3), pp349–362.

Russell, K. (2018) *Principles of Structure Clinical Care, Forensic Network*. Available at: https://www.forensicnetwork.scot.nhs.uk/wp-content/uploads/Principles-of-Structured-Clinical-Care.pdf?x82981 [Accessed: 10 June 2020]

Rüth, U. (2009) Classic Balint group work and the thinking of W.R. Bion: how Balint work increases the ability to think one's own thoughts. *Group Analysis*, 42, pp380–391.

Rutherford, M. & Duggan, S. (2008) Forensic mental health services: facts and figures on current provision, *The British Journal of Forensic Practice*, 10 (4) pp4–10.

Ryle, A. & Kerr, I. (2002) *Introducing Cognitive Analytic Therapy*. London: Wiley.

Ryle, A. & Kerr, I.B. (2002) *Introducing Cognitive Analytic Therapy: Principles and practice*. Chichester: John Wiley.

Ryle, A. (1978) A common language for the psychotherapies, *British Journal of Psychiatry*, 132, pp585–94.

Ryle, A. (1982). Cognitive theory, object relations and the self, *British Journal of Medical Psychology*, 58, pp1–7.

Ryle, A. (1990) *Cognitive Analytic Therapy: Active participation in change. A new integration in brief psychotherapy*. Chichester: Wiley.

Ryle, A. (1994) Projective identification: a particular form of reciprocal role procedure. *British Journal of Medical Psychology*, 67, pp107–113.

Ryle, A. (1997) The structure and development of Borderline Personality Disorder: A proposed model, *British Journal of Psychiatry*, 170, pp82–87.

Ryle, A. (1998) Transference and countertransferences: the cognitive analytic therapy perspective, *British Journal of Psychotherapy*, 14 (3) 1998.

Ryle, A. (1998) Transferences and countertransferences: the cognitive analytic therapy perspective, *British Journal of Psychotherapy*, 14 (3) pp303–309.

Ryle, A. & Kerr, I. B. (2020) Introducing *Cognitive Analytic Therapy: Principles and Practice of a Relational Approach to Mental Health* (2nd edition). Chichester: Wiley.

Ryle, A. & Kerr, I.B. (2002, 2020) *Introducing Cognitive Analytic Therapy*. Chichester: Wiley-Blackwell.

Ryle, A. (2002) Differences between borderline and narcissistic personality disorders, *Reformulation*, Autumn, pp16–17.

Safran, J. (2000) *Negotiating the Therapeutic Alliance*. New York: Guilford Press.

Scanlon, C. (2012) 'The traumatised-organisation-in-the-mind: opening up space for difficult conversations in difficult places', Chapter 14. In: A. Aiyesbusi, P. Kleinot, A. Motz, L. Scanlon and J. Adlam (2012) *The Therapeutic Milieu Under Fire: Security and Insecurity in Forensic Mental Health*. London: Jessica Kingsley Publishers.

Schon, D. (1983) *The Reflective Practitioner: How Professionals Think in Action*. New York : Basic Books.

Shannon, K. (2017) 'CAT supervision in forensic practice: working with complexity and risk.' In: D. Pickvance (Ed) *Cognitive Analytic Supervision: A relational approach*. Abingdon: Routledge.

Shannon, K. (2020) Email to David Harvey, 20 June (Personal communication).

Shannon, K., Butler, S., Ellis, C., McLaine, J. & Riley, J. (2016) Use of CAT concepts; a relational framework for organisational service delivery and working with clients with multiple complex needs at the Liverpool YMCA. *Reformulation*, Winter, pp12–20.

Shannon, K., Butler, S., Ellis, C., McLaine, J. & Riley, J. (2017). 'Seeing the unseen': supporting organisational and team working at YMCA Liverpool with multiple complex needs clients. The use of cognitive analytic concepts to enhance service delivery. *Reformulation*, Summer, pp5–15.

Shannon, K., Willis, A. & Potter, S. (2006) 'Fragile states and fixed identities: using cognitive analytic therapy to understand aggressive men in relational and societal terms.' In: P. Pollock, M. Stowell-Smith and M. Göpfert (Eds) *Cognitive Analytic Therapy for Offenders: A New Approach to Forensic Psychotherapy*. New York, NY, USA: Routledge/Taylor & Francis Chapter 17, pp295–314.

Shannon, K.L., Willis, A. & Potter, S. (2006) 'Fragile states and fixed identities: using CAT to understand aggressive men in relational and societal terms.' In: P.H. Pollock, M. Stowell-Smith and M. Gopfert (Eds) *Cognitive Analytic Therapy for Offenders: A New Approach to Forensic Psychotherapy*. London: Routledge, pp295–314.

South East Coast Strategic Health Authority (2006) *Report of the independent inquiry into the care and treatment of Michael Stone*. Available at: http://hundredfamilies.org/wp/wp-content/uploads/2013/12/MICHAEL_STONE_JULY96.pdf [Accessed on 15 February 2020]

Staunton, G. Lloyd, J. & Potter, S. (2015) Relational patterns amongst staff in an NHS teams, *International Review of Psychiatry*, 19 (1) pp63–80.

Staunton, G., Lloyd, J. & Potter, S. (2015) Relational patterns amongst staff in an NHS Community Team. *Reformulation*, Summer, pp38–44.

Tetley, A., Jinks, M., Huband, N., Howells, K. & McMurran, M. (2012) Barriers to and facilitators of treatment engagement for clients with personality disorder: A Delphi survey, *Personality and Mental Health*, 6, pp97–110.

Thompson, A.R. (2008) Multidisciplinary Community mental health team's experience of a skills level training course in cognitive analytic therapy, *International Journal of Mental Health Nursing*, 17 (2) pp131–7.

Thompson, A.R., Donnison, J., Warnock-Parkes, E., Turpin, G., Turner, J. & Kerr, I.B. (2008) Multidisciplinary community mental health team staff's experience of a 'skills level' training course in cognitive analytic therapy, *International Journal of Mental Health Nursing*, 17, pp131–137.

Timmins, N. (2016) *The Chief Executive's Tale*. Kings Fund and NHS Providers. Available at: https://www.kingsfund.org.uk/sites/default/files/field/field_publication_file/The-chief-executive-tale-Kings-Fund-May-2016.pdf [Accessed : 10 March 2020]

Trevarthen, C. B. (1979) 'Communication and cooperation in early infancy: A description of primary intersubjectivity.' In: M. Bullowa (Ed) *Before Speech*. Cambridge: Cambridge University Press.

Tuck, G. (2009) 'Forensic systems and organisational dynamics.' In: A. Aiyegbusi and J. Clarke-Moore (2010) *Therapeutic Relationships with Offenders: An Introduction to the Psychodynamics of Forensic Mental Health Nursing*. London and Philadelphia: Jessica Kingsley Publishers.

Tuck, M. (2017) A Mixed-Method Service Evaluation of 'Map-and-Talk' – A Cognitive Analytic Therapy (CAT) Model of Reflective Practice in a Medium Secure Unit. *MSc Clinical Forensic Psychology Dissertation*, Institute of Psychiatry, Psychology and Neuroscience, Kings College London.

Tucker, S., Iqbal, M. & Holder S. (2012) College Centre for Quality Improvement – Standards for Low Secure Services. *CCQI130*. London: Royal College of Psychiatrists. Available at: http://www.rcpsych.ac.uk/pdf/QNFMHSStandardsLowSecureServices.pdf [Accessed: 10 June 2020]

Vachon, B., Durand, M.J. & LeBlanc, J. (2009) Using reflective learning to improve the impact of continuing education in the context of work rehabilitation, *Advances in Health Sciences Education: Theory and Practice*, 15, pp329–48.

Völlm, B. A., Edworthy, R., Huband, N., Talbot, E., Majid, S., Holley, J., Furtado, V., Weaver, T., McDonald, R. & Duggan, C. (2018) Characteristics and pathways of long-stay patients in high and medium secure settings in england; a secondary publication from a large mixed-methods study, *Frontiers in psychiatry*, 9, p140.

Vygotsky, L. S. (1978) *Mind in Society*. Cambridge: Harvard University Press.

Vygotsky, L. (1978) 'Interaction between learning and development.' In L.S. Vygotsky (1978) *Mind and Society*. Cambridge, MA: Harvard University Press, pp79–91.

Vygotsky, L. S. (1986) *Thought and Language – Revised Edition* (Revised); The MIT Press.

Walker, J., Amos, T., Knowles, P., Batson, S. & Craissati, J. (2012) Finance: putting a price on psychiatric care, *The Health Service Journal*, 122 (6296) pp-24.

Walsh, S. (1996) Adapting cognitive analytic therapy to make sense of psychological harmful work environments, *British Journal of Medical Psychology*, 69, pp3–20.

Walsh, S. (1996) Adapting cognitive analytic therapy to make sense of psychologically harmful work environments, *British Journal of Medical Psychology* 69, pp3–20.

Walsh, S. (2019) 'Infamy, Infamy, they've all got it in for me': exits in organisationally informed CAT supervision, *Reformulation*, Summer, pp6–8.

Walsh, S. & Freshwater, K. (in press) 'Struggling Well': Using CAT to make sense of organizational hurt. In: L. Brummer, M. Cavieres and R. Tan (Eds) *Oxford Handbook of Cognitive Analytic Therapy*. Oxford: Oxford University Press.

Warman, A. & Jackson, E. (2007) Recruiting and retaining children and families' social workers: the potential of work discussion groups, *Journal of Social Work Practice*, 21 (1) pp35–48.

Zagier Roberts, V. (1994) The Organisation of Work: Contributions from Open Systems Theory. In: A. Obholzer and V. Zagier Roberts (Eds) *The Unconscious at Work: Individual and Organizational Stress in the Human Services*. Routledge: London.

Appendix 1

The helper's dance list – a checklist of interactions when helping others www.mapandtalk.com

The helper's 'dance' list

A checklist of interactions when helping others

Our efforts to help each other usually go well enough, but there are some difficult patterns of interaction which we can be part of, despite our best intentions. These patterns can be called dances to capture the whole interpersonal and social interaction summed up by the adage: *'it takes two to tango'*. If we can notice and map out all the steps to these patterns, we have a chance to discuss them and re-negotiate them in a more reflective way.

Each item in the list is a prompt for an open and compassionate conversation. The list is not set in stone. Our aim is to understand the pattern with compassion and curiosity. Rate your responses to each item. Along the way, cross out or add words to help each item fit your experience. Not all the items will strike a chord with you. Go through your responses and discuss how to change the dances by changing your thinking, your behaviour or your expectations of how others will interact with you. The aim in knowing more about our own and other people's patterns of relating is summed up as *'name the dance, don't blame the dancer'* which is to say: 'be kind enough to name the dance, but wise enough to not blame the dancers.' The other rule of thumb is what has been dubbed the *'thirds rule'* which is to keep in mind that one third of what is happening when we are helping is coming from the person being helped, one third from the helper and one third from the system or context they are in. Keep this *'thirds rule'* in mind for each of the statements.

Appendix 1

Tick if applies to me: never 0, rarely ✓, sometimes ✓✓, often ✓✓✓, often ✓✓✓✓	
Never good enough: I have high expectations of myself which makes me think my help will not be good enough, others will be disappointed, and I will cope by trying even harder.	
The blame game: When trying to understand why something went wrong, I expect the finger of blame to be pointed directly at someone and everyone hides from taking some responsibility.	
Out of my depth: If I get involved, I fear I will get out of my depth, so I back off and keep distant.	
Super sponge: When people are demanding, I feel put upon but soak up the pressure, and will not complain through fear of making things worse.	
Genuine and vulnerable or safe but less real: Either I show feelings and feel genuine but somewhat vulnerable or I safely hide feelings, appear professional but less the real me.	
Either it is my way or the wrong way: If I am sure I am helping in the right way I can stick to it stubbornly and find it hard accepting other views.	
Fear of prejudice: If I feel someone is very different to me, I will back off for fear of embarrassment or criticism for saying the wrong thing.	
Lose perspective: I can be drawn into the detail of the moment and forget the bigger picture or main purpose.	
Let it be and wait and see: When I am not sure what to do, I let things be and wait and see.	
Tell me what to do: When uncertain about how to help, I rely too much on reassurance and guidance.	
Switch off: When I am upset by the suffering of those whom I help I cope by switching off.	
Who is who? If I help too many people in a day, my feelings and understanding of one person can get mixed up with another person.	
Jump in or hold back: As a helper I am in at the deep end giving my all or I am not so involved and hold back and then miss the moment to help.	
My hands are tied: With a freer hand, I could be more helpful, but I must follow the rules.	
If I do not help no one will: Other people won't see the need, or know how to help, so it is up to me to provide the help that someone needs.	
Lack of resources frustrates me: I know what needs doing to help but the treatment or support is not available. I feel frustrated, angry or helpless.	
Looking after others means neglecting myself: I put so much into looking after others that their needs take over and I forget to look after myself.	
Not here, not now: I see the need to talk about what is happening between us but just now often seems the wrong time.	

Appendix 2

THE COVID STRUGGLES LIST

Many of us are facing unprecedented challenges in our work. This is a list of common experiences and dilemmas described by staff in a mental health and disability setting in the wake of the pandemic. The aim is to illustrate how many of these struggles are normal, and shared between us – we are all human and doing the best we can. It has been informed by the theory and practice of Cognitive Analytic Therapy (CAT).

Written by Dr Steve Jefferis, Consultant Clinical Psychologist, CNTW Cognitive Analytic Therapy Service, Newcastle-upon-Tyne. With contributions from colleagues in the Centre for Specialist Psychological Therapies, the CAT Service, and ACAT. Contact steve.jefferis@cntw.nhs.uk. Last updated 20th April 2020. Inspired by Steve Potter's "Helper's Dance List"

How do we talk about it? There are stresses around but people are not talking about it. What are people feeling? How do I ask?

Who am I going to be? I want to do my bit, but my normal job may not be possible or may not be needed now. How long will I have to wait to find out? Who will I be then? Was my old job not important? Will I be able to do the new one?

Too much change. So much has changed, in my job, my family and the world, without time to adjust or say goodbye, that it can all feel too much.

Where did the team go? Some of the things that held us together have gone now, because we changed roles, or aren't in the same place now. I miss the team.

How can I help when we're this far apart? I try to adapt and help from a distance but can't be sure if I'm getting it right.

The lost connection. I can feel isolated by my new working life. How do I stay connected with people?

Soldiering on exhausted. The changes to my work have left me tired and drained. I must keep going because others need me.

If I put myself first I feel guilty. I might know I need to put myself first eg by having downtime, or protecting myself better from risks, but it's a crisis and if I do that I will feel guilty (or the organization might make me feel like that).

The 'overwhelmed' dilemma. The volume of information and instructions changes so quickly, and different sources conflict. It is too much. Sometimes I don't know what to do or what to believe. I either cut off from the flow of information (but something important might get missed) or immerse myself in it (and get exhausted again – perhaps I have trouble switching off).

The 'boundaries' dilemma. The world has changed so maybe we need to be flexible. But it can seem like either I stick to what I would normally do (but someone's needs don't get met) or I change the boundaries but then it doesn't feel OK.

'In the line of fire.' My job means I can't socially distance, and may be at risk of being infected or infecting others. I try to rise to the challenge but it might mean I'm putting me, my family, or other patients at risk, which worries me.

The 'authority' dilemmas. With so much uncertainty, I know people want clarity and simplicity. But:

1. I don't always have the answers, and don't know what to say to help; and
2. I can be torn between either telling people what to do (which they may find too controlling) or trying to make decisions together but risk spreading the uncertainty.

All of these may lead to problems in the relationships with people over whom I have some authority.

The 'rush or reflect' dilemma. There is so much pressure to get things decided and done now, I may rush into things without thinking it through. However, if I stop and reflect, I fear it may then be too late.

Are YOU a hero? I may be invited to be a hero: by the world around us (clapping for the NHS), by my organization, by myself. That can feel good, exciting, special. But:

1. If not a hero, I may feel overlooked, left out, even resentful
2. If I can't be a hero (for instance if I need to stay out of things for my own health) I may feel guilty
3. No one can be a hero all the time. What happens then? It may feel like we are never allowed to make mistakes, to not know the answers, or not to be firing on all cylinders.

Absorbing the stresses of others. People I am trying to help might be very stressed and struggling to cope. I do my best to help manage their anxiety but then I am left with the anxiety myself, which can take its toll.

Work or home? Home is topsy-turvy because of money, children, people close to me who are vulnerable, or all of these. I can feel split between putting my time and effort into what's needed at home, and what's needed at work. I might feel confused or overwhelmed, or feel guilty about having to put one set of needs above the other; or feel guilty about not meeting either set of needs.

The hairline cracks. At work, if relationships have been difficult before the crisis, the extra pressure that everyone is under may make it even harder now. Communication between us might be difficult, or we get locked in argument on bones of contention.

Who is to blame? When things are less than perfect we may want to find someone to blame. That can feel good but may make others less able to do their jobs well, and may not help us when it is our turn for some compassion.

IDEAS WORTH TRYING. What helps to manage these struggles will differ for each of us as people, and differ across our work settings. This is a developing list of general strategies which people we have spoken to have found helpful at times. In Cognitive Analytic Therapy these are known as 'exits'.

- Voicing the struggles, without shame
- Recognise this is a process – have permission to take one day at a time
- Normalising – recognise the struggles are universal and normal: we are all human and all in it together, and we can support each other
- Organise yourselves for connection
  - For remote workers – extra check ins, virtual coffee time, WhatsApp groups – but discuss what people find useful and what is too much
  - For present workers – creative ways to do things together eg socially distanced lunches; explicitly ask how each other is doing
- Create space for yourself and each other, and give permission to use it (eg use physical and virtual 'wobble rooms')
- Keep some 'anchors' to your familiar working life (eg start and finish work times, team rituals such as regular team meeting times; use 'setting events' for working at home eg use a specific chair/desk)
- Reconnect with things that have meaning and set simple goals
- Attend to the basics: sleep, food, physical safety
- Pay attention to boundaries and what feels comfortable; give yourself permission to separate work and home
- Shift your focus – remember the world is bigger than Covid